Shaped by the Shadow of War

by Don Catherall

Acknowledgements

This memoir focuses on the male relationships in my life and is thus incomplete, as I was greatly influenced by my mother, my sisters, my wife, and my daughter. Their absence in this volume does not reflect the important roles they've each played in my life.

I thank my wife, Kim, and my children, Kate and Cody, for their patience and support over the many years I spent pursuing this project. Kim's father was badly wounded in World War II, and her family lived with the consequences of his wounds for the remainder of his life. Thus, Kim also grew up in a world that was shaped by the shadow of war, as have our children.

I began putting my memories on paper when my children were still small, and I shared my first draft with my late brother-in-law and writing coach extraordinaire, Jerry Cleaver. Jerry showed me what I needed to focus on and what I could do without. He helped set the path I took, and this book is much improved as a result of his guidance.

Preface

Most people don't know what it really means to be a survivor. They know the myths—the dedicated Lone Ranger whose life is a mission to right the wrong that took his comrades or the tormented Ahab who takes everyone with him in his suicidal pursuit of vengeance. While such extremes occur, surviving is usually a more mundane experience. Indeed, the challenge for many survivors is simply to be able to resume ordinary life after extraordinary experience. You are changed by that which you survive. For the rest of your life, you evaluate events from the perspective of that extraordinary experience. When you or someone you know is in distress or fear or danger, you compare that experience to what you've witnessed and experienced yourself. You hear others' complaints from the perspective of one who knows a great range of what can be endured. That sense of perspective helps you maintain an appreciation of what matters and what is trivial, which can make difficult things easy but can also make ordinary things excruciating.

Whereas the business of surviving may be mundane, the internal experience is not. Survivors are forever different from those whose security has never been challenged. War veterans are a group unto themselves. It is difficult to articulate what it does to a person to see and experience the horrors of war, perhaps because many of the most horrifying experiences are internal. War leaves a lasting imprint on the human spirit. For some, that imprint leads to better choices and a more meaningful life. For many, the wounds of war throw a shadow over all that follows.

In my career as a psychologist, I specialized in treating people who have been traumatized. Our rational Western culture uses the term *posttraumatic stress disorder* to refer to those who've been traumatized by war. But in Vietnam, where such categorizing is less developed, traumatized people have been referred to as suffering from *spiritual sadness*. For me, the Vietnamese view holds greater meaning. Rather than a mental disorder that satisfies objective criteria in some formal text, the term spiritual sadness describes the experience of being touched by the shadow of war.

I think every survivor of war carries sadness, though some may not recognize their sadness and mistake it for the things they cover it with—anger, numbness or the perpetual pursuit of excitement. It is important for those of us who've been touched by the shadow of war to honor our sadness. Monuments and memorials serve that function, providing a safe place for veterans—and their families—to honor their sadness.

Telling one's story is another way to honor one's sadness.

The sadness of my own spirit mostly derives from my tour of duty in Vietnam. I saw more death and pain than I ever would have imagined. But my spiritual sadness didn't start there, it started in my childhood growing up with my father. I was born nine months and fifteen minutes after he returned from fighting in the South Pacific. I grew up in a world that was shaped by the shadow of war. My father is at peace now—he died in 1987—but I wrote this book for him as well as for myself. The Navajo concept of ancestral healing suggests that healing in the current generation can have an impact as far as seven generations back and another seven generations into the future. I think I know my father's wounds better than anyone—his wounds are an important part of my story, and my healing is an important part of his.

Dedicated to

Lyle Albert Johnson, Captain, USMC

- KIA October 5, 1967

William Edward Rees, Lance Corporal, USMC

- KIA October 5, 1967

Richard Roy Catherall, (formerly) Corporal, USMC

- deceased March 31, 1987

Prologue

Christmas, 1954, Santa brought me boxing gloves, two pair of boxing gloves—a single pair isn't good for much. The year before, he brought me a BB gun. The year after, he brought me my first real gun, a single-action .22 rifle. The year after that, he brought me a belt with a hunting knife and hatchet holstered on it. The year after that was my first shotgun and two years later, a .22 revolver.

I don't recall expressing any interest in boxing gloves, but I was always interested in the guns. You do have to wonder, though, if Santa was trying to tell me something.

A few days after Christmas, my dad and I were home alone, and he suggested we go out in the yard and try out the boxing gloves. I was eight years old, and I was not aggressive. He kept trying to get me to punch him, but my efforts were half-hearted. I didn't really want to hit him. He grew frustrated with my lack of aggressiveness and started jabbing at me faster and faster, telling me to hit him. Finally, he punched me in the nose. I was stunned by the punch; it hurt worse than I expected. But more than that, I couldn't believe that my dad actually hurt me for no reason that I could see.

So I started crying.

When I was small, I cried easily. Mostly, I would cry if I felt I was disappointing the two most important people in the world, my parents. My dad was an easygoing man most of the time, but he had a bad temper, and I lived in fear of displeasing him. My crying always had a terrible effect on my dad—he absolutely hated it when I cried! That particular day, I couldn't stop crying, and that made him angry. He said I'd better stop crying or he would give me something to cry about.

I tried, but I couldn't stop the tears. The more I cried, the harder he yelled at me. I could see the anger and disappointment written on his face—which made me cry harder. Finally, he slapped me. That only added to my inability to stop crying—not so much because of the physical pain but because I was disappointing him so badly—so I cried even harder. That day, he lost control and began to slap me repeatedly until I finally stopped crying.

After that day, I pretty much stopped crying altogether. When I felt like crying, I found a greater feeling of quiet distress that stifled the urge and helped me to choke back the tears.

Part I

The Shadow of War

Chapter 1

To be a Man

"And please, God, let me grow up to be six feet tall."

That's the way I ended my prayers every night as a child. I was a runt, much smaller than other kids my age. In most of my class pictures from elementary school, I am kneeling in front of the other kids—this was an act of kindness by the teachers who engineered the photo sessions. If I'd been standing alongside the others, I'd have looked like a child from a lower grade who'd inadvertently wandered into the photo session. At home, I was surrounded by sisters and they towered over me—even my younger sister. My parents were both tall—especially my dad—and they kept reassuring me that one day I would grow. I lived for that day.

My diminutive size was not such a big deal in the lower grades—I didn't become acutely aware of it until I changed schools in the sixth grade. At the new school, a lot of my classmates were sprouting physically while I was still years away from puberty. I became aware of many differences between me and these kids. The school drew from a wealthier part of town, and I was dimly aware that I came from a different background. I didn't dress the way they did, and I couldn't figure out what to wear. I convinced my mother to buy me some slacks, but then I felt weird sitting on the floor of the gymnasium and I wanted to wear my jeans again.

One day, shortly after I had started at the new school, someone tripped me as I was walking down the hall. I landed on my face right in front of a group of the most popular kids in my class, and they all laughed at me. It seemed like every time I encountered those kids after that, they were laughing. I was pretty sure it was one of them that had tripped me, but no one seemed concerned about it.

The only thing positive about that year in the sixth grade was the flag. Somehow, I got a position on the safety patrol. I wore a white Sam Brown belt with a strap that looped over my shoulder and crossed my chest. It was a military looking badge of authority—the safety patrol kids manned the crosswalks near the school and had the power to stop traffic. I didn't get crosswalk duty; my job was raising and lowering the American flag in front of the auditorium. This was a position of responsibility—and it brought privileges. Any time it started raining, I left my classroom and sprinted outside to save the flag from getting wet. The flag was sacred—it must never touch the ground, be left up during rain, or flown lower than another flag. I treated it with the utmost respect, the same way I saw my father operate. Whenever he encountered a flag being raised or lowered, he removed his hat and put his hand over his heart. I even saw him stop the car and get out to show respect for a flag that was being lowered.

I took very good care of the flag, and no teacher ever questioned me when I had to go retrieve it in the rain.

My flag duties made me feel important, but there was far more evidence that suggested I was not in the same league as my classmates. I heard two boys on the playground talking about "jism" and "coming" and I had no idea what they were talking about. They were in my class but they each stood a head taller than me—they were talking over my head both figuratively and literally. Many of my classmates towered over me in those years, especially the girls.

My favorite sport was baseball, and we played just about every day. I was generally playing with kids bigger than myself, so I was always among the last ones chosen when they picked teams. I was accustomed to being an afterthought, but I still tried to move myself up the status ladder. One day, I hit a home run. I don't know how I did it—I swung and somehow caught the ball just right. It took off like a rocket, and I was as surprised as anyone on the field. I stood there amazed for a moment, while the other guys on my team were all yelling at me to "Run, Run". So I ran the bases and then savored the admiration of my teammates. The next day, I was chosen early in the picking. Hooray, I was finally moving up! That day, I swung as hard as I could at every ball pitched to me. And struck out every time.

Within a few days, I was back to standing with the other unwanted players as the team-picking made the shift from who is wanted to who is acceptable.

One day, my mother said, "You know, your Daddy would love to see you play football."

He would? I didn't know that; I'd never seen him show much interest in football. Certainly, I had never taken much interest in football myself. It seemed like it was only the biggest kids that played football, and that sure didn't include me. But if it would please my dad...so I joined the football team. There were no tryouts; everyone that wanted to be on the team was accepted. Of course, that didn't mean that everyone played equally. I shared a jersey with the other runt on the team, and we would trade off wearing it so that we each got in for a minimum of one play per game.

When I went out for my one play, it was always on defense, and I would try to tackle boys twice my size. On one of those rare plays, I tackled a boy who was running straight at me—it may have been my only solo tackle—and he nearly trampled me to death. Coach slapped me on the shoulder pad as I limped off the field afterward, "That's what we like to see out there." I hurt, but I was filled with pride. I looked to see if maybe my dad had taken off work and come to see me play, but he wasn't there.

That day, I swaggered into the locker room with the real players—the ones with the stained jerseys and the sweaty hair pasted to their heads—and I swung my helmet by the plastic face guard, just like the big seventh grader with the pubic hair. That was another unexpected facet of playing football—dressing with other boys. The first time I saw that seventh grader getting into his jock strap, I was floored. He looked more like my dad than a kid; I had never even considered the possibility that a kid could grow that stuff.

My small size and lack of pubertal markings were not the only evidence that I didn't belong in this world. Another unexpected result of switching schools was the change in my academic performance. I had been a good student at my previous school, but I became one of the worst in the new school. I found it impossible to concentrate in class, except when I was daydreaming. I would imagine being able to climb through the transom over the door or out the windows and down the exterior walls. Sometimes, I fantasized about making a big play on the football or baseball fields, but most of the time, I was just off in Neverland. When my daydreaming was interrupted by the teacher asking me a question, I never knew the answer.

Nor did I ever do my homework. My language arts class required us to do a year-long project, a composition book reflecting all the things that had interested us in the class throughout the year. At the end of the year, I turned in a folder containing two pictures of jet planes glued to a single sheet of notebook paper.

Nowhere was my academic failing more pronounced than in Mrs. Alexander's math class. Every day, she had us pass our homework up from the back of the class to the front. And every day, when the papers reached me, the process would come to a stop while I searched through my notebook, declaring that my homework was "in here somewhere". I never had it, of course, but I could come up with nothing better than this pitiful charade. Mrs. Alexander played out her side of the charade as well; she would wait a few minutes as though she actually expected me to find it this time.

Eventually, she would remark, "It looks like you don't have it."

"Oh, yes ma'am, it's in here somewhere. I did it. I know I did it." Then I would try to make a joke of it, "Maybe I turned it in for my language arts homework and Mr. Siedel didn't notice all the numbers." That might get me a giggle from somewhere in the room, which was about the only thing I could salvage from the situation. Mrs. Alexander never saw any humor in my remarks; her response was to send me to sit in the broom closet in the hallway.

I spent much of that year studying janitorial supplies.

If humiliation could kill, I never would have gotten out of the sixth grade. I would have been struck dead on the floor of Mrs. Alexander's classroom, my undersized body covered by a pile of other people's homework papers.

Chapter 2

Shadows

My grandfather was a bitter and cynical man. He had a successful business that went under during the Great Depression. He was hard on my dad, and I guess my dad developed an attitude because he got into a lot of trouble with authority at school. He eventually had a showdown with his high school principal, who was going to give him a paddling for some infraction. My dad, who was physically larger than the principal, picked up the paddle himself and announced that he was not going to accept any paddling.

After he was kicked out of school, he left home and joined the Merchant Marines. He was fifteen years old.

Chapter 3

Something to Prove

I finally entered puberty my sophomore year of high school, about a century behind the rest of my classmates. I was fourteen. I got my driver's license when I turned fifteen at the end of the first semester of my sophomore year. I was still so short that I couldn't see over the top of the steering wheel—I had to look under it. It helped to be able to drive and things improved even more when I started to grow, but throughout late elementary school, junior high, and much of high school, I devoted myself to trying to make up for being small and unworthy.

My primary means of compensating was to prove how courageous I was. I became a daredevil. I discovered that nothing impressed my peers more than my willingness to try something that was likely to get me killed—and which most of them had better sense than to try at all.

I was the first to climb up onto the roof of the elementary

school with the ropes from the flagpole and then jump off and swing like Tarzan. No one knew whether we would swing around the pole or right into it.

One day, my grandfather caught me climbing on the roof of his house. He yelled at me to "get down offa there". I was barefoot, but the grass in his back yard looked pretty soft, so I just walked over to the edge and jumped. I limped for a week before my mother took me to see Dr. Beckering, who x-rayed me and then put a cast on my broken foot. I saw Dr. Beckering regularly thoughout my childhood. Most kids have a pediatrician that is their regular doctor; I had an orthopedic surgeon. It got to where my mother would bring me in the door and Beck would look up, shake his head, and say, "Well, what's he done this time?"

Basically, I approached every situation looking for an opportunity to fly in the face of fear. I would climb to the highest point in the tree, swim the farthest out into the lake, and climb the steepest cliffs. By the time I reached high school, I had broken several bones, sustained a lot of stitches, and begun a series of concussions (eight) that continued into my twenties.

Life was not easy in a world of giants, but I wasn't the only midget. I saw other small boys suffer. Some of them became targets for the school bullies, those slow-witted guys whose only claim to prestige was their larger size. Fortunately, I never ended up as one of their targets, possibly because of my compensatory attitude—they usually preferred more passive victims. But these were not the most troubling aspects of my size problem anyway. No, the hardest thing about being so small was that I was such a disappointment to my dad. He didn't come out and say that, of course, but I could tell.

At times, I felt my slight size disgusted him.

Chapter 4

Shadows

When my dad was young, he was on his way home from school when three other boys started chasing him. I never got the details but apparently he had said or done something that justified their desire to catch him and give him a beating. He had almost reached his house when his father looked out and saw what was happening. My grandfather got up and locked the door so my dad was forced to turn around and take his beating.

He never did anything quite like that to me. I guess he figured just telling me the story was lesson enough.

Chapter 5

Influences

The summer after my sophomore year of high school, it finally happened. I grew. Sure enough, by the time I was a senior, I made it to six feet. My prayers had been answered, and it was probably the single greatest thing that happened to me in high school. But something else happened senior year, something that left a different kind of mark.

Like many members of my high school class, I was a fan of our youthful, heroic president. In November of my senior year, President John F. Kennedy made a trip to my hometown—Dallas, Texas. It was a Friday, and I took the day off from school. Since I lived right outside Love Field Airport, I went to meet his plane, along with my sister, Beth, my best friend, Carl, and my sister's friend, Sally. The president's plane taxied up to a stop right across from the fence where we were standing in a crowd of people. President Kennedy came down the steps from his plane and walked toward the black Lincoln Continental convertible that would take him downtown. We were all cheering. As he approached the car, he suddenly swung around it and came over to the crowd lined up behind the fence. Then he walked along the fence and shook some of the many hands extended toward him. I was in the second row of people pressed against the fence, but along with getting tall and gangly, I had grown some long arms. I stretched my arm way out there and President Kennedy gripped my hand.

It was an exciting moment; I had shaken the president's hand. Twenty-five minutes later, President Kennedy was assassinated, and the world changed forever.

For me, Kennedy's assassination probably produced the opposite effect from what the assassin intended. What Kennedy stood for was now the only thing I had to hold onto. I could find no better principle to direct my choices than Kennedy's inaugural dictum, "Ask not what your country can do for you, but what you can do for your country."

Years later, that dictum would become the most common explanation given by those who volunteered to serve in the Vietnam war.

Chapter 6

Shadows

In our living room, we had a large green book titled, "The Old Breed"; it was a pictorial history of the First Marine Division in World War Two. This was a sacred text. I spent many afternoons on the living room floor reading that book and studying the pictures. At the back of the book was an appendix containing the citations for all the Medal of Honor winners, most of whom received the award posthumously. I read those citations many times. The only medal my father brought home was a Purple Heart, but that medal is earned at a greater price than any other.

Medals didn't matter anyway; my father was a hero to me, through and through.

Chapter 7

"I Joined the Marines"

It was August of 1966, and I was returning from College Station where I had been trying to make up some of the courses from when I flunked out the year before. My ride dropped me off, and both of my parents came outside and met me in the front yard. I wasted no time in telling them.

"I joined the Marines."

My mother burst into tears, while my father beamed and slapped me on the back. As we went into the house, she said to my dad, "This is your fault, you know."

"What do you mean, 'fault'? This may be the best thing he's ever done!"

"Oh yeah? Dropping out of college and joining the Marines? That's the best thing he's ever done?"

"Well, he sure as hell hasn't been setting the world on fire in college. The Marines'll make a man of him."

"If they don't get him killed."

"The country's at war. It's his duty to serve."

"He could serve without being in a foxhole getting shot at. He wouldn't be going there if it wasn't for you."

"So it's my fault if our son joins the Marine Corps. What about his bad grades, are those my fault too?"

At about that point, I disappeared into my bedroom and listened to their muffled voices get louder as the argument escalated. I understood that my mother didn't want to wait anxiously while another loved one went off to war. But my dad had been watching me stumble through life for years. From his point of view, I had finally taken a positive step.

As for myself, I was feeling kind of numb. Some little voice in the back of my head told me that I was about to step into a world of shit, but I didn't want to listen to it. I knew that the reality was going to hit me in the face soon enough; I didn't want to give it any more time in my head than I had to. I had just spent the better part of two years at a military college, I had a pretty good idea what was coming. I knew that Marine boot camp would be far worse than the hazing of freshmen in Texas A&M's Corps of Cadets, but then it wouldn't last for nine months either.

Besides, there wasn't much I could do about it.

Chapter 8

Shadows

My father's intense identification with the Marine Corps shaped my childhood. I was indoctrinated in things Marine from an early age, and my view of manhood was indelibly chiseled in the form of the disciplined, steel-willed Marine. The Marine Corps is a unique culture—everything in the Marine Corps has its own unique approach, its own language, its own meaning. I grew up inundated in Marine rules like "Take all you want but eat all you take", Marine rituals like having my fingernails inspected before meals, and Marine values like never submitting to fear, standing up for the powerless and forever pushing to expand my personal limits.

They say that there is no such thing as an ex-Marine, and my father was a living example. From his grooming to his personal bearing to the discipline with which he worked, he continued to abide by the best of the Marine culture. He had no respect for a man who had poor posture, poor hygiene or poor character.

This was my life with my father. I was not permitted to have bad posture; I had to eat everything on my plate; and I knew that there was only the Marine Corps and the other services.

Chapter 9

Rites of Passage

Aside from my childhood indoctrination, my introduction to the Marine Corps began with the meeting with the recruiter when I signed up. I had received a 1-Y draft status because of knee surgery a year earlier. The 1-Y classification was a temporary status, usually a prelude to getting classified 4-F—permanently unfit for duty. I was due for another physical to determine whether I would be classified 4-F, but the recruiter wasn't concerned; he assured me they could take care of any difficulties with passing the physical. He was more interested in getting me to sign up for more years.

"I can get you aviation. You'll be on the best posts in the Marine Corps, eating the best chow and sleeping in the best beds. No slogging through the mud."

I explained that I was satisfied with the brief, two year enlistment that had been developed to provide extra troops for the escalating war in Vietnam.

He shook his head solemnly and said, "There's only one place you're going with a two-year hitch, and that's infantry and Vietnam."

I shrugged my shoulders like I didn't care, but the truth was I would have considered a longer enlistment in order to get into the infantry and Vietnam. Why else would any fool join the Marines in 1966? As far as I was concerned, being in the infantry was the only genuine form of being a Marine.

A few weeks later, after I'd gone home and told my parents, I went to Houston for a follow-up appointment with the Marine recruiter there. They put me in a staff car and a corporal drove me to the office of an orthopedic physician. I filled out some forms in the waiting room and then they took me into an office. The doctor came in and told me to take off my pants. While I was removing my jeans, he asked, "Which knee did you have the surgery on?" I showed him the scar on my left knee.

He gripped my leg and started pushing and pulling on it while he continued to ask questions.

"It used to pop out on you?"

"Yes, Sir."

"Had any trouble with it since then?"

"No, Sir."

"Does this hurt?"

"No, Sir."

"How about this?"

"No, Sir."

He nodded, said "Okay", turned away and filled out a form. Then he handed the form to me and said, "Give this to the corporal in the waiting room." That was all there was to it, no x-rays or fancy tests. The whole examination lasted about two minutes.

After that, I got on a plane and flew to New Orleans where my dad was on a business trip. I was nineteen years old and could legally drink in Louisiana because the age limit there was eighteen. So my dad took me out on the town. First, we went out for a lobster dinner, and then we hit Bourbon Street for some grownup drinking. I did okay after my first Hurricane at Pat O'Brien's, so I insisted I could handle another.

I got so drunk I could barely stand up.

I ended up with my dad holding me up by the shoulders while I puked that lovely lobster dinner into the street. Then we walked slowly back to the hotel, with my dad holding my shoulders and telling me to "just take deep breaths". He made me brush my teeth and clean up a bit in the hotel room. I felt a little better, but when I went to bed, the room was spinning wildly and I started getting nauseous again. My dad had me put a foot on the floor to stop the bed from spinning, and somehow I eventually went to sleep.

Chapter 10

Shadows

Before I departed for boot camp, my dad had a talk with me. I remember his last words. "Remember, Son, thousands of guys have made it through boot camp. They weren't any tougher than you. The hardest part is in your mind. If you know you can do it, then it's just a matter of putting one foot in front of the other."

I reflected on that thought more than once during the months to come.

Chapter 11

Boot Camp

Boot camp was not all that bad, considering its intimidating reputation. I already knew how to march and do the military thing, and, for the most part, I wasn't really too intimidated. I had experience as both an underclassman and an upperclassman in the Corps of Cadets at Texas A&M, so I had been on both ends of the military status thing. I understood the game. You act like the guy giving the orders is passing on God's word from on high. Many guys seem to experience that as demeaning, but it serves a purpose. You just do what you're told, and the guy giving the orders accepts responsibility for what you do. That's actually an appealing setup for a lot of people in this world.

Even though the guy giving the orders often yells at you, it's not really personal. That's a lesson the Marines are particularly good at teaching, but I had already learned it at A&M. Of course, they are a bit tricky in the way they teach this lesson, and it started as soon as we got off the bus.

"Stand on the yellow footsteps. What the fuck are you doing, you idiot? That's a right footstep and that's a left. Didn't your mother teach you the difference between your right and your left? What kind of mother would not teach her son the difference between right and left? What else did she leave out of your education? Did she let you go to the bathroom by yourself? Are you toilet trained?"

We were labeled on the basis of our most superficial appearances—our race, weight, height, accents, haircuts, blemishes, whether we wore glasses. The lesson was clear; this man doing the yelling didn't know anything about me; so he was just trying to find something that would get to me. Unfortunately, some guys didn't get that and would take it personally when the drill instructors focused on them.

Another reason that I was not too intimidated was because my dad had been a drill instructor. I knew he was basically a good man, and so I figured the same was true of the men in charge of us. They yell at you because that's their job. You try to do exactly what they want, of course, but you don't take it too seriously that you're being yelled at.

During that first week of being examined, prodded and probed, they gave us a battery of intellectual tests. I received the high score in my platoon, and that resulted in my being assigned the position of "schoolteacher". I coached the guys who were struggling with the academic side of boot camp, especially the required test on the U.S. Constitution. Every time we took a break, it was my job to step out of formation and read aloud from a set of papers I carried inside my shirt. Sometimes I took the guys who were struggling aside, and we would have a question and answer session.

"Who wrote the Declaration of Independence?" "What are the first ten amendments called?"

Virtually all of the guys who had a hard time with this had dropped out of school at a young age. One guy named Jimmy Smith hadn't finished eighth grade, but he had worked as a construction supervisor. He was obviously plenty smart about how to do things, but he had great difficulty memorizing verbal material. He probably had an undiagnosed learning disability. He worked really hard at learning the material, but it was painful to watch him struggle so much with stuff that was so elementary to everyone else. He and I spent many hours drilling on the same questions over and over. When Jimmy finally passed the test, the whole platoon cheered. We were all proud of him.

It would be crazy to say I enjoyed boot camp, but there were some things I liked about it. I was finally on a par with my peers. I had been tall for a couple of years, but I was awfully skinny the way I shot up overnight in high school. During the year prior to entering the Marine Corps, I finally began to fill out and put on some muscle. I was still skinny but I could hold my own in physical tasks. I even excelled at some of the physical challenges of boot camp. I always liked climbing and swinging on things, so I looked forward to the obstacle course.

One day on the drill field, our platoon made a number of mistakes in close order drill. Sergeant Gorman started yelling at us, "I don't think you people are motivated. Maybe we can help you find some motivation tonight."

That sounded ominous. Sure enough, after dinner we

picked up our M14's and Staff Sergeant Gorman and Sergeant Bailey marched us over to a big empty gymnasium. We filed inside and then formed ranks in the middle of the gym floor. Then Sergeant Gorman stood in front of us.

"I saw a lack of motivation in this platoon today on the drill field. A lack of motivation! I don't like to see my platoons lose motivation; it makes me feel like we're not making progress, like maybe we should transfer the whole bunch of you to Motivation Platoon. But Sergeant Bailey and I didn't want to start over with a new bunch of recruits, so we decided to bring you over here for a little extra dose of close order drill motivation."

"Platoon, Tench Hut."

Right Shoulder, Arms."

"Right Face,"

"For Ward, Harch."

"To the rear, Harch."

"To the rear, Harch."

And on it went. Close order drill is kind of cool when everyone gets it right; you move around like a perfectly functioning machine. Unfortunately, there is only one way to do it right and a whole lot of ways to screw it up. The harder they pushed us, such as taking only one step in one direction before being ordered to reverse direction, the more mistakes we made. This went on for about an hour until one particularly fast set of changes had us all turned around and bumping into each other.

Sergeant Gorman started yelling, "Whoa, whoa, whoa, just stop, you bunch of uncoordinated morons. Just stop where you are." He yelled at the top of his voice, "Freeze", and everyone froze.

Then his voice got softer, "I told Sergeant Bailey you poor things must be getting tired. Is that it, are you getting tired?"

"No sir!" we all yelled.

"I can't hear you; I guess you are getting tired. Is that right?"

"No sir!" we all yelled again, louder.

"Good, then I'm sure you are ready to do some double time." He paused, "Well, are you ready to do some double time?"

"Yes Sir." we all chorused.

"All right, Everyone, rifles over your head, arms extended. Now, start running in place. Let's go, I want to see those knees in the air."

We held our rifles over our heads and started jogging in place. Then they turned us and we started running laps around the gym. Now holding your rifle above your head, your arms go numb and weak in no time, and this probably affects your whole circulatory system. Before we had gone half a dozen laps, a guy passed out.

Sergeant Gorman yelled at us to just run around him, and Sergeant Bailey dragged him into the center of the gym floor. Soon guys started collapsing all over the place, within minutes there were more guys on the floor than on their feet. But most of them were not really passed out unconscious. They didn't just smack the floor with their faces; they just sort of swooned and fell, usually catching themselves on their hands. This was not the same as passing out; it was more of a decision to quit trying. I'm sure the drill instructors knew the difference, but they didn't seem to care. They just kept pulling all the guys into the center of the room.

I started thinking about when I would swoon and fall. At the same time, I found myself doing the same thing I always did when running long distances. I would make deals with myself about making it just a little further. I would decide I could make one more lap before I gave it up, so I would make that lap and then I would decide I could do another one more. My arms were totally numb but somehow they stayed up there and I kept going. After a few minutes, there were only two other guys running with me. Then, on the same lap, they both gave out and I was the only one still on my feet.

I understood that crapping out was psychological. If you didn't really pass out, then the decision to give up was arbitrary. Whenever you chose to do it, you could have gone a little bit further. I kept going. I did a couple more laps, then Sergeant Bailey had me stop and run in place. My rate of jogging had gotten very slow and I wasn't lifting my knees the way they liked, but I was still going. Sergeant Bailey finally ordered me to stop jogging and go to "order arms" and stand at ease. I lowered my rifle and tried to snap it over to where the stock is on the ground and my right hand holds the end of the barrel between my fingers. But the rifle just slid on through the fingers of my numb right hand and fell clattering onto the floor.

One thing you never do is drop your rifle.

Sergeant Bailey said, "Well, you almost had that one, Catherall. Almost." He stepped toward me and said, "But close only counts in horseshoes and hand grenades."

"Yes sir."

"Pick up your rifle, numbey."

"Aye, aye, sir."

I didn't have the most glorious ending, but at least I had remained on my feet through the crap-out session. I knew I wasn't any stronger than anyone else; it was simply that "crapping out" is more of a psychological mechanism than a physical one, and I guess my stubbornness got activated. I view the whole experience of Marine boot camp as more of a psychological challenge than a physical one—unless you're in really bad shape.

Finally, I was not the smallest kid, the last one chosen or the first to strike out. In fact, I had it relatively easy. The drill instructors tended to pick out a few individuals to heap their abuse upon, mostly as a lesson to the rest of us. They usually picked the smallest guys, the least athletic, the fat guys, the uncoordinated ones who couldn't march, and the ones with an attitude. I was big enough, athletic enough, coordinated enough, and most importantly, I knew enough not to piss off the drill instructors—they never singled me out for abuse.

Chapter 12

Shadows

My dad used to take me out to the dump where we would set up tin cans and shoot them from various distances with the .22 rifle. He taught me how to shoot accurately—centering the target on my sights, taking a breath, blowing half of it out, and then gently squeezing with my whole hand so that the trigger got pulled along the way.

On one of our shooting forays he found a small glass ashtray and set it on top of a post. Then he walked back to where I was, a long ways away. He said, "Let's see you hit that ashtray."

I squinted at the post and said, "Daddy, it's so small I can't even see it. There's no way I can shoot it."

He snorted at me and said, "You don't have to be able to see it to hit it; you just have to know where it is. Let me see the rifle."

I handed him the rifle and he lay down prone. He aimed, there was a moment of silence, and then the rifle fired.

The ashtray exploded into a cloud of tiny fragments of glass. I stood there with my mouth open; I didn't know that such a thing was possible.

After that, I knew better than to tell my dad that something couldn't be done.

Chapter 13

Every Marine is a Marksman

One curious thing about boot camp was that I couldn't see most of what I was shown there. Literally. I wore contact lenses for the year previous to entering the Marine Corps, and when I arrived at the Marine Corps Recruit Depot, they made me remove my contacts and send them home. They said contact lenses were too vulnerable to dust and other problems, and that I would have to wear glasses.

When I had my eye exam, the doctor explained that I would have to wait several weeks before I could be fitted for glasses because my eyes needed to readjust after wearing the contacts. So I went through six or seven weeks of boot camp unable to see any distant details. This didn't actually pose much of a problem for most things, like close order drill or running the obstacle course. It was when I sat in a class and had to see charts or a blackboard—things like a picture of the inner workings of the .45 pistol—that I couldn't see. At first, I would say something and be allowed to sit up close in the classes, but I soon gave up on that because I still couldn't see—even from the front row.

It didn't seem to interfere with my being able to learn what I needed to learn.

About the sixth week of boot camp, we went to the rifle range. We would live there for two weeks while we learned the art of marksmanship. I began to get agitated. I had been fitted for glasses but I still had not received them. I sure wasn't going to be able to shoot a rifle without them. Fortunately, I still had some time after we arrived at the rifle range. You learn to shoot in the Marine Corps by spending a full week "snapping in" before you ever put a bullet in the rifle. First they teach you how to use the sling of the rifle to stabilize it, then you spend days snapping in—standing, sitting, kneeling and laying prone for hours in the sand while you aim at a post. All the instructor does is walk around and correct your posture.

My glasses arrived while we were snapping in.

You spend the second week firing live ammo at the rifle range. Again, you fire from the various postures, starting with firing in the prone position from a distance of five hundred meters.

Then you move closer for the other positions. At 500 meters, you cannot see the bullseye on the target; in fact, you can barely see the target at all. But if you center the whole target on your front sight, and you hold the rife perfectly steady, you can still hit the target in the bull—if you're firing a reliable weapon like the M14. We practiced with live ammo all week, then on Thursday we went through a practice test of scoring our shooting to determine whether we would qualify as marksman. Friday we would repeat the qualification process for real.

Marksmanship is a very big thing in the Marine Corps. There are three levels of qualification for marksmanship: Marksman, Sharpshooter and Expert. I was shooting well all week, so I had my eye on winning that Expert badge. On Thursday, I got the highest score in the platoon—well into the Expert range and just four points off a perfect score.

I was psyched.

Then on Friday I choked and missed Expert by one point. I was glad to get a sharpshooter badge, but I knew I could shoot Expert and the only reason I hadn't was because I couldn't handle the pressure. I lost all my points on the standing position; I had still hit ten out of ten bullseyes from 500 meters in the prone position.

I felt like I did as a kid when I kept striking out after my first home run. Would I ever stop choking? And what about when it really counted, like when someone was shooting back at me?

Chapter 14

Shadows

The Marine Corps has a tradition of awarding the top graduate from boot camp with the title of honorman.. My dad was honorman in his platoon when he went through boot camp. Towards the end of boot camp, they start putting the top recruit in charge of the other recruits. So he must be strong enough to take charge and get the others to do what he tells them to do. Some of that involves being tough enough to back up your orders with a physical presence. My dad was 6'3" and was physically intimidating enough.

He joined the Marine Corps early in 1943, a period when the overall size of the Corps was expanding drastically to deal with the demands of World War II. They were short on experienced personnel and occasionally took an exceptional recruit and promoted him into a position that far exceeded his level of training. As soon as my father completed boot camp, he was made a drill instructor and started taking new recruits through boot camp. He served as one of two junior drill instructors under Gunnery Sergeant Ryse, who had been his own drill instructor when he was a boot. After two cycles as a junior drill instructor, my dad became a senior drill instructor. My mother moved to San Diego and they settled into life as a stateside Marine family.

Chapter 15

Honorman

By the time we returned from the rifle range, I was doing so well that I started entertaining fantasies of becoming honorman. The path to honorman is to first be appointed a squad leader and from there to right guide, which you then have to be able to hold onto through the end of boot camp. The drill instructors usually experiment with several different people as squad leaders and right guide before they settle on their final choices. Those guys all get a PFC stripe at graduation from boot camp.

The right guide marches at the head of the rightmost file when the troops are in formation. Everyone else is supposed to match their stride and their speed to his. The three squad leaders march at the head of the three columns to the left of the right guide, so the front rank of the formation is composed of the three squad leaders and the right guide.

I was made a squad leader while we were at the rifle range.

At the rifle range, each squad had an ammo can full of materials for cleaning our rifles and we had to have that can with us wherever we went with our rifles, which was practically everywhere. Sergeant Bailey, in his drill instructor wisdom, decided the squad leaders should each carry the ammo cans for their squad. This was supposed to teach us the importance of keeping our weapons clean. As if that wasn't bad enough, Sergeant Bailey was obsessed with running. He was an exercise fanatic, one of the few people in the Marine Corps to score a perfect 500 on the physical exam. Not only did we run back and forth to the range every day, but he liked to take us out in the evening and just go for a long run—with our rifles, of course, which meant we had to bring the cleaning materials. Not that we were going to shoot the rifles and actually need the cleaning materials or anything like that, this was just an object lesson typical of Marine Corps mentality.

So we spent our time at the rifle range running with our rifles. Everyone in the platoon ran with their rifles held at an angle across their chests—known as port arms—except the three squad leaders in the front rank. We three—I was the one next to the right guide—each ran with our rifle slung from our right shoulder and an ammo can hanging from our left hand. That can kept banging against my leg and bumping into the squad leader to my left. After several days of this, we all had bruises on our thighs. I think this was the only time in boot camp that being a squad leader constituted a form of punishment.

Still, I was a squad leader and we only stayed at the range for two weeks before we returned to San Diego. That's about when the fantasies started up. Then, one morning shortly after our return, Sergeant Bailey removed the fellow serving as right guide and put me in his place. This was getting close to the end of our training—all I had to do was hold onto the position for the few remaining weeks and I would graduate as honorman. My fantasy blossomed, and I imagined inviting my parents to the graduation ceremony.

The fantasy lasted less than an hour. After breakfast, we marched over to the base store where I was left in charge while Sergeant Bailey went off for a few minutes. My job was to monitor how many guys went into the store at a time; I was to make sure that everyone got their turn without overcrowding the store. One guy came to me after his turn and asked to go back in because he had forgotten to get something. I exercised my new authority and let him go.

Sergeant Bailey returned and asked, "Catherall, is everyone present and accounted for?"

I replied, "Sir, all but one, he's still in the store, Sir."

Sergeant Bailey frowned and walked over to where I was standing. In a deceptively casual tone, he asked, "And why is he still in the store, Catherall?"

"Sir, he forgot to get toothpaste, Sir."

Now Sergeant Bailey got right up in front of me. He stood about five feet, five inches tall and had to tilt his head back so that he could properly glare at me out from under his Smokey the Bear hat. His tone was even quieter.

"He forgot to get toothpaste. And how would you know what he forgot to get, Recruit?"

Uh oh, now I saw it coming. "Uh, Sir, because he came to me after his turn and told me, Sir."

Now Sergeant Bailey adopted that super sweet tone that indicated that what he was saying was not to be interpreted as what he was saying. "So you, Recruit Catherall, decided to change the program and give him a second turn back into the store. How nice."

Then he yelled at me at the top of his lungs, "Who fucking put you in charge of my Marine Corps?"

I stared hard at the horizon and answered loudly, "Sir, no one, Sir."

"Then who the fuck told you that you could give people extra turns because they were too fucking stupid to get what they needed when they went through?"

"Sir, no one, Sir."

Then he lowered his voice, which was somehow more ominous than the yelling. "Then give me one reason why I should keep you as right guide."

I continued to stare hard at the horizon and said nothing because I could think of no reason why he should do anything to confirm my worth as a human being, much less allow me to continue as right guide. He continued to stare at me for a while just to make sure I felt sufficiently stupid. My ability to remember that it wasn't personal wasn't holding up so well right then.

Finally, he said, "Okay, Numbey, back in the ranks."

I not only lost the right guide position, but I didn't even get to return to being squad leader. So much for my fantasy.

Chapter 16

Shadows

My dad worked as a traveling salesman and was gone from Monday to Friday most weeks. I lived for when he would come home because I always wanted to do stuff with him. Yet it seemed that soon after he appeared, he would find something wrong with what I was doing. I didn't stand up straight enough. I came to the dinner table with dirty fingernails. I didn't eat everything on my plate. If I had done something really bad, like break something or fail to do a chore, then he would confront me.

"Don, didn't I tell you to get your fishing tackle out of the garage so we could get the car in there?"

"Yes Sir."

"Well, I just went in there and the corner is full of cane poles."

I stood mute.

"Well, what do you have to say for yourself?"

I muttered, "I forgot to do it."

"You always forget to do it. Forgetting is no excuse. I think everything we tell you goes in one ear and out the other."

"Yes Sir."

"Well, what are you going to do now?"

I didn't know what to say, so I just stood there and looked at my feet.

"Look at me when I'm talking to you, young man."

I looked up at him, "Yes Sir."

"Go put that stuff away. Right now!"

"Yes Sir."

At Texas A&M, underclassmen had only four answers they could give upperclassmen: "Yes Sir"; "No Sir"; "No excuse, Sir"; and a lengthy way of saying "I don't know, Sir." I was a proper cadet long before I ever reached the campus.

Chapter 17

Choking Again

During the final weeks of boot camp, we began to be assigned duties that were more like some of the things we would be doing after graduation. One of these was a turn as a sentry, guarding empty warehouses from enemy agents. I was doing my sentry gig, walking back and forth in the dark, when Sergeant Bailey appeared with an older man. This man was several inches taller than me; he had broad shoulders, a lean, flat stomach, and he stood straight as a flagpole.

He looked a lot like my dad.

When they came closer, I saw that he was wearing gold bars—he was a lieutenant. Since he was older, I presume he was a mustang—an enlisted man who had worked his way up to become an officer. This was the first time I encountered a Marine officer.

The lieutenant came up in front of me and I came to attention, holding my rifle in the proscribed position that constitutes attention when bearing arms. The lieutenant stared straight into my eyes and asked, "What's your fourth general order, sentry?"

There are twelve general orders for sentries, things like "I will walk my post in a military manner." and "I will not quit my post until properly relieved." As the schoolteacher in the platoon, I had these things memorized backwards and forwards. So when the officer asked me to recite a general order, no problem. All I had to do was spit it out.

But instead of spitting it right out, I just stood there staring at him. I went completely brain dead. I could not even open my mouth to start the sentence, "Sir, my fourth general order is—".

I just stood there and stared at him. He asked me about a different general order, but I was still unable to fire up a single neuron.

He gave me another moment, and then he just wheeled around and walked off without saying a word. But Sergeant Bailey was at no loss for words—his were brief and exquisitely to the point. He stepped up and whispered in my ear, "Catherall, you suck", with emphasis on the "suck". Then he walked off after the lieutenant.

As soon as they left, I remembered my fourth general order. But mainly, I just felt like an idiot. I figured Sergeant Bailey had told the lieutenant he was going to show him one of his sharper men, since he knew that I had all the "academic" stuff down stone cold. Instead, he showed the lieutenant one of his more dysfunctional idiots. I had let him down and I was disappointed in myself as well—a familiar feeling.

No matter how much I seemed to improve, some things refused to change.

Part II

War

Chapter 18

Historical Note

On November 22, 1943, the Second Marine Division made the Marine Corps' first large amphibious landing against a strongly defended beach. The island's name was Tarawa, a tiny 300-acre atoll surrounded by coral reefs. They conducted the landing with two kinds of landing craft. The largest number of men were in the old "Higgins boat", those open shoeboxes that pull up on the beach. The leading wave was in a newer type of landing craft, the amphibious tractor or amtrac, a boat with tracks that would allow the craft to climb over the reefs. The plan was for the amtracs to return from the beach and ferry more men ashore, while the Higgins boats would float over the reefs at higher water points.

The Marines learned valuable lessons in this large amphibious assault. Unfortunately, lessons learned in combat are always costly. The first lesson the Marines learned was that the heavy pre-landing bombardment did practically no damage to the Japanese positions. The Japanese had been building up their emplacements on the islands in the Pacific for years. Many of their pillboxes and blockhouses had fortified walls six feet thick and were impervious to anything less than a direct hit from a very large piece of ordnance.

At Tarawa, the Marines also learned what it means to land on a fiercely defended beach held by a foe who is committed to win or die trying. There is no retreating from an amphibious assault. Either you succeed or you die.

Another important lesson learned at Tarawa involved the use of the landing craft. The amtracs managed to get most of the first wave of Marines to the beach but there was no ferry service. As soon as their bows touched the sand the amtracs became easy targets; most of them were hit and disabled at the water's edge. Few amtracs ever left the beach. The plan for the Higgins boats to float over the coral reefs ran into even uglier reality. The Higgins boats were unable to get across the reefs; many hung up as far as 500 yards from shore. The gear-laden Marines had to climb over the sides into neck-deep water and slowly slog their way to shore holding their weapons above them. The Japanese had an unimpeded field of highly visible, slow-moving targets. The

Marines from the boats that hung up the farthest out were easy targets in the water for as long as an hour.

The Japanese defenders poured a steady stream of heavy machine gun and mortar fire into the long line of men loaded down and wading through the water. The closer they got to shore, the better targets they provided the Japanese gunners. The men on shore and in observation planes overhead watched in horror as this slaughter continued through much of the day.

There was never a break in the fighting during the 76 hours that it took the Marines to capture Tarawa—they slept little or not at all. The Marine Corps made this assault with a single reinforced division and lost over a thousand men and another twenty-five hundred wounded.

The Japanese had regarded Tarawa as impregnable and its fall was a major blow to their morale. But it was equally regarded as a disaster by the American public—they were shocked by the newspaper photos of bloody beaches and dead Marines floating in the water. The costly lessons of Tarawa galvanized the Marine Corps to develop new strategies before they would assault another heavily fortified island surrounded by barrier reefs.

The First Marine Division established their reputation early in the war when they persevered against a fiercely resistant Japanese force to take the island of Guadalcanal. But the landing on Guadalcanal was uncontested. The only casualty was a Marine who cut his hand trying to open a coconut with a machete. The division's next big landing was nearly a year later—at Cape Gloucester in New Britain. Again, the resistance was deeper into the island. Only twenty-one Marines were killed on D-Day at Cape Gloucester. The Second, Third and Fourth Marine Divisions made numerous landings after Tarawa, but none were mounted against a beachhead as heavily defended as Tarawa.

On September 15, 1944, three months after the landing at Normandy in the European theater and almost a year after the Second Division's battle at Tarawa, the First Marine Division made an amphibious assault on a heavily defended coral atoll surrounded by barrier reefs. This time, the entire landing force arrived in amtracs—no more Higgins boats. Nor did they bring a bunch of photojournalists; they didn't want to publicize another potential slaughter.

This assault received little publicity back in the states. To this day, many Americans do not know of this island and the battle to take it. Yet there are those who say that this was the fiercest battle of the Pacific island campaigns. The First Marine Division awarded nineteen Medals of Honor during World War II. Eight of those Medals of Honor were awarded for actions on this small island, more than any other campaign in the Pacific theater, including Guadalcanal, New Britain and Okinawa.

The name of the island was Peleliu.

Chapter 19

Hearts and Minds

I stepped out of the cabin of the plane into a sensory onslaught. Heat waves hanging over the baking concrete of the Danang airstrip severely distorted the images of the crowded lines of F4 jets, helicopters, and huge transports. They looked like shimmering pictures on some outdated piece of film; it was difficult to believe they were real. The noise was relentless; I could barely hear a human voice over the whine of the jets and the punctuated roar of the helicopters flying overhead. Worst of all was trying to breathe. I felt like I was drowning as I took in the stifling hot, humid air, heavy with the smell of diesel fuel and burning rubber. Stepping from the cool atmosphere of the plane into that air was like taking a physical blow. Already my clothes stuck to my skin like I'd walked into a steam room fully clothed.

The whole situation was surreal.

Our commercial airliner looked very out of place in the sea of green and brown camouflaged warplanes. And I felt just as out of place. We were replacement troops. We wore the same green as everyone else, but the similarity stopped there, for we were green on the inside, and it was obvious. The men who scurried about at their tasks wore faded jungle boots and jungle utilities with their shirts hanging outside their pants. Most of all, they didn't have the look of scared and lost children. They moved about with confidence, while we stood around in a group and waited to be told whether to sit or stand.

One of the NCO's yelled at us to pick up our seabags. We scrambled through the pile of green bags, each us of searching for the one stamped with our name. I found my seabag, heaved it onto my shoulder and, again following orders, walked over to a Quonset hut where we laid them back down, no longer in a pile. Then we lined up before a folding table that was parked outside the door. A corporal sat at the desk and was sorting through our orders as we handed them to him. As each Marine reached the table, the corporal would take that individual's papers and staple a new page on top. Then he stamped the paper and directed the individual somewhere behind him. As we got closer to the table, I realized he was alternately stamping our papers for the First Marine Division or the Third Marine Division.

I had no idea what difference it might make if I went to one division or the other. But it made a difference to me. I was well acquainted with the blue and red Guadalcanal patch with the big numeral 1—it adorned the sleeve of my father's uniform that continued to hang in the back of the hall closet—and it was on the cover of that big green book in our living room. I counted down the people in front of me and discerned that I was due to be assigned to the ThirdMarDiv. So I turned around and spoke to the guy behind me.

"Hey, do you mind if we trade places?"

He looked at me suspiciously, "How come?"

I said, "Well, he's sending every other guy to the First Division, and that's where I want to go."

He continued his suspicious look, "How come?"

I said, "My old man was in the First Division….So I want to be in the same outfit."

He shrugged and said, "Okay", and we traded places in line.

This arbitrary action caused me to go south from Danang to

the Seventh Marine Regiment in Chu Lai, while the guys assigned to the ThirdMarDiv went further north. It seemed like the heaviest action was occurring in the north, near the DMZ, so the guy behind me may have ended up in a worse situation.

I left the airbase in the rear of a truck—a six-by— traveling down Highway One to Chu Lai with several other new troops. A staff sergeant hitched a ride on the truck, and he was enjoying his seniority over a bunch of FNGs.

"Just got off the plane, didn't you. You guys still smell like soap, like your mamas just gave you a big old bath." He pinched one guy on the cheek, "Soft as a baby's ass. Don't they even train you guys outdoors anymore?"

He was smiling as he spoke but I didn't know whether I was supposed to smile back or not. He told us stories and went on about how dangerous the place was. I noticed he was wearing a clean uniform, and his boots weren't faded like some of the guys I'd seen at the airstrip. I wondered about the veracity of his stories and his point of view. Still, it was nice to have a guide. He introduced us to the countryside. It was amazingly green, more shades of green than I had ever seen before—rice paddies everywhere and tree-covered mountains in the distance further inland.

The whole picture was foreign, not just another place but a whole other world. We kept passing peasants clothed in black pajamas and big conical straw hats. Some of them were on bicycles and motor bikes, but most were out working in the rice paddies, standing barefoot in the water with their trouser legs rolled up. I saw a couple of old women whose teeth were completely black. They were smoking short cigars and they looked pregnant.

I said, "Look at those old women with the black teeth. They look pregnant."

The staff sergeant laughed and said, "They ain't pregnant. They're just fulla shit." He laughed at his own joke and said, "They got the worms, intestinal parasites, that's why they got those guts on 'em." He smiled at me and added, "And their teeth are black from chewing betel nut. Real pretty, huh?"

I grimaced and tried to focus on the kids; they looked a lot healthier than most of the adults. One young boy was riding on top of a water buffalo and wielding a switch to direct the animal. He looked like he was having the time of his life. Maybe life wasn't so miserable for everyone here.

As we passed through one region, the staff sergeant told us how some of our South Korean allies—the ROK soldiers—had recently been ambushed there.

"Yeah, about two weeks ago a ROK convoy got hit right along here. Command-detonated mine." He waved his arm at the field of rice paddies. "There were gooks all over the field there—no way the ROKs could tell who set that mine off."

He gave us an intense look and said, "So you know what those ROKs did?" He paused, making sure he had our full attention, "They blew away every gook in sight. They opened up on 'em and killed every swinging dick. They even killed the water buffalo and the geese in the ditch."

He shook his head in admiration, "You don't fuck with those ROK soldiers."

No one said anything; we all just stared at the peasants in the rice paddies. This whole world was different, and that included us as much as them.

Eventually, we stopped on the outskirts of a village, and

several local Vietnamese approached the truck. They were trying to sell cokes and bread and various goods. It was the first time I had seen them up close and heard them talk their strange sounding language. They would start a sentence in a normal tone and then get louder and end the sentence with a higher tone—like they were asking a question. One old gray haired woman climbed up on the side of the truck and was waving a mirror around that she had for sale. She didn't speak English and she was talking loudly in Vietnamese as she waved her mirror at us. She had climbed up near the cab, right in front of the staff sergeant. He started yelling at her.

"I don't want your shit, Mamasan, get off my truck."

She didn't seem to understand and just kept squawking at him. He said, "I said get the fuck off my truck, you old bitch." He waved his arms at her and yelled, "Off, off, off!"

She just kept up her sales pitch. Then he reached out, put his hand in the middle of her chest and shoved. She fell backward off the truck and landed flat on her back, hard. She laid there for a moment, then she got up and limped off without looking back.

I felt like a complete jerk. I was pissed as hell, and I wanted to say something really angry to this sonofabitch, but I was scared to start anything with a staff sergeant. Staff sergeants were minor gods during my training, and I was still afraid of them.

Several of the villagers had watched the old lady get knocked from the truck. No one said or did anything but I felt their eyes on us. I felt guilty and embarrassed; I was disgusted with this abusive man and with myself as well. We were supposed to be there to help these people. This was the first time in my life that I had ever seen an elderly person treated with that kind of contempt.

This couldn't have been the way American troops treated the civilians in World War II. I had seen the pictures of Americans liberating towns in Europe and being warmly greeted by grateful civilians. Wasn't that the way it was supposed to be here? But when I thought about it, I had also seen film of natives throwing their children and themselves off of cliffs on Saipan. The narrator of that film explained that the natives chose to die rather than submit to the Marines because the Japanese told them that the Marines would torture them. I always just accepted that explanation; now I wondered if there could have been more to the story.

In our training, we had been told that our goal in Vietnam was to win the hearts and minds of the people. That sergeant sure didn't care about winning over the people. To him, the people were dirt.

I wondered how common that attitude was.

As we drove off from our little rest stop, I couldn't get my mind off that old woman. Where must her sympathies lie in this war?

Chapter 20

Shadows

In late spring of 1944, my dad's tenure as a drill instructor ended and he shipped out to the Pacific. He was assigned to the First Marine Division, which had lost many men in the battles for Guadalcanal and Cape Gloucester (New Britain). The division was pulled back from combat and rebuilding with new personnel and supplies. They were bivouacked on the island of Pavuvu, not far from Guadalcanal, and preparing to start intensive training for amphibious landings.

The ability of the division to perform well in combat was compromised by the heavy losses they'd taken, forcing them to add large numbers of inexperienced troops. This made the veterans very valuable. My dad came in with these inexperienced troops, but he had been a drill instructor and, consequently, he was assigned to the cadre of instructors helping to train the new troops in amphibious assaults. He knew nothing about amphibious operations, but in typical Marine Corps fashion, he trained others even as he was learning about it himself.

Living conditions on Pavuvu were poor. The Marines lived in small tents and the wet ground was a perpetual mudhole infested with land crabs, rats and endless mosquitoes. Dysentery was epidemic and many of the men, including my father, acquired malaria on Pavuvu.

But they were getting a rare opportunity to acclimate to the hot, humid climate; they had enough to eat; and no one was shooting at them. Relatively speaking, Pavuvu was a piece of paradise.

Chapter 21

Disgusting Conditions

I stood my first 'hole watch' at battalion headquarters—manning a bunker on the perimeter. As soon as it started getting dark, I was engulfed in a thick swarm of mosquitoes. They were all over me. I would reach up to swat them, and my hand would crush several at once and then smear blood across my face. They were so thick in the air around my head that I couldn't breathe in without sucking mosquitoes into my nose. I tried to breathe shallowly, but it was suffocating. I wanted to scream. By an hour after sundown, my face was swollen from bites all over it. The mosquitoes slowed down then. They were probably all so engorged with my blood by that point that they were too heavy to fly off and tell their friends that they'd found the mother lode of A positive.

I began to relax a bit. Maybe the worst was over. The mosquitoes hadn't disappeared entirely, but I no longer felt like a glazed donut abandoned on an anthill. There was no moon, and it was extremely dark. I couldn't see a thing, so I sat down crosslegged in front of the sandbag bunker where I could peer into the darkness over the rice paddies in front of me. Suddenly, I heard something hissing very close. I literally jumped up and backwards onto the bunker in one move. I crouched down and pointed my rifle towards whatever was in front of the bunker. At first, I thought it was a cobra because it sounded snake-like and I could see something reared up in the air. It took me a while to make out what I was looking at in the darkness. I finally realized it was a mongoose, reared up on its hind legs and showing no fear.

I can't say the same for myself; I was petrified. When it came my turn to sleep, I didn't sleep well at all.

So passed my first night on hole watch. The thought of enduring thirteen months of that misery was very depressing.

Two nights later, I still hadn't left Battalion HQ to join the company. The company clerks offered to let me sleep in the back of the company office on a cot. It looked more comfortable than the transient tent, so I took them up on their offer. In the middle of the night, I suddenly awoke with something on my face. I reached up with my hand and grabbed a big rat that was squatting square in the middle of my face. I instinctively threw it across the room.

When it hit the floor and rolled, I could hear its companions as they squeaked and scampered about. It sounded like the floor was covered with rats! After that, I could not get back to sleep. I kept hearing the rats and imagining them climbing up onto my cot. I pulled the blanket over my head and clutched it tightly. I was hot inside the blanket, breathing the stale air I had just exhaled, but I sure as hell was not going to leave any opening for something to get inside that blanket with me.

And this was the rear; I hadn't even gotten out into the field yet. I could only imagine what yet awaited me.

Chapter 22

Shadows

My father gave me one directive before I went off to boot camp. "Don't tell them you can type. If they find out you can type, they'll make you a clerk. So just keep it to yourself."

I understood. I didn't join the Marines to become a clerk.

Chapter 23

They Also Serve

During those few days at battalion headquarters, I borrowed the use of one of the typewriters in the company office so that I could type some letters. Sergeant Rodriquez, who ran the clerical office, saw that I could type, and he recruited me to do some work for them while I was there. I was firmly entrenched in my infantry MOS (Military Occupational Specialty) so I didn't see any problem with doing their typing.

I was there for four days before it it came time for me to join the company in the field. The morning I was due to get my ride, the company First Sergeant, called me in.

Top said, "I understand you did some work for us over the last two days. We appreciate it."

I nodded, "No problem, Sir. I didn't have anything else to do. I've just been waiting to get a ride out to the company." Strictly speaking, you don't call enlisted men "Sir", but senior sergeants like Top rate a "Sir" whether the Marine Corps mandates it or not. I always called Top "Sir" and he never corrected me. More junior sergeants usually respond with, "Don't call me Sir; I work for a living."

Top nodded. "Sergeant Rodriquez tells me you're a good typist. He said you're fast and don't make many mistakes."

I smiled and shrugged, trying to be humble. I thought this was just his way of being appreciative. Aw shucks, it ain't nothing, Ma'am.

Then he said, "So I talked to the captain, and he agreed that it was a good idea for us to have a new position. We're going to call it clerk in the field." He smiled at me.

I was dumbfounded. Was he saying what I thought he was saying? I fumbled with words, "Uh, what....I mean, are you saying that you're, I mean that I'm going to be—

"Working as a company clerk but out of the combat base instead of back here. Yeah, you'll be performing clerical duties from that end. Handling the mail, typing the daily reports, that sort of thing. The skipper said it sounded like a good idea, make things work a little more smoothly between the company and the office back here."

All my infantry training didn't matter; I was going to be a pogue, a noncombatant in a bureaucratic position. Such positions are not highly valued in the Marines—candy, for example, is referred to as poguey bait.

I felt a tightness in my stomach. I had joined the Marines to serve in the infantry and see combat. But at the same time, I was beginning to appreciate that people were actually getting hurt and killed in combat. The prospect of seeing combat was not as glamorous as it seemed in the recruiter's office, and part of me was relieved to think that I was going to be in a non-combatant role.

But I also felt guilty.

So I finally headed out to the combat base, but in a much different role than I ever expected. When I arrived, the gunny assigned me to sleep in the tent with the rest of the guys from the command group—mostly the radiomen—and he showed me where to set up my clerical area to sort the mail. He was very happy to have someone to take over the mail and administrative stuff—he had been doing most of it himself. I felt like a fish out of water—or perhaps a lamb in with a pack of wolves. Not only was I a new guy—a position that never commands any respect in a combat unit—but I was a pogue in amongst the guys doing the fighting. And I was on my own; there was no group of other guys doing the same thing.

It was a lonely feeling.

Two days after I arrived, we went out on a company-sized operation. It was a minor one; we didn't use helicopters to reach the area of the operation—we just walked out from our firebase. It was not a big deal as operations go, but it was the first time I had stepped foot into the countryside of Vietnam.

We walked in single file, a line of maybe a hundred men, and I was somewhere in the middle of the file. It was very hot, and my pack weighed a ton. During one of the breaks on the first day, I complained about how hot I was. A grunt standing nearby gave me one of those looks that goes from head to toe and takes the full measure of the person. I could practically hear his thoughts categorizing me as an FNG (fucking new guy). Then he asked, "Are you wearing underwear?"

I was surprised at the question but replied, "Sure." I gave him a quizzical look and wondered where the heck this was going.

Probably to a smart-ass comment.

He smiled and said, "You're the only guy out here in underwear. That'll get you overheated faster than anything." He paused and continued watching me. When I did nothing, he said "You better get rid of 'em."

For a brief moment, I considered that he was putting me on. What a hoot to get the new guy to start removing his underwear in the midst of an operation. My dad told me of gullible new guys who were ordered to watch for the mail buoy when their ships were crossing the Pacific. But something about this guy's demeanor told me that he was not fucking with me. Still, I had difficulty rising above my civilian (i.e., civilized) state of mind.

I stammered, "Maybe I should wait until tonight. I don't want to get caught with my boots off if we start moving again."

The grunt smiled again and shook his head. "Fucking new guys." He pointed at my web belt, "Just use your bayonet. Cut 'em off. You'll get a rash if you don't."

I nodded. Then I lowered my pants and cut my underwear off and discarded the remains. Sure enough, I felt better immediately—I was still hot as hell but I didn't feel oppressed by it as I had moments earlier.

At the end of the first day, one of the radiomen went through my pack with me and helped me sort out a bunch of stuff that I shouldn't have been carrying. Since I wasn't in a squad, I'd had no squad leader to direct me in how to pack. The radioman thought it was hilarious that I had done things like actually put the C-ration box into my pack—rather than just the cans.

Obviously, I didn't know what I was doing. I felt like an idiot for only about the hundredth time since I'd arrived in-country.

The second day, we took automatic weapons fire as we were walking through tall grass. It was the first time I experienced incoming fire. The sound of the firing came from somewhere in front of me, but I had no clue where it was directed or whether we were firing at someone or being fired upon by someone. Everyone got down when we heard the sound of the firing. I squatted there and looked around me at the other Marines. There was no cover to get behind in the grass, certainly nothing solid enough to stop bullets. But none of the guys around me seemed particularly upset, so I just squatted there and waited until the situation was resolved. Soon enough, we got up and started moving again. I later heard it was incoming fire, but I never heard any of the details.

On the third day, one of the platoons went off on a patrol and returned with three VC prisoners. They were clad in black pajamas—no gear and just a couple of M2 carbines for weapons. I heard one of the grunts that escorted them to our area talking to the gunny. He said, "We looked for weapons around where they were, but all we found was those carbines. None of 'em has marks on their shoulders, so they haven't been carrying a pack any distance. They probably live nearby and waved at us when we walked past their hooches yesterday."

The gunny grunted, "Yeah, probably not NVA, just local VC. But that older one, he looks like he could be cadre or something."

I studied the one older guy; he was definitely different from the two younger VC. He didn't have that intimidated look that the other two had. I could see where he might be some kind of senior officer or something. I found myself feeling a certain respect for him; it takes balls to remain poised when you're surrounded by a hundred hostile Marines. Especially when you're about five feet tall and weigh a hundred pounds soaking wet—a condition I may appreciate better than most people.

We kept the prisoners overnight, with the intention of sending them out in a chopper the next morning. Since they were left with the command group, I was one of several people who took a turn guarding them that night. The prisoners were tied up and lying on the ground. For some reason, someone covered them up with some ponchos, and I took my turn watching the lumpy ponchos in the middle of the night. I never even looked under the pile to check on the prisoners; I just assumed all was okay.

The next morning, all three prisoners were gone.

The gunny came over to me and the two radiomen who had taken turns watching the prisoners. He said, "Those guys escaped during one of your watches."

One of the radiomen spoke up fast, "It wasn't during my watch, Gunny, I never took my eyes offa them."

The gunny snorted and looked at me, "Maybe somebody fell asleep."

Now I felt defensive!

"I didn't fall asleep, Gunny, no way. I know I didn't. Those ponchos didn't move during my watch. I mean, I didn't look under the ponchos to see if they were still in there, but…but I know I didn't fall asleep."

Shit, I was just making it worse, making it sound like maybe the guy before me lost them, or acknowledging that I should have checked on them. I stopped talking and just sat there wishing I had the good sense to keep my mouth shut.

The gunny gave another snort and walked off. No one knew when they got out or whose fault it was, and there was no more finger pointing.

It gave me a really eerie feeling to know that those three VC had managed to free themselves from their bonds and had crawled out from the center of a large group of Marines without getting caught. They might have cut a few throats on the way, but they didn't. I couldn't ignore the obvious implication: If they could crawl from the center of our perimeter to the outside, then they could do the same thing in the other direction. It was an unsettling thought.

The day before we started back to our base, some of our people took fire from the other side of a large river. It was basically harassment, since the VC didn't pose much of a threat shooting across a wide river. Our people shot back at them, but no one was in much danger of getting hit on either side. I was with the command group on higher ground back a ways from the river; we had a nice view of the whole thing. The captain called in an air strike, which was delivered by a single jet, a silver Phantom F4.

We were all lined up looking over the crest of the hill. The gunny was nearby, and he provided a running commentary.

"That's an Air Force jet; you can tell because it's unpainted....Here comes the napalm, we'll probably be able to feel the heat all the way up here."

The jet flew down over the surface of the river and dropped a long silver canister that tumbled over once and hit the surface of the water. It exploded like it had been dropped on a concrete parking lot. The napalm flared into a high sheet of flame that spread out over the surface of the river, but it didn't touch either shore. In fact, it came as close to getting our side of the river as it did to reaching the VC on the other side.

The gunny had plenty to say about that.

"Fuck, get that guy out of here! He damn near cooked our platoon. We don't need that kind of help."

The jet was called off after one run and we sat around for another fifteen minutes, with no idea what the captain had planned. Then another Phantom came by. This one was painted green and brown camouflage colors.

The gunny said, "Now that's a Marine jet. He'll know something about close air support."

The river curved away from us on our left. The Phantom made a dry run first. He came zooming down the river just about at tree height, flying out of the curve with the plane canted over on its left side, the belly pointed toward us, and then he straightened out and went roaring up into the sky.

Somebody said, "Shit, here we go again."

The gunny didn't say anything, and the captain passed the word for everyone to get down.

On his napalm run, he again came flying out of the curve on the river. This time he was tilted toward us even more prominently, his left wingtip just above the surface of the water. As soon as he made the turn, he flipped the other way and released his napalm at the same time. Now his right wingtip was close to the water, and he went flying by in front of us with his canopy pointed at us. The result of his fast flip was that the napalm canister was thrown sideways even as its momentum carried it down the river. It hit the water just short of the opposing shore and exploded into flames; its momentum then spread it far downriver, where it obliterated a long stretch of shoreline.

We took no further fire from the other side of the river.

The gunny said, "Now that's Marine flying, by God", and several guys spoke up with similar expressions of admiration.

Though dropping napalm is an act of tremendous destruction, I found that whole scene to be incredibly beautiful. The sheer power of that jet flying several hundred miles per hour right above the surface of the river and performing those maneuvers was breathtaking! I thought about the jet jockey; he didn't even have any of his buddies around to see his incredible maneuver—just a bunch of grunts who would never know his name.

The next day, we walked back to our combat base—all the way in one day. We hadn't been out long on the operation, less than a week. When we returned, my dilemma about serving in a non-combatant role was resolved for me. Captain Poole called me in and said he couldn't afford to waste an "oh-three hundred" (the number for the MOS of infantry) in a clerk position, and I was going to go to Weapons Platoon.

My MOS was 0331, machine guns, and Weapons Platoon was the usual assignment for machine gunners. The rifle platoons didn't have machine gunners of their own; they borrowed personnel from Weapons Platoon when they needed a gun team. At that point, I'd been around this captain for about a week, just barely long enough for him to get my name straight. But I took advantage of my slight familiarity and dared to speak up.

"Sir, could I make a request?"

He crossed his arms and said, "What?"

"Sir, I'd really prefer to go to one of the rifle platoons. I never much cared for the M60; I was a lot better with the M14." Actually, I was pretty fair shot with the M60, but I didn't figure he was likely to honor my request if he knew I just hated carrying the heavy machine gun.

He gave me a long look that said, "Who gives a shit what a PFC prefers?" But then he shrugged and said, "What the hell, we've got a lot of machine gunners. Go tell the gunny I said you're to go to Third Platoon."

So I almost became a clerk despite my efforts to be an infantryman, and then ended up carrying a rifle instead of that damn 25 pound machine gun. Basically, things turned out better than I could have hoped. So why wasn't I happy? This was what I wanted…wasn't it?

Chapter 24

Shadows

During the amphibious training at Pavuvu, my dad's job was to prevent accidents as much as possible. When they trained for going over the side of the troop ship to the landing craft, he constantly yelled at the men to keep their helmets unbuckled, grab the vertical ropes and not the horizontal ones, and keep up a steady pace.

In the Marines, yelling is viewed as the best way to keep a large group in tight control. A man with a deep, strong voice has a definite advantage. My dad had such a voice and knew how to use it. When he was a drill instructor, he once yelled so hard at his recruits that he broke the little flap of skin that anchors your tongue to the bottom of your mouth.

Chapter 25

My Squad

A Marine rifle company has three rifle platoons and a weapons platoon. The rifle platoons are organized into three squads each, and each squad is supposed to be broken down into three fire teams. However, since every company in Vietnam was perpetually undermanned, we never had enough personnel to maintain more than two fire teams in a squad and most of the time just operated as one group, the squad. When I arrived at Third Platoon, I was assigned to the third squad.

I was the most junior member of the last squad of the last platoon in the company.

My squad leader was Alan Cowardin. He was 18 years old and had a perpetual smirk on his face. He took me to the tent that the squad lived in and introduced me to the other guys. Then he sat down on a cot across from me and explained a few things.

"We're going out on an ambush tonight. No sense you waiting around to get out into the field. Now 'Nam is a war of ambushes. Most of the time, the people on the giving end come out a whole lot better than the people on the receiving end. So we want to be on the giving end whenever we can. Unfortunately, the VC are guerillas; they're the ones who get to hide while we walk around in plain sight. That means that we're on the receiving end a lot more than the giving end."

He smiled, "When we go out on ambush, that's a chance for us to be on the giving end, but it's not always that simple. They're out there setting up ambushes too. So we gotta sneak out to our site. The most dangerous part of night ambushes is getting to the site and getting back in the morning."

He leaned toward me and lowered his voice, "The most important thing you've gotta remember is", he paused, put his index finger up before his mouth, and whispered, "to be realllly quiet."

He leaned back and continued, "So get dressed for an ambush. No pack, helmet or flak jacket—just your weapon and web gear. Wear your cover, it'll break up the outline of your head. The whole point is to travel light and make sure nothing is making noise."

I nodded, "Do I have to grease my face?"

Cowardin laughed, "Naw. I mean, you can if you want to, but I'm not worried about it—it's going to be darker than the inside of a cow out there. There won't be any moon. Nobody's going to see your face."

"Okay." I hesitated, I still didn't feel like I really had a clear idea of what I was supposed to do. "Is there somebody I should, like, stick close to or something?"

Cowardin got a big laugh out of that. "Yeah, me! You're going to carry the radio, and you're going to walk right behind me. But you're not going to talk on it; you just carry it. If anybody calls on it, you just tell me. But don't talk loud; whisper if you need to get my attention. And don't key the handset. I'll show how to do that when we're set up. Don't you touch it till I tell you."

He gave me a quizzical look and asked, "Are you following all this?"

I nodded again, "Yeah, I got it."

I felt about as stupid as I did my first night in boot camp, like I had to be told how to breathe. Except it seemed everything he told me was what *not* to do.

He said, "Okay then. Now it's going to be dark out there, so don't lose sight of me. You hear? Don't lose sight of me and start calling out in the dark. You gotta keep up."

I nodded, "I understand."

I met the other guys in the squad. A lance corporal named Redke told me that Cowardin was not the regular squad leader. The regular squad leader was a corporal named Feller. He had been wounded and was in the hospital. Redke said that this was the first time Cowardin had taken out a patrol as patrol leader. That sounded a little ominous, but Redke didn't seem to be concerned.

At dusk, we saddled up, checked each other to make sure no one had a piece of gear that would clang about and make noise, and then we quietly walked out of the company perimeter in single file. I had the radio on my back and immediately began to sweat beneath the radio pack. We walked along in the darkness for about forty minutes and then came to our ambush site, which was just a point near a trail that led into the local ville. We quietly established ourselves off to the side of the trail.

Cowardin taught me to sit by the radio and answer when the company would call for a situation report. They would say,

"Echo Three Charlie, this is Echo Six. Sit rep, over." I would respond by keying the handset twice without saying anything. This was how the company command checked in with us to make sure all was okay. We responded to their query for a sit rep by just keying the handset so that no one would speak aloud and run the risk of revealing our presence.

Keying the handset was pretty much all I learned that first night on ambush. I didn't even know that "sit rep" stood for situation report until later.

Chapter 26

Shadows

Climbing down rope netting in a heaving sea with a 70 pound pack on your back is not only extremely difficult, it's downright dangerous. If you lean out too far, the pull is even harder to control and grabbing a horizontal handhold is such a better way to get control of all that weight. Except if you have another Marine right above you who steps on your hand with a size 10 boondocker bearing all of his weight, including the 70 pound pack that he's wearing.

It was considerably harder when the seas were not calm. Some of the Marines fell from the netting and were crushed between the landing craft and the troop ships. Some drowned. The training was truly dangerous, and the seriousness of it helped the inexperienced Marines begin to get a sense of what they were facing.

Chapter 27

Moving North

One afternoon, around the beginning of April, our platoon sergeant stuck his head in the door of our hooch and said, "Tonight's ambush is cancelled. We're moving tomorrow, so pack up everything into your seabags and your packs. The whole battalion is going to Danang. The trucks will be here first thing in the morning."

Medina said, "Everything, Sarge? Man, we got a lot of shit here." He swept his arm toward the cots, big empty spools serving as tables, melted candles in C-rat cans, and other junk filling up our tent.

"Everything but the cots. Leave anything you don't want to lug with you. All you're going to have is what's in your pack and your sea bag. You'll wear your helmet, flak jacket, web gear, and your pack, and you'll carry your rifle and sea bag. If you got extra bandoliers or grenades, go turn those in at the ammo bunker. We don't want nobody wearing grenades aboard the aircraft."

Aircraft? I said, "We're flying to Danang?"

He gave me a dumb look, "That's what most people do with aircraft, they fly in 'em." Then he softened his tone, "Okay, get moving. Put all the shit you're throwing away in a pile in the middle of the hooch. We'll pick it up later. The whole platoon's got to fall out and police the area before we can leave.

Somebody asked, "This isn't like an operation, is it?" Thank God I wasn't the only one asking stupid questions. Even I knew we wouldn't be taking our sea bags on an operation. So the sergeant's answer surprised me.

"I don't think so; I think the whole battalion's just going to take over a new area of operation. But they haven't told us for sure…I know the battalion afloat stores their sea bags on a ship when they're in the field. But I don't think that's what's going on here." He paused and then said, "All I know for sure is that we're moving North, and we're flying to Danang tomorrow morning."

He ducked out and the speculation immediately launched into high gear as we started getting our gear together.

"North! Shit, man, that could mean the DMZ."

"Con Thien, man, that's where they been taking it in the

shorts. They got overrun; you know they need troops there."

"No way, he said Danang. We'd be flying to Dong Ha if we was going up close to the DMZ."

"Yeah, Danang is like safe. They already cleared all the gooks outta there."

"Ain't no place safe in this fucking country."

"Danang is safe, man; that's where China Beach is. And Headquarters is there. You know it's safe if that's where they put Headquarters."

And on it went. Nobody knew what was going to happen, not even our platoon sergeant and maybe not even the C.O.

All I knew for sure was that it was goodbye to the rice paddies and little villages in the immediate vicinity of our combat base. I had learned the basics there—how to keep the right distance on patrol, how to speak over the radio, how to look for booby traps, and just generally how to operate outside the wire—and I was finally starting to feel somewhat comfortable. Now we were going to go start over again someplace else. I began to get a tight feeling in my stomach.

The next morning, we boarded trucks and drove to the

airstrip. We got out and formed up lines to lug our shit aboard C-130 Hercules transport planes. We were in full combat gear, carrying all our worldly possessions in our packs and sea bags. This was typical Marine thinking—just have each man carry everything he owns. Imagine trying to walk in helmet, flak jacket, web gear, full pack and carrying a rifle and a big heavy sea bag. I could barely move; I had gear sticking out in every direction. My sea bag was dragging against my leg with every step, and I couldn't turn to right or left without bumping into someone else. Finally, it was my squad's turn to board our plane. We were the last, of course, being the third squad of third platoon. I made my way up the ramp at the rear of the plane, waddling like a dung beetle bearing too much dung.

Since we were among the last to board, they sent us up high in the tail, above the ramp that drops down from the rear end. We had to climb over people, dragging our sea bags, and trying to squeeze into what little space was left for us. I couldn't sit easily or even have a comfortable handhold. I think we had the worst seats (I use the word loosely) on the plane. And the atmosphere inside the plane was really awful; the heat was unbearable, and it reached its zenith up high in the tail. The trip probably only took about 30 minutes but I was aware of every breath I drew in that oppressive heat. I felt close to passing out by the time the plane set down at Danang.

We landed at the airstrip in Danang (the same place where I'd landed in February), boarded trucks and headed out to the new battalion area. We didn't drive very far from the airstrip, so we figured we must be in a pretty secure area. Along the way, we drove past some of the whorehouses that surrounded the battalion area—they called it Dogpatch—and the ladies came outside and greeted us. Some of them pulled up their shirts and gave us a visual taste of what they had to offer. The Marines cheered.

We cruised right past the battalion area and ended up on Hill 60, in a valley northwest of Danang. The hill was apparently one of the longstanding ones; it was covered with wooden bunkers dug deep into the hillside. The bunkers looked especially safe, and the hill had a commanding view of the surrounding countryside. Overall, the position didn't look too vulnerable.

Maybe this change was going to be okay.

Chapter 28

Shadows

Living on the island of Pavuvu prepared my dad and his comrades for the side of war that most folks don't tend to think about. They learned to live with the filth and the vermin and the wet and the hot and the crummy food and the loss of most of the things that our civilized society takes for granted. He learned to pay little attention to these things; his focus was on the training because he had some idea what was coming. Of course, when the First Marine Division landed at Peleliu, it turned out that no one had known what was coming.

My dad never knew if the Marine Corps did it on purpose, but he felt that life on Pavuvu helped prepare him to do whatever it takes to stay alive.

Chapter 29

Hill 60 Rats

One of the first things we discovered about Hill 60 was that those nice strong looking bunkers were full of rats! The bunkers were made of big timbers, and they were strong and virtually impervious to a mortar attack. They had wooden bunks built into the sides of the walls, which was nice, but the walls were constructed with big hollow spaces, and the Marines had been eating and dropping empty—and half empty—C-Ration cans down into those hollow walls. A fundamental rule of life is: Where there be food for the taking, there be rats taking it. I didn't see many of them, but I could hear them all night long as they scurried about and fought over the scraps. Needless to say, I employed my blanket over the head sleeping technique every night, regardless of how hot it was.

After about two weeks of living in this rat-infested filth, our platoon commander called a meeting of the platoon. We clustered outside in front of one of the bunkers.

The lieutenant said, "How do you guys feel about living in these bunkers?"

There was a chorus of people saying basically the same thing, "We hate these fucking rats!"

He nodded, "But these bunkers are secure. Would you be willing to give up that security to get rid of the rats?" He paused. A few guys muttered that they would, but we were waiting to hear what he was getting at.

He continued, "The last company here tried to get rid of the rats, and it's pretty clear that nothing worked. If we really want to get rid of them, we're going to have to tear down the bunkers and live in tents."

I didn't mind living in tents; we lived in them in Chu Lai and I never felt particularly vulnerable. I looked around me and saw that most everyone was nodding.

The lieutenant nodded, "Okay, well the skipper has made arrangements for bulldozers to come out and flatten the top of the hill. But it's up to us to tear down the bunkers and get rid of the rats. We can't just burn 'em out because these timbers would burn for days. We have to tear them down."

So that's what we did, but I still hadn't understood what was really involved.

It took two days to tear down the bunkers. The first day, a large work detail pretty much destroyed the whole complex of bunkers. I missed out on that detail, 2nd Platoon supplied the people for it. They actually did burn most of the timbers, but only after they had torn them out and dragged them off to a big pile. They left the final walls—the ones that were built deep into the side of the hill—for the following day.

The next day, we gathered in front of the remaining structure with our entrenching tools. The lieutenant, the gunny, and several others were waiting in a group. The gunny stepped out in front with an entrenching tool in his hand. Then he launched into that formal tone and cadence that Marine NCOs use when they're giving instructions. It is some kind of tradition in the Corps to speak this way, because everyone adopts that same tone when they are giving a class. It's sort of a combination of speaking in a loud, clear tone, using words with the fewest syllables, speaking in short phrases, using the full official name for tools, weapons and forms, and using a volume that is somewhere well above speech but below yelling.

The gunny held up his entrenching tool and commenced. "This is an entrenching tool. Do you know what it is for?"

No one responded for a moment, and then some wiseass yelled, "Digging holes for burying rats."

The gunny proceeded as though he had not heard the wiseass, "You probably think this is for digging holes. Well, you're right. An entrenching tool can be used for digging holes." He unscrewed the end of it and flipped the shovel part from straight to an L shape. "As you see, it can be used as either a shovel or a pick. But an entrenching tool is a multiple purpose instrument, especially in the hands of a resourceful Marine."

He shifted the shovel back to the straight design and began to tighten the screw assembly. "Who can tell me what other purpose the common entrenching tool has served in the Marine Corps?"

No one said anything, and the gunny shook his head in mock sadness. "I don't know what they're teaching you young people these days." He raised the e-tool and brandished it like a club, "A weapon! During World War I, the Marines sharpened the ends of their entrenching tools and used them for close in-fighting in the trenches." He swung the e-tool sideways, "It can be more effective than a bayonet in crowded situations."

He scanned the crowd, and then added, "A resourceful Marine can use anything as a weapon—even your Aunt Fannie's bloomers." That got a few smiles, no laughs.

He straightened his frame and proudly held up his e-tool, "Today, we introduce a new use of the entrenching tool weapon. You will each adjust your entrenching tool to its full extension and tighten it in place." Several guys started unfolding their e-tools. He continued, "We are going to start pulling down the final walls in these bunkers, and they are full of rats. Every time we get a wall down, we're going to have rats all over the place. Your job..." He paused, looked us over carefully, and then smiled and said, "is to hammer the shit out of 'em!"

People made all kinds of sounds: laughter, groans, cheers. Someone asked, "Why can't we just shoot "em, Gunny?"

The gunny smiled again, "Because we don't want you goofballs shooting each other. And when a rat starts running all over the place, that's just what's likely to happen."

He paused and then added in a more serious tone, "That's probably the most common kind of hunting accident, when the game tries to escape and runs between two hunters. So we're not going to shoot 'em; we're going to whack 'em. And for crying out loud, watch out, and don't whack each other."

So we formed in a semi-circle outside while they started pulling the final timbers down. Soon rats started running out of the ruin, sometimes it was a single rat, but most times it was several at once. The rats ran all over the place, and we screamed and yelled, while we chased them down and pounded them to death with our entrenching tools. The carnage went on for hours. By the end of the afternoon, there were dozens of flat rats lying around the side of the hill. A detail picked up the carcasses and burned them in a diesel filled drum.

It was fun—sort of. Here we were, a couple dozen bare-chested, adolescent Marines, chasing rats and hollering and screaming the whole time. That day, we were boys—big boys, of course, big enough to drink and pursue the services of the local whores. But boys nevertheless. My dad was twenty-seven when he went into the Marine Corps during World War II; he was married and already had a child. He was probably older than anyone on my firebase but the gunny. And the gunny sure wasn't chasing any rats; he just stood by and watched the boys have their fun.

That day, the rats were our enemy. We were afraid of the rats, and we channeled our fear into hating and killing them. I guess it wasn't so different from dealing with the VC.

Chapter 30

Shadows

The amphibious training at Pavuvu was deadly. Transferring large numbers of personnel from a troop ship into a much smaller landing barge—while both craft are at sea—is a very challenging maneuver. Such transfers don't take place in protected harbors; they have to be conducted on the open sea. And calm weather cannot be guaranteed, because too many variables are being juggled to allow for the flexibility to choose the perfect moment for an assault. To prepare adequately, the Marines on Pavuvu went out in some of the worst weather and climbed down the cargo nets into the open barges. They tried to start off with calmer weather and carrying less gear, but they quickly moved toward circumstances that approximated what they might encounter on the real assault. It was dangerous work and men were injured and died in the process.

My father said that it brought a dimension of reality to what they were facing, and he could see it in everyone's faces as they climbed over the railing and clung to the nets in heaving seas. They didn't know where they were going yet, but their commanders began to warn them that this was going to be a resisted landing, a fiercely resisted landing.

Chapter 31

Shit Details and Shitty Details

After we tore down the old bunkers and cleared out the rats, bulldozers came out and flattened the top of the hill for us. Then we had to rebuild the base. The biggest part of that was filling sandbags. Whenever we weren't out on patrol, we filled sandbags. And don't let the name fool you—there was no sand in those bags—just dirt or, much of the time, mud. For all our vaunted technological superiority, our approach to filling sandbags was not very high tech. One guy holds the empty bag while the other guy fills it with a shovel. Then you tie it closed and stack them. Eventually, when you have enough, you stack them around the positions you want to protect. Since they were full of dirt and mud, they dried hard as rocks. So they turn into big heavy, cloth covered bricks.

I hated filling sandbags!

Part of reworking the base entailed clearing new fields of

fire for the machine gun positions and other bunkers on the perimeter. This meant clearing away the vegetation in front of those positions. We chopped down some of it but we got rid of most of it by pouring diesel fuel on it and setting it afire. This was a dangerous way to operate; after the first burning, we had to carry open cans of fuel among bushes that were still smoldering.

Sure enough, wouldn't you know that I was the one to run into trouble. I was carrying a 5-gallon can of diesel fuel in my hands when a spark drifted into the opening and set the can on fire.

Watson and Medina saw the flames and they both started yelling at me.

"Look out, you're on fire."

I was in the middle of a group of Marines so I couldn't throw the can down right there. I ran toward the edge of the group to where I could throw the can into the bushes. While I was running, fuel sloshed out of the can and ran down onto my right arm and shoulder. I caught fire from my shoulder to my wrist as I was getting rid of the can.

Still on fire, I ran to the edge of the hill where the bulldozers had pushed a huge pile of fresh dirt. I dived over the edge and rolled in the loose dirt and put myself out. I was on fire for only a couple of seconds, but, boy, did it hurt! I jammed my thumb pretty bad when I made my swan dive into the dirt, but it was the pain in my arm that told me I had a serious problem. They medevaced me by truck to the Aid Station, which was located in one of the many big framed tents at the Battalion area.

There wasn't much the docs could do but cover my arm with salve and wrap it with gauze. The whole time they were working on me, my arm was shaking uncontrollably. I had to hold it out straight in front of me while they tended to it, but I could not hold it still. It was shaking so badly, it looked like a blur. They warned me that I would have bad scars but they turned out to be wrong about that. I lost all the skin on my arm but, after it healed, there was no scarring.

I went around with my arm wrapped up for a couple of weeks, but otherwise things didn't change too much. I was on light duty and didn't go on patrol for about ten days, but I still sat hole watch at night. The best part was that I didn't have to fill any sandbags. But I discovered a big downside to being on light duty. When my squad went out on patrol without me, it made me feel like I was no longer part of the group. I didn't like that feeling at all, and I was glad when I was returned to full duty.

My light duty status didn't last for long. My squad was rapidly evolving into a new group and I had a more accepted role in it. When Corporal Feller returned from the hospital, a lance corporal named Ramsey came with him. They had both been in third squad and had been wounded. Ramsey was promoted to corporal right after he rejoined the squad. He was a big, easy-going guy with a wry sense of humor. We used to spend a lot of our free time together, playing chess and shooting the shit.

Shortly after he returned, Corporal Feller rotated home. Ramsey and Cowardin had both made corporal, but the lieutenant made Ramsey the new squad leader. By the end of May, my squad had shrunk down to just six guys: two corporals, Ramsey and Cowardin, two lance corporals, Medina and Ray, and two PFCs, myself and Watson. Mike Watson and I were the lowest members on the totem pole, and we were the ones who got stuck with every unwanted job. We spent our days filling sand bags and going on patrols and then at night, we either went on ambushes or sat hole watch. My cot was practically untouched.

One morning, a funny thing happened when we came in from our night ambush. Medina and I went to the ammo bunker to put away the pop flares and claymore mines. A pop flare is a little aluminum tube with a firing cap in the bottom. To fire it, you take the top off and put it on the bottom and then you slam it against the palm of your hand (the top has a small pin in it that hits the firing cap in the bottom of the tube). Medina was dropping some pop flares into the slotted box in which they were stored. He didn't realize it but the top was on the bottom end of one of the flares, so when this flare was dropped into the box, the flare went off.

Of course, this occurred in the ammo bunker. That meant it could conceivably set off all the ammunition stored in the ammo bunker.

As soon as it happened, we took one look at each other and then we both hauled ass out of there as fast as we could go. We ran toward the edge of the hill, yelling, "Fire in the ammo bunker!" at the top of our lungs. We reached the area where the bulldozers had pushed the fresh dirt and we leaped out into the air, landing a moment later twenty-odd feet down the side of the hill. A lot of the guys were either still in their cots or just sitting around their hooches, but it was amazing to see how fast they reacted. I looked up from my perch in the loose dirt and all I could see were bodies launching into the air as every Marine on that hill followed us. It was hilarious!

Somehow, no one got hurt and the ammo bunker didn't blow up. But I will never forget the sight of all those bodies popping into midair above me.

Chapter 32

Shadows

Often when my dad would talk about the war, he would get a particular look on his face, It's hard to describe the look: He mostly just gazed off into the distance and had a hard set to his mouth, but it conveyed a lot. It wasn't an angry look or a mean look or a look of disgust or pain, but it was part angry and part mean and part disgust and part pain and part something more. It was a hard look. It always gave me a creepy feeling when I saw that look on my dad's face. Whatever was behind it, it seemed like he was seeing something too ugly to describe.

He was especially prone to get that look if he'd been drinking and started talking about the war. I saw the look emerge many times when he drank, but I also saw it at times when he wasn't talking about anything, like when he would sit out on our porch in the dark. Sometimes, I would go outside and sit near him, but he never said anything, and so we would sit together in the dark.

There were times when he talked about the war without getting the look, but there were two topics that always evoked it: an incident that occurred when he was manning the lines on Okinawa and anything that had to do with Peleliu.

Chapter 33

Beauty and Ugliness

Late that spring, we began making trips into the jungle area Northwest of Danang. We made platoon-sized patrols out to the end of Happy Valley and up into the mountains near the valley. It was different from the developed areas around our combat base. When we walked patrol in the rice paddies, we were visible from a great distance and so we kept very large distances between ourselves. But in the jungle, you often couldn't see beyond the guy in front of you and you had to walk closer. We could walk into the enemy with very little warning.

At first, it was really eerie to walk down the jungle trails. There was a thick canopy of trees high overhead so we were always in deep shade. Everything took on a different kind of look in that dim light. The jungle has its own distinct smells and sounds; even the air is different—more still and humid. In places, we would have to hack our way through the thickness with a machete. But other times, there were roomy trails you could practically stroll down. Those were usually animal trails that had been used by woodcutters; they were like super highways through the jungle.

We learned to be really quiet in the jungle, sometimes staying off the trails and walking for hours down the middle of streambeds or keeping parallel to the trails. The whole goal was to be able to surprise anyone you came upon and not be the ones that got surprised.

Later in the year, during the monsoon season, the jungle was treacherous—muddy and slippery and subject to flash floods in the valleys. But during the dry season, the jungle could be relatively easy to navigate. And it had a magical quality.

When you walk silently, taking each step very consciously, constantly looking around you, tuned into every sound, every sight and every smell, you are about as alive as it is possible to be. You are completely outside your self—no thoughts, no past or future, just fully attuned to your senses and your immediate environment. It wasn't being in a state of fear, just a state of complete, total attention to your surroundings. These days, people pay for mindfulness training to learn to do the same thing.

I loved that part of the job—when there was no immediate

thing to fear and yet we had to stay fully alert for possible danger.

The prospect of encountering the enemy was only one of the dangers offered by the jungle. There were also more ordinary dangers. I saw many snakes and other weird critters, but the most consistent annoyance was the leeches. These were land leeches, not the big flat kind that live in water. These were more like little fat worms; they were pinkish and grey, about an inch long, and crawled by inching along like an inchworm. There were areas of the jungle where you always had leeches on you; if you stopped walking and looked down, you would see some crawling up your boot. You generally could not feel them crawling around on you but you would discover them in their favorite spots, such as the armpit. They would find a spot and suck blood until their bodies would swell up to capacity.

We got them off by spraying mosquito repellant on them and by holding lit cigarettes to them. When you used the lit cigarette technique—usually the more effective method—you could feel the heat as the leech spurted the hot blood back into your body. When we took breaks, we would check each other for leeches—one of those personal intimacies that harsh conditions can produce.

On one particular walk in the woods, I had my worst experience with the leeches. I could tell that I had something in my crotch, so when we took a break I lowered my trousers. My scrotum was not visible; it lay within a solid ball of leeches!

I was stunned when I saw this ball of leeches. "Oh shit" I exclaimed, "I can't believe this."

Medina was standing near me.

"What are you talking about, man?" Then he exclaimed, "Holy Shit! Wow! Hey, you guys, come look at this. Man, Catherall's got his balls fuckin' covered with leeches."

Several others came over and examined my leech infested crotch. Meanwhile, I was acutely uncomfortable. It hadn't bothered me so much when I had my pants on, but now that I had seen this infestation, I wanted those leeches out of there!

"Fucking help me, goddamit."

"Yeah, yeah, we'll get 'em. Watson, gimme your insect repellant." Mike had a bottle of insect repellant strapped to his helmet with a thick black rubber band. Medina took it and sprayed it all over the mass of leeches and said, "Here, this'll get some of them, then we'll get the ones that don't fall off with cigarettes."

None fell off.

Medina and Mike Watson took lit cigarettes and helped me to remove the leeches. We counted them as we got them off. We removed twenty-three leeches from my balls. It was not easy getting them all off and when we finally succeeded I continued to bleed, because the leeches put some kind of anti-coagulant substance in the blood. My trousers turned red from crotch to ankle on the inside of each leg.

One morning the platoon sergeant caught us at the chow hall. He said, "Eat your breakfast and then go get saddled up; we're going on a mission and the choppers are picking us up at oh eight hundred." Someone asked what was up and he said something about VC being seen doing something with boats.

The rumors flew as usual, but we got the general idea that VC were spotted unloading or loading boats and we were therefore going to the ocean's edge. Sure enough, we were choppered to a beach. It felt very strange to come into the landing zone over the water—a bit like an amphibious landing. But there was no incoming fire and we never saw any VC. It was a mountainous peninsula and we spent the day climbing from the water's edge all the way up to a road that crossed over a pass at the top.

Unlike the mountains that surrounded our valley, this mountain was rocky and didn't have many trees. It was not difficult to climb; it was simply a case of walking up a very steep hillside. The lower portion had some trees and vegetation, but as we got higher the trees thinned out and I got glimpses of where we had climbed from. The view was stunning. You could see the peninsula jutting out into the green water, with thin sandy beaches in places surrounded by the many greens of the vegetation. There were some sanpan type sailboats out at sea leisurely going about their business. It was like a picture postcard of a gorgeous vacation spot. This was a Vietnam that I had never seen before; indeed, a Vietnam that I had no idea even existed.

It was totally beautiful.

Climbing the hillside was hard work, of course. We were all huffing and puffing and drinking up our water. About two thirds of the way up, we found a spring pouring out of the side of the mountain, and the water was cold and delicious. I drank my fill and filled both my canteens. It made the rest of the climb more bearable, and I still had water when we finally reached the roadway. Then we parked ourselves on the road and waited for trucks, which were not long in arriving.

On the drive back to our combat base, we crossed over the top of the mountain and stopped in a small ville located at the top of the pass. As usual, the villagers came out to the trucks and sold us cokes. Whenever they sold us cokes, they would stand around and wait for us to drink the whole thing so that they could get the bottle back. I think the bottles were more valuable than the cola inside. The trucks were stopped for a few minutes; I assume the stop was just so we could all get a cold drink. So here were three trucks full of Marines all finishing their cokes at the same time, and a bunch of peasants all nervously requesting their bottles back.

As the trucks started up and began to pull out, there were still Marines with empty bottles, and some of them were taunting the peasants who were so concerned about retrieving the empties. Now our cruelty emerged. Bottles started being pitched into the air. As the trucks began to pick up speed, we all saw one bottle go sailing high into the air. Then it came down and hit a young woman square in the head and knocked her off her feet. She was a pretty young woman dressed finely in the traditional ao dai. When the bottle hit her, a cheer went up from all the trucks—as though our team had just scored a goal.

I don't even understand why, but I joined in that cheer. It just sort of emerged from the energy of the moment. As the trucks threaded their way down the mountainous road, my thoughts stayed on that young woman and how I had cheered when she was hit.

I discovered something very ugly in myself that day, something that I had not known was there. I thought back to that disgusting staff sergeant my first day in-country.

Was I becoming like him?

Chapter 34

Shadows

The landing at Peleliu was as fiercely defended as Tarawa, but the exclusive use of amtracs did allow more of the Marines to make it to the beach. However, as soon as the amtracs reached the beach and became sitting targets, most of them were promptly hit. The Marines didn't get stalled out on the reefs, but what they did encounter was a beachhead that was completely controlled by the enemy. They could not progress inland and the entire division was exposed to heavy fire, the worst of it coming from a mound of coral on their left flank. The sandy beach offered no natural cover, so the Marines had to improvise with what little they could find; some found positions behind their own ruined amtracs; most could only burrow into pitiful little depressions in the sand.

Chapter 35

Hot LZ

In June, the war opened up in earnest for me and my squad. Up until then, I'd encountered little more than snipers and booby traps. But we were in full-fledged firefights and mortar attacks throughout June. It all started on the afternoon of June 3 when the platoon sergeant stuck his head in our hooch.

"Saddle up! We're going out as soon as the choppers get here. Full packs, helmet and flak jacket. Ramsey, you come with me. Bring some people to carry gear. Get moving, this is no drill! The shit's hit the fan and we're being called in."

Ramsey said, "Catherall, Watson, come with me."

We joined Ramsey and followed the platoon sergeant to where several bare-chested Marines were stacking cases of C-rations in a big pile in the middle of the hill. A crowd of PFC's was forming as everyone hurried to grab cases of rations. Mike and I made several trips carrying cases of C-rats back to our hooch while

Ramsey went off to meet with the platoon commander. After carrying the C-rats, we reported to Ramsey at the ammo bunker where he had a new pile for us to carry. This time it was bandoliers of M16 ammo, grenades, claymore mines, and two LAW's, Light Antitank Weapons, which were little short single shot bazookas that we rarely ever used.

By the time we had all the cases open and everyone was stuffing their packs with green cans of C-rats, Ramsey returned and told us what the scoop was. He wasn't sure about some of the details but it didn't sound good.

"Fifth Marines was on a big operation somewhere south of Danang. They ran into a couple battalions of NVA, and they're surrounded and pinned down. If we got the right skinny, there's like a thousand NVA pounding the shit out of 'em."

Cowardin sounded dubious, "Yeah, we heard that story before. Last time we went out on one of these things, we didn't see shit."

Ramsey shrugged, "We'll see. But we're definitely going in, choppers start arriving at 1700. Everyone carries two extra bandoliers. And the captain wants every squad to carry two entrenching tools and two LAW's."

Medina said, "Aw shit, what are they loading us down with all this stuff for, man? I got a full pack already. Where we going to put all this shit?" There were still unopened cans of grenades and claymore mines that someone had to carry. "Shit, they're making us carry as much as the other squads. We're the smallest squad, man."

Ramsey said, "Cool it, Medina. Everyone carries bandoliers. Everyone but the corporals carries a claymore in their pack. PFC's carry the LAW's and the entrenching tools. Let's move it."

Great, we had exactly two PFC's. That meant Mike Watson and I would be carrying extra bandoliers around our necks, claymores in our packs, entrenching tools mounted on the back of the packs and LAW's strapped over our shoulders—all of that on top of the normal amount of food, ammo, etc. By the time we had loaded our packs, strung extra bandoliers around our necks, strapped on the e-tools and hung the LAW's over our shoulders, we looked more like traveling supply depos than infantrymen. I hated carrying all that stuff. The other squads all had more PFC's than us, so the extra stuff was distributed more widely. All we had was me and Mike.

As soon as we were all loaded up, we hiked up to our LZ to wait for the helicopters. Since our squad was the 3rd squad of the 3rd platoon, we were literally on the last chopper. The helicopters were ferrying us in waves, so we had to sit and wait while the rest of the company flew off into who knew what. While everyone was sitting in little groups around the LZ, the scuttlebutt was running rampant. The gist of it was that we were headed into something heavy. But that was always the scuttlebutt, you never knew how much credence to give it.

After hurrying to get ready, we sat out at the LZ for a couple of hours, smoking cigarettes and eating a bunch of apples that the cooks brought out to us. Two waves of choppers loaded up and left with virtually everyone in the company, except 3rd squad of 3rd platoon. There still wasn't room for our squad so we ended up sitting on the hillside all by our lonesome, just the six of us. Finally, a lone chopper arrived—another Chinook, the double bladed craft that was the standard assault chopper used by the Marine Corps.

We flew off blind, just the six of us in this chopper. We had no radio, so we had no way of even knowing what was going on while we flew unless the helicopter crew were to pass on something that they'd heard over their radio. We only knew that we would link back up with the rest of the platoon, and the whole company, when we landed.

The whole affair took a bizarre turn when the chopper made an unexpected landing at the Danang airstrip. Normally, we'd have flown directly to wherever we were going. At Danang, we were required to unload from the Chinook. This was totally bizarre; we had no idea what was going on. We stood around for a few minutes; then we were told to reload aboard a different chopper, a big Sikorsky 56. The Sikorsky looks like a big flying beetle; it has short choppy wings and is much bigger than the Chinook. It was used for ferrying personnel and equipment, not for combat assaults. The Chinook was armed with two side gunners firing .50 caliber machine guns. The Sikorsky also had side gunners but they were armed with the smaller M60 machine guns (only .30 caliber, or to be more exact, 7.62 millimeter), and the aircraft is more ponderous and difficult to maneuver.

When we boarded this big chopper, a group of five combat engineers was loaded along with us. We were quite puzzled by this switch of helicopters; I still don't know why they did it though we later figured it must have been because the LZ had already been established and wasn't hot (receiving incoming fire), though that doesn't really explain why they took the Chinook out of the operation. There would have been room to add the engineers aboard the Chinook, so it wasn't for the extra room. Maybe the Chinook was running low on fuel.

In any case, we finally headed off to join the rest of the company. As I learned later, the company was unable to land near the 5th Marines' position because the fire was so heavy, so the first wave of the company landed and established an LZ miles away. It was getting dark, so they put out a strobe light to guide the choppers to this secure LZ. That's where we were headed with the engineers.

But that's not where we arrived.

Instead of joining the company, my squad ended up in the hot LZ where the remnants of the 5th Marines had been battling all day long. These guys were surrounded in an area of dried rice paddies. They were under extremely heavy fire, including a barrage of mortar fire from multiple mortar tubes. The explosions of the incoming mortars created a series of flashes that were so rapid that the pilots of our chopper mistook them for the strobe light! So they flew in toward these flashes and, when they realized their mistake, it was too late. We were hit in the air by explosives and machine gun fire. The explosives were either mortar shells that happened to hit us in the air or else rockets aimed at the chopper.

I was seated in the first seat, next to the open window areas where the two machine gunners were stationed across from each other. I watched in fascination as arcs of machine gun tracers reached out for us. Then they found their target; bullets started flying through the fuselage around us. Something vital was hit and the chopper was going down fast, the pilots jerking it back and forth to slow its fall. We hit hard, and everyone was thrown onto the floor. The compartment was filled with smoke and tracers continued to come through the fuselage. I didn't see it but Mike Watson was across from me and able to look into the cockpit. He saw a lot of blood and thought one of the pilots had been hit in the head. I believe one of the door gunners was also hit but kept firing his machine gun.

We needed to get out of the aircraft as rapidly as possible, but the ramp wouldn't go down, and there was a moment of near panic. The machine gunners were firing, and the smoke and noise inside the compartment was overwhelming. We were trapped inside a steel coffin. I had the urge to climb out the window where the gunner was firing, and I might have done so, but about then the crew chief took an ax and chopped some hydraulic lines. The rear ramp fell open and Ramsey yelled at us to get out fast. Everyone ran out of the chopper. Since I had been sitting in the most forward seat, I was the first man to board and the last one out.

When I got outside, there was smoke everywhere, and I couldn't see more than a few feet in any direction. The guy in front of me disappeared into the smoke, and I started after him. Then a line of tracers passed between him and me. The tracers were coming from my right so I turned left—I sure didn't want to run right into a stream of bullets. I went about ten or fifteen yards but I didn't want to run in the dark, and I didn't want to get further separated from the rest of the squad, so I crouched down and began to move slower. I knew they wouldn't have gone far; as soon as they were clear of the helicopter, they would get down and Ramsey would try to get oriented. He needed to know where the Marines were and where the enemy was. I thought maybe I could turn back to my right and find them, but as I started to turn there was a sharp explosion—a mortar shell had landed behind me on my right side—and I went face first into the ground, mostly taking cover but I was also pushed by the concussion of the mortar blast.

Then everything got very quiet, like I was in some tiny place far away from the war.

Chapter 36

Shadows

The three regiments of the First Division—the 1st, 5th, and 7th—landed abreast on the long stretch of beach at Peleliu. Colonel Chesty Puller's First Marines held the left flank, which abutted the jagged coral mound that jutted thirty feet into the air and thirty yards out into the sea. The Japanese gunners positioned in the mound, which came to be known as the Point, were wreaking havoc on the landing amtracs. If the Marines could not find a way to silence the guns on that coral mound, the beachhead was going to be as thick with dead Marines as the beach at Tarawa.

The pre-landing bombardment had not touched any of the five pillboxes that were built into the Point; they had been constructed to withstand the worst kind of punishment. The Japanese had blasted huge holes in the coral and then covered them with reinforced concrete six feet thick. Tunnels ran between the positions so that the Japanese defenders could move about and shift the focus of their resistance. A 40 mm anti-tank gun was wreaking the worst damage on the amtracs; the other four pillboxes were manned with heavy machine guns that were chewing up the personnel on the beach. Each pillbox was surrounded by light machine guns set up in coral emplacements, as well as riflemen in hidden spider traps.

Assaulting such a fortress—held by dedicated troops commanding tremendous amounts of firepower and offering precious little cover to the troops making the assault—is as formidable a challenge as an infantryman ever faces. The only way to take such a position is with the most daring of all infantry maneuvers—the frontal assault.

Chapter 37

The Taste of Fear

I was in a deep, dark quiet place—a place far away from the noisy, smoky, chaotic world where I had just been. I don't think I was knocked unconscious, but it felt like I was trying to wake up from a dream. I was sprawled on the ground with my face in the dirt, my pack jammed up against my helmet and my helmet cutting into the back of my neck. For a timeless moment, I couldn't move. My body didn't seem to want to respond to the commands coming down from my brain.

Was I hit?

Finally, my head began to clear, and I rolled over on my side. I had landed with my head jammed into the side of a small rice paddy dike, so I must have been coming from behind me, except I'd been trying to turn back to my right toward where I figured my squad was located. Or did I fall to the side? The explosion was kind of on my right side, so maybe I fell to the left.

Or maybe I had already crossed this dike and I didn't notice it. My heart sank—I wasn't sure which way was which, and I couldn't get my bearings.

I didn't appear to be wounded, so I got up on my hands and knees and tried to look around. I thought the helicopter should have been behind me but I could see nothing through the smoke. I turned a full 360 degrees, peering into the smoke around me and trying to see something.

All I could see were lots of tracers and the white flashes of mortar explosions.

When we first took fire in the air, and I felt the explosions shake the chopper and saw the tracers coming up at us, it seemed too incredible to be real. But smashing the ground on our landing was very real. When the ramp wouldn't open and I felt trapped in the chopper, I had a panicky feeling of desperation—followed by a huge wave of relief when the crew chief dropped the ramp. And as I lay in the dirt after getting knocked down, I mostly felt numb. For a moment, it was like I was no longer in my body, then I started to feel the pain in my neck.

But now I was scared, really scared.

I had no idea where the rest of my squad was, or even where I was relative to the helicopter, if it was still on the ground. I was disoriented and alone, and I was afraid to move for fear I might go further in the wrong direction. I needed to find some kind of landmark so I could figure out where I was, but I dared not rise up too high because the air was full of bullets, all of which seemed to be flying a few feet above the ground.

I peered into the smoke around me. All I could see were white flashes of mortar shells exploding and lines of tracers streaking through the smoke. The tracers were coming from several different directions. It looked to me like they were all incoming, but I couldn't really tell which fire was from the enemy and which might have been from my guys. Sometimes the VC used green tracers, which made it easy to identify them at night, but these were NVA and they were using red tracers like ours.

This was the scariest moment I had ever experienced in all my life. I could taste the fear.

I have no idea how long I was there, though I think it was only a few moments. Then I saw a helmeted figure moving through the smoke low to the ground. It had to be a Marine.

"Catherall"

It was Ramsey, God bless him. Out of nowhere, he had found me. I was sure glad to see him. He didn't even say anything about my getting separated from the squad.

"You hurt?"

"No."

"Follow me, we're set up over here."

We both low-crawled and he led me to where our squad was set up on the perimeter. My mind was still foggy but I think it was only about forty yards or less from where I'd been. He placed me with Mike Watson and told us to dig in deep.

Guess what, suddenly our entrenching tools were in big demand—everyone wanted to dig in as deep as they could get. Worse yet, the privileges of rank were asserted and the corporals and lance corporals demanded our entrenching tools. Mike and I had to dig our hole with our helmets! That's right, we carried them but we didn't get to use them when the shit started flying.

After that, we settled in, and I engaged in my first intense firefight—one that lasted most of the night. Once I was dug in with Mike, however, I was no longer so scared. I was still scared, of course, but not like when I was alone and disoriented. Now I knew where the enemy was, and I could shoot at them. Being able to shoot back made a tremendous difference—I no longer felt helpless.

Except for the mortars. The NVA kept up a steady barrage and walked their mortars around on us for hours. This turned out to be the longest mortar barrage I would ever endure. In the coming months, I would be mortared many more times, but it was usually just ten or twelve shells, before we fired counter-mortar fire and the attack would end pretty quickly. This was nothing like that— we had no counter to their mortar fire, and they just kept it up for hours. There was also a lot of automatic weapons fire but we avoided that by staying close to the ground. Mortars come straight down from above, so you can't get low enough to duck them. At one point, Mike said, "Look how those last two shells landed in front of us. They're walking 'em back and forth toward us."

"Yeah; they could drop the next one right on top of us," I looked at Mike, "Whatta we do?"

"Be a really small target, I guess."

We hunkered down and got right up against each other. It

wasn't planned but we were literally hugging each other; about all that was showing was our helmets and the backs of our flak vests.

A shell exploded on the other side of the dike we were set up on; it rang our bells but didn't hurt us, though it was probably closer than the one that knocked me down earlier. The next shell landed to our right. The other guys in the squad were all on our left side; I didn't know who was on our right side, but I knew it had come awful close to whoever was there.

Chapter 38

Shadows

Because the twelve rifle companies in Puller's regiment were spread across the beach and pinned down, the job of taking the Point fell to the single company that held the left end of the line—K Company, Third Battalion, First Marine Regiment (K 3/1)—my father's company. My father and the other men in the first and third platoons of K Company assaulted the Point and fought their way from pillbox to pillbox. Within about forty-five minutes, they had taken the Point, but dead Marines littered the ground in front of every position.

Chapter 39

The Taste of Death

A few minutes after the mortar rounds landed near me and Mike, Ramsey crawled up to our hole from the right side. He was moving down the line, checking on everyone.

Ramsey said, "There's five dead guys in the next hole."

I was still having a little trouble taking it all in. I asked, "Are you sure they're all dead?"

Ramsey grinned at me, "Deader'n shit, man. They're all dead. One of those mortar rounds took 'em all. Five guys in one hole, man—all fuckin' wasted."

We all had different ways of being affected by fear. My particular manifestation was that I would have an intense need to urinate. It didn't matter what the situation was, I would find some way to pee. Still, it gave me a weird feeling to see Ramsey smiling as he talked about the guys in the next hole all getting killed. I knew he'd have done whatever he could to save them, so it wasn't that he didn't care, it was just his particular reaction to the intensity of combat. But it was weird, all the same.

The five guys in the next hole were the engineers who joined us in Danang. They'd been on the chopper with us, and had set up in line with my squad. I don't know why all five of them stayed together in the same hole; that was one of the things we were trained not to do. The non-coms were always yelling at people to spread out because "one grenade could get you all".

As far as my own peculiar manner of manifesting fear, I never needed to pee worse than I did that night. While the mortars continued to explode all over the place, I had to take a leak something terrible. However, I was afraid to get out of our shallow little hole.

"Mike, I gotta take a piss bad."

Mike laughed at me. "Yeah, you get out of this hole and you'll get the piss blown out of you."

"I'm serious, man, I really gotta go."

Mike shook his head. "If I were you, I think I'd just go in my pants, man. You do not want to be outside of this hole." He looked around at our shallow little foxhole and added, "such as it is".

I said, "Look, I'll lay on my side and do it without standing up."

Mike shook his head again, "Man, you do have a serious case. Okay, go ahead. But I'm not coming out there to drag you back in if you get hit."

As I rolled out of the hole, Mike grabbed my arm and said, "That's far enough, partner." He held onto my arm so he could pull me back if he needed to. I clumsily laid on my side and relieved myself. Then I crawled back into the hole.

The firefight stretched on for hours. This was the first time that I had targets to aim at, even though I couldn't actually see them in the dark. I had laid down covering fire and returned fire into treelines in the past, but I had not fired at specific targets until this night. After Mike and I laid there about an hour, I noticed that there was a machine gun out in front of us that was trading fire with a Marine machine gun down the line to our right.

"Hey Mike, you see that automatic weapon that's firing from over there? He's been firing every few minutes toward the guys to our right."

"Yeah, looks like a machine gun."

"We've got a better angle on him. I'm going to try to hit him."

"It's worth a try, but you can only see him when he's firing. And then he's going to be a little behind his flash."

"Yeah, I've got some magazines loaded with a tracer every third round. I'm gonna sight on him when he fires."

I carried some of my magazines loaded with tracers every third round, rather than the usual method of every fifth round, because I thought they would be more effective at night. It allowed me to fire three round bursts and adjust my fire more effectively in the dark. Since I was trained as a machine gunner, I'd had a lot of practice firing tracers at night and adjusting my fire by watching the tracers, rather than by aiming the weapon.

I inserted one of the tracer magazines. He soon fired again, and I sighted on him but held my fire and waited for him to fire a second time. When he started firing another burst a moment later, I carefully dumped twenty rounds on him in seven quick bursts.

There was no further fire from that position.

The battle raged on for hours; it seemed endless. Spooky,

the flare ship, was firing support fire all around us. Spooky was a C-47, the old reliable cargo plane from WWII that they used to call a gooney bird. They had mounted one of the new mini-guns in the open doorway of the plane. The mini-gun was a contraption that involved six M-60 machine gun barrels in a rapidly rotating mount and fed by a constant flow of ammunition. It allowed an incredible rate of fire. When they fired the mini-gun, it looked like a water hose of red fire raining down from the sky. I heard that a one-second burst would place a bullet in every square foot of a football field. This flare ship was dropping flares and pouring tracers all around our position.

    The most incredible sight of the night, however, was when a jet, probably a Marine Phantom, was shot down. Several jets had been dropping napalm out in front of us, and Mike and I were watching carefully. Every time a load of napalm burst into flame, we had a chance to get a better look around us. This allowed us to get our bearings and to spot any enemy in the vicinity. So we were both watching closely when this plane went down and slid across the horizon. It lit the area up like day. We figured he must have still had his load of napalm aboard as well as tanks full of jet fuel, because it made an enormous fire that covered like a thousand meters. That was the only time I ever saw a jet go down, and I have no idea whether the pilot got out.

The firing finally stopped around four a.m.

When the sun came up, the area around us looked like something out of Dante's Inferno; everything in shades of gray. Everyone had soot on them from the napalm and the endless smoke. And the group of Marines that had fought together all night was pitifully small—it seemed to total only about thirty guys. There were dead Marines on the ground, still in the positions where they'd died—I'm not sure how many but they made a long line when we lined them up side by side. There were no dead NVA; they had dragged off their dead.

About an hour after sunrise, the rest of Echo Company arrived. They had marched all night but missed the entire battle. The six of us in my squad were all okay. As far as I know, we were the only part of 7th Marines to actually participate in that dreadful firefight at Operation Union II. Years later, I learned that everyone involved received the Presidential Unit Citation.

I felt lucky to be alive.

Chapter 40

Shadows

The Marines of K Company actually took the crest of the Point before they had knocked out all the positions, including the 40 mm anti-tank weapon—it was still firing from a large pillbox near the base of the cliff. My father was among a group of Marines who reached the top and saw a large number of Japanese soldiers running away from the mound. All of the Marines got into kneeling positions and started firing at the retreating Japanese. They shot down a considerable number of enemy soldiers. For a brief moment, they felt like the battle was over and they had taken the island.

Then they heard the anti-tank gun still firing below them. My father turned and gazed down the length of the beachhead. For as far as he could see, the white sand was littered with the broken bodies of dead Marines. The live ones were clustered along the edge of the beach.

The battle for Peleliu had only just begun.

Chapter 41

Turning Point

When the sun came up, we stacked the bodies of the dead Marines. We had no enemy bodies, only Marines—more dead people than I had ever seen before. They were lifeless, their limbs twisted in directions that limbs are not supposed to twist. Their green uniforms were black with blood, and one body was opened up in the middle. When we carried that body, a long black string of something from the depths of the intestines dragged behind it. I couldn't decide whether I should cut it free from the body or just leave it. I left it but later wished I had cut it off.

Once they were all laid out, I stood there and stared at those bodies, studying the faces of each of those young men. I think, for the first time in my life, I understood the true finality of death. The faces were still young boys, but they were dead, and they would be dead forever. It was permanent, irrevocable. Five of them had sat across from me on the helicopter the night before. I hadn't known them, and I couldn't have told you which five they were. But it didn't matter, those young Marines had been alive the night before, and now they were dead forever. Their families didn't even know yet. I felt a cold, heavy feeling in my gut.

I had never felt anything this real before.

I stood there looking at those bodies for several moments, unable to stop thinking about how their lives had just ended forever. I now recognize that when I turned away from those bodies, I was a different person. I left something there that morning; my life was changed forever, and I no longer lived in the world I'd known. The terrible things that happened to some people in the world had always been removed from my life, lifeless images in a newspaper or on the screen of a television. No more. Maybe that was the moment when I picked up my thousand-meter stare—everyone seemed to get it sooner or later—for I saw many more dead bodies after that, but it was never the same. I learned to look without seeing, to be unaffected. But not that morning, that morning I felt the pain, the permanence, the senselessness of those deaths, and I felt it to the marrow of my bones.

It made me sick, and I wanted to throw up. I felt like I'd

been punched in the stomach. Never in my life had I seen anything as awful as those dead boys laid side by side.

After we stacked the bodies, my company formed up, and we started walking off. My squad was at the end of the long file of Marines, so we had to wait and allow everyone to walk out and establish their distance. I was standing near a hooch that was only a few hundred yards from where we'd been pinned down in the nightlong firefight. The house had a bomb shelter in the front yard, like all the houses in this part of Vietnam, and an old lady in black pajamas was working in the garden adjacent to it. She was working with a hoe and her back was to us, so I couldn't see her face, but she seemed totally oblivious to the presence of a long line of heavily armed men in front of her home.

I stood very still and stared at her, just as I had stared at the dead Marines a few minutes earlier. She had a way of moving the hoe with her hips without moving her arms. Her hips swiveled and the hoe rose and fell, yet her back remained stationary, her arms pinned to her sides. It looked like she'd been jerking that hoe her whole life.

As I stood there watching her, I imagined her spending the previous night in the safety of her bomb shelter while those men were dying in the dry rice paddies adjacent to her home. The battle would have been impossible for anyone to ignore—a jet and helicopters shot down, the whole world nothing but smoke and tracers and napalm and mortar explosions. And I imagined that this old woman was safely underground—probably in the company of North Vietnamese soldiers—throughout the battle.

Now she looked as though she could care less. We'd come halfway around the world to fight and die for her—and she could care less. The disinterest that I attributed to her felt like the coldest attitude I'd ever encountered. To me, it meant that all those people had died for nothing. Not just the Marines, but everyone—the NVA soldiers, her neighbors, the guys flying those jets—all kinds of people were dying and this old woman could care less. She just stood there, rhythmically dipping and pulling on her hoe.

I clicked off the safety on my rifle and raised it to my shoulder. I carefully sighted between her shoulder blades and put my finger on the trigger. Then I took up the slack in the trigger and stood there unmoving for an interminable moment.

I wanted to shoot her very badly. She seemed so completely unconcerned; I wanted to blast through that apathy and force her to know what was happening all around her.

I had just witnessed the worst kind of horror imaginable, and I was enraged at a world that allowed such horrors to exist. Some tiny part of me knew that it would be wrong to kill her, that this would do nothing to change that horror in the world. Indeed, it would have been adding to the horror, but I was only dimly aware of that.

I'd found a focus for the intense feelings that had filled me ever since I stood over those dead Marines. I wanted so badly to be able to release those feelings, to have something or someone that I could destroy—as though that would somehow transform the hell that was raging inside me.

The old lady never looked up nor gave any indication that she knew I was aiming my rifle at her. The rhythmic swinging of her hoe never faltered. Finally, I lowered my rifle and put the safety back on. The long file of Marines stretched out in front of me, and it was time for my squad to start moving. I turned and walked on.

She never looked up.

And no one ever said a word to me about how close I'd come to killing that woman. I don't know if anyone even noticed. Perhaps my squadmates were filled with their own feelings about what we'd just seen. What I do know is how utterly senseless it would have appeared if I had pulled the trigger and committed that horrible act. Who would ever understand? Yet it made complete sense to me in the state of mind I was in—after seeing so many people die for no reason that made any sense to me.

I now understood how war atrocities happen. We came here to save these people, and some of us were making the ultimate sacrifice of our own precious lives. Where was their appreciation, their gratitude for what we were giving up for them? And where was my compassion, my outrage at the way I'd seen that old lady treated my first day in-country? Now I was prepared to kill an old lady no different from her.

Something profound had changed in my life. The previous night I'd experienced a level of fear beyond any I'd ever known before. But it was the morning—after the danger was past—that made the difference. I'd come face to face with death, and I was changed by that encounter, but the most disturbing part was what I'd encountered within myself. I didn't just come close to killing that woman; I wanted to kill her—I fiercely wanted to kill her. I wanted the satisfaction of being able to strike out against everything wrong with the world, and somehow that act of murderous violence felt like the only way I could do it.

I never imagined I was capable of anything remotely like that, and even though I managed not to do it, I knew I was capable of it.

Carl Jung said the personality of every person has a hidden side, a side that dwells in the shadows. It is the place where our most vile, reprehensible impulses lay in wait. I had come face to face with my own shadow, and it was more disturbing than anything the NVA could throw at me.

Chapter 42

Shadows

An hour after hitting the beach, K Company had taken the Point. The Japanese had retreated, and my father and his comrades held the high ground. For a period of time, no one was shooting at them.

Maybe the worst was over with.

But when they looked down at the long stretch of beach, they began to realize that the battle for Peleliu was not going as expected. Across the entire beachhead, the fighting was still so intense that no one had progressed more than a few dozen yards beyond the beach.

The Point still had the greatest strategic value of any position along the entire line held by the Marines, which meant the Japanese could not afford to allow it to remain in the hands of the Marines.

Chapter 43

The Aftermath

After we had walked a short distance, they told us to fix bayonets. I knew there was a huge number of NVA in the area, so that was a bit creepy. We kept walking past bomb shelters but we didn't go down into them. We dropped some grenades in a few but that did nothing but make noise. The general feeling was that they were probably full of NVA soldiers waiting to come springing out at us. Yet nothing appeared.

It was deathly quiet. All of those troops the night before and now nothing. We stayed in the area for three days and had no significant contact. It had seemed like the whole North Vietnamese Army was up against us the night we arrived. Now it was deserted, except for the peasants. We found some uniforms in one of the bomb shelters, and Mike Watson captured two NVA soldiers he found in a large spider trap. But overall, the enemy had disappeared. It was very creepy.

Chapter 44

Shadows

Out of more than two platoons that had taken the Point, there were only thirty-two Marines in any shape to defend it. Second Platoon was cut off; they had gotten caught in a large ditch intended to stop tanks, and they had taken heavy casualties from machine gun positions built into the ditch. K Company was separated from the rest of the division by a gap of nearly two hundred yards. The next company down the line, L Company, was supposed to move across the gap and connect up with K Company, but L Company had their hands full and the gap remained.

If the gap was not filled before nightfall, the Marines on the small mound of coral would be vulnerable to attack from all sides.

Chapter 45

The Arizona Territory

We were only back from Union II a couple of days when we got word that we were going out on another op. It was named Operation Arizona because it was in an area Southwest of Danang that was much like the climate of Arizona, extremely hot and arid. The land was absolutely parched; the earth was cracked apart in places and the most valuable thing around was water. This area eventually became known as the Arizona Territory. Even though it was south of Danang, it was full of NVA.

We boarded helicopters and flew to the base in An Hoa. It was in the middle of nowhere, surrounded by barbed wire and watch towers. All we did was get out of the choppers and walk over to a bunch of amtracs, a more modern version of the ones in which my dad made his beach landings. These were enclosed on top, like tanks except with more empty space inside. We then rode to the area of the operation in these amtracs—actually *on* them since we sat on top of them and didn't ride inside. I preferred to ride on the outside, after my experience in the helicopter in the hot LZ. I didn't like the feeling of being cooped up inside a big target. We rode on the amtracs until we came to a river that bordered the Arizona territory. The amtracs ferried us across, and then we got off and walked. The amtracs bivouacked somewhere near where we crossed, and we didn't see them again until they showed up a few days later.

It was really hot. As usual, I was loaded down like a pack mule, and I was drenched in sweat. Whenever I leaned over, my glasses would get steamed up from the humid air pouring out from under my flak jacket and helmet. The worst part was that we were sweating away our water faster than we could replace it. Water was a constant concern. We all wore two canteens, each of which held a quart. Usually when we encountered water, most of us would hold our positions away from the water and just pass our canteens down the line of Marines to the guys who were at the water. They would fill all the canteens and then pass them back up the line. You never got the same canteens back that you'd passed down, but that didn't matter—you just wanted water.

On the second day when we stopped at a water source and passed our canteens to be filled, I made a really big mistake—I was so thirsty that I drank up both of my canteens as soon as I got them back. Normally when we were on squad-sized patrols, or even out with the platoon, I could drink my fill at the water source and still leave with full canteens. But when we were out with the entire company, I wasn't able to even get close to the water source. I told Ramsey that I had just drunk all my water and asked if I could run down to the water source and refill my canteens. He couldn't let me because we were leaving right then. We headed away from the water, and I was carrying two empty canteens!

Within an hour, we were spread out in a horizontal line, sweeping a large open area, when a VC ambush opened up on us. They had machine guns in front of each end of our line and they were sweeping us with interlocking fire. There was no place to take cover so everyone—the entire company—had to run to an area straight ahead that was between the VC gunners but had some cover to hide behind. The run was probably a hundred and fifty yards, which might not sound like much but I was carrying my usual 75 pounds of gear, and I was super thirsty to start with. In that oppressive heat, I could barely walk fast, much less outright run. I doubt if I would have been able to run at all if I hadn't had the adrenaline rush from someone shooting at me. Even as it was, the shooters were a distance away, and my fear of getting shot just barely outweighed my exhaustion as I tried to run in that heat.

When I finally reached cover, I was more thirsty than I could ever imagine. I watched Ray drain his canteen.

"Ray, you got any more water?"

"No, man, that was all I had. That run about killed me; I could drink another full canteen."

"I drank all my water up an hour ago. Man, I'm so fucking thirsty; I feel like I'm gonna die if I don't get something to drink."

He said, "Look in your pack, maybe you got a fruit cocktail or something."

I hadn't even thought about the stuff in my C-rats. I tore off my pack and dug in it looking for anything moist, and I came up with a can of pears. I opened up those pears and ate them and drank the juice. It was the greatest thing in the world; it totally revived me. That can of pears saved my life!

The whole time I was devouring the pears, we were being

shot at, and I barely noticed. All I could think about was how thirsty I was. Maybe if the shooting were closer, I'd have been more concerned about it. But getting shot at was becoming such a common experience that its impact had diminished, especially when the enemy was shooting from a long ways away.

The operation lasted about ten days, and it was filled with action. We were in a bunch of firefights and were mortared every night. Phantom jets dropped bombs really close to us when we were in big firefights. For such close-in bombing, they used snake-eye bombs. These were bombs that had large fins that popped out right after the bomb was released, which caused the bomb to stop all forward motion and drop straight down right beneath the release point. The snake eyes were for precision bombing, such as when we were in very close to the people we were targeting. Often the bombs would hit so close that big bomb fragments would sail over our heads and land among us or behind us. These fragments were usually quite large, red hot, and very jagged. You could hear them making an irregular swooshing sound as they spun through the air. Generally, no one got hit but, now and then, someone would get burned by one of those hot fragments.

The Arizona territory was controlled by the NVA. We were just visiting and had no bases in the area, so the NVA easily followed our every move. At night, they hit us with their mortars and each day they sniped at us and sprang ambushes on us. We got used to it and soon learned to throw off the mortar gunners. We would dig our holes and look like we were digging in for the night, then after dark, we'd move our location slightly and dig in a second time. The firefights were also to be expected. I got to the point where I really wasn't paying much attention if my squad wasn't involved. Several times, we would get a break while we could hear firing a short distance away.

That was the situation on June 15, which was about the third day of the operation. My platoon had set up temporarily for the afternoon in a small graveyard. The graves in Vietnam were not like in America—they were mounds, usually rising about two feet above ground level. I was playing chess with Cowardin—he carried a little magnetic chess set that gave us something to do when we had down time. There was firing going on behind us and we could hear rounds going over our heads but there was nothing we could do about it as our platoon had been given a break and First Platoon was dealing with the problem. So we just stayed down behind the graves and played chess and smoked cigarettes.

Then the lieutenant came up and yelled at us, "Third Platoon, saddle up. First Platoon is pinned down, and we're going to help them. Leave your packs here."

It turned out that First Platoon had been lured several hundred yards away from the body of the company as they pursued some VC, and now they were pinned down and calling for help. We left our packs in the graveyard and gathered up to go into the firefight. For some reason which I don't recall, the platoon got split up into squads and my squad ran right over to a big open area that we had to cross to get to the firing.

We lined up to run across the open area toward a tree line that would provide cover for us as we moved toward the firing. We understood that there were none of our troops in the treeline, and the VC might have infiltrated into it, so I was going to lay down some cover fire before running across the open area. My M16 jammed on the first round I fired.

"Ramsey, my rifle just jammed."

He looked over at me, thought for a moment, then said, "You stay behind. We don't have time to fix it right now." Then he turned to the rest of the squad and said, "Let's go" and they all got up and ran across the open area.

I was left on my own.

I turned around and ran back to the command group. I found the company top sergeant; I hadn't even realized he was out on the operation with us.

He was smiling as he spoke first, "What's your hurry there, Private?"

"Top, my rifle just jammed, and my squad took off without me!"

Top was cool. He just handed me his rifle and said, "Here, take mine. I'll get yours unjammed, and we'll trade back later."

I said, "Thanks, Top", and took off at a run.

I ran back to where my squad had left to cross the open area without me. They were nowhere in sight, and the amount of firing was now considerably heavier. There was no one else in this area now; I guess the other squads had already run across as well. I took a deep breath and ran across the open area all alone. This was very scary; I felt incredibly alone out in the open, and I couldn't tell if anyone was on the other side of the open area. After I got across the open area, I moved along the tree line looking for my squad. I found other Marines who were also moving toward the firing. My squad had to be further ahead, so I kept moving fast in hopes of catching up with them.

We were in a grove of small trees—a rare sight in the Arizona territory—and rounds were hitting the trees all about us. These were not a few sporadic rounds; it was a steady stream of bullets coming into the area we were in, and I could tell it was from a lot of different weapons shooting at once. As I got closer to the center of the firefight, it grew increasingly chaotic. Those of us in the trees were running as low to the ground as we could get. Marines were trying to find some cover behind the trees, but these were skinny little trees. I was still not with my squad, but I had a lot of Marines around me. I assumed they were from Second Platoon because I didn't recognize anyone. I saw no officers or non-coms, just a lot of Marines moving toward the firefight, and the closer we got to the firing, the more chaotic everything became.

Bullets were snapping all around, explosions were erupting out in front of us, but we couldn't see them, and everyone seemed confused about where First Platoon was actually located. I hoped the NVA didn't decide to drop some mortars into these trees because they would get airbursts, and they would have hit a lot of people. Everyone kept moving toward the firing, and as we got closer everyone got down lower and lower. Soon, we were all bent over, trying to move fast but be only about two and a half feet tall at the same time. The VC couldn't see us in the trees, but they were shooting a lot of rounds into them. Fortunately, the bullets were high enough off the ground that we were steadily moving under them. It was very loud, you could tell we were moving into a total shitstorm of a firefight. I still hadn't found my squad, so I just followed the crowd toward the firing.

Suddenly, we ran out of cover and I was on my belly.

I'd reached the end of the grove of trees. Marines were scattered along the edge of the treeline aiming at a line of dikes and shrubs about 200 yards away—where all the firing was coming from. I was off a good ways to the left, and First Platoon was to my right. I still couldn't see them, but the word was they were pinned down directly out in front of the NVA trenches. Despite all the firing, it was difficult to see any targets. I crawled up to where I had room to shoot and aimed at the base of the shrubs, assuming the NVA were in a position similar to my own, which was lying as flat on the ground as I could get.

For the second time that day, my rifle jammed on the first shot. This was not even the same weapon; this was the one I'd gotten from Top. I was totally frustrated and yelled to no one in particular, "Shit, my rifle just jammed again!"

Somebody nearby said, "No shit, Sherlock."

I looked around me, and that's when I realized that no one was firing their weapons. All the firing was coming from the NVA positions because every M16 around me was jammed! I felt like I'd been dumped in the middle of the freeway with cars flying at me from every direction.

First Platoon had engaged with a reinforced company of NVA that was dug in to trenches in the relative shape of a giant horseshoe. The NVA had a .50 caliber machine gun—I actually heard there were two but who knows—and a .57 recoilless rifle. First Platoon had been lured right into the kill zone of that horseshoe-shaped ambush. I was outside the horseshoe and well off to the left side of it. First Platoon got lured in by an age-old trick. When a few enemy soldiers show themselves and then run, you better be damn careful about where they're leading you.

The worst thing about that day, however, was not how the enemy outsmarted us. When First Platoon engaged the enemy force, every Marine's M16 jammed as soon as he first tried to fire it. We were all carrying useless weapons! The only weapons that were working were the M60 machine guns, the sniper rifles and the M79 grenade launchers.

Once I knew my weapon was jammed, I crawled back into the trees and tried to find someone with a cleaning rod to help me get the jammed cartridge out of my weapon. My own cleaning rod was in my pack, which was back at the graves. Meanwhile, someone started yelling for those of us in the trees to come help with the casualties. First Platoon had taken heavy casualties. So I followed a group of Marines back through the same trees, angling toward the area behind First Platoon. We came out of the area of cover but we weren't directly in the line of fire. Bullets were still flying overhead, but nobody around me was getting hit.

Eventually, we found a group of casualties and people yelling for corpsmen.

I spent the afternoon packing a worthless rifle and helping carry the wounded out of the firefight. The only way we got out with as many people alive as we did was that the amtracs arrived and were used to shield the guys from First Platoon as they retreated, while F4 Phantoms dropped bombs and napalm. There were a lot of casualties! The platoon commander, Lieutenant Lyons, was dead, and the platoon sergeant was very busy trying to get all his casualties carried out. The lieutenant was killed as he ran around with a cleaning rod trying to unjam the rifles of his men. He received a posthumous Silver Star.

The amtracs put up a valiant fight and one of their crewmembers was killed in the battle. They had working machine guns and one track had a .106 recoilless rifle mounted on it, but the NVA knocked out two of the amtracs and inflicted damage to the others. Four people were killed from Echo Company, and we were medevacing casualties into the evening.

I didn't see my squad all through the firefight. In fact, I

didn't see much of anything after my second rifle jammed. I made two trips helping carry casualties. The whole time, I kept looking for someone with a cleaning rod to help me unjam my rifle, but that never happened. At the end of the afternoon, I eventually found my way back to where we'd stashed our packs, and my squad was already there. I got my cleaning rod out and dislodged the spent cartridge in my rifle and then went looking for Top to return his rifle. When I found him, he wasn't smiling like he had been earlier.

"Top, I brought your rifle back."

Top was sitting next to a radio; I guess he was monitoring the medevacs. His head was kind of hanging. He said, "Yours is right there," indicating a rifle that was propped up next to the radio.

I said, "You better make your first shot count, Top. Yours jammed too. First shot."

Top nodded, "Every rifle in the company jammed." He raised his eyes and gave me an intense look, "Every fucking one of 'em."

I nodded in response and stayed quiet. I had never heard

Top swear before; he was a very gentlemanly guy, and I thought of him as old. I don't know how old he was, but I thought of him as being like my dad's age. He wore his hair very short, but you could see that he didn't have much to start with.

He continued, "Somebody let us down, Son. Somebody let us down big time. If an infantryman can't trust his weapon, he's no longer a threat to the enemy. He's not a threat to anybody. He's just a target."

I didn't know what to say, so I didn't say anything. I just nodded and walked back to my squad. Top was really sad, and I had never seen him look anything close to sad. He was one of those guys that is always upbeat, smiling and taking care of everybody.

We were all disheartened. It was simply unbelievable that every M16 had jammed. After that, we didn't trust them. We'd been told that they could jam if they were dirty but that was not what happened in this case. The jams occurred because the extractor on the bolt ripped the lip off the cartridge casing when it was supposed to pull the spent casing out of the breech after the round had been fired. Normally, the extractor hooks the lip of the cartridge and flips it out of the receiver as the bolt goes backward. Then when the bolt goes forward again, it pushes a new round into the breech. But if the metal lip on the cartridge rips off, then the spent casing remains in the breech and the new bullet jams up against it when the bolt is pushing it into place.

We had received fresh ammo before the operation and everyone had replaced the ammo in their magazines with fresh rounds. Many people figured the problem was that the ammo was defective, that the brass had been made with insufficient nickel so it wasn't strong enough, and that was why the lips ripped on the cartridges. The defect apparently didn't show until we were using the rifles in such extreme heat, which may have caused the casings to swell excessively. After the operation was over, armorers came out and replaced the buffers in our M16's to slow them down so that they didn't rip the cartridges out so fast. They said this was the source of the problem; the weapon was just too fast.

Perhaps.

I was never convinced that the problem was the buffers. Our weapons had fired okay before the operation. I still tended to think the problem was the ammunition; i.e., that the heat caused the casings to expand enough in the breech to require additional force from the extractor and that put greater demands on the metal of the casings. If the problem was the ammo, was it an honest mistake or had some unscrupulous defense contractor scrimped on materials? Or was it simply that the rifle fired too fast and was consequently more vulnerable in a variety of conditions; i.e., being dirty, too much heat, less than perfect ammunition. In any case, one thing was clear: We had been issued a weapon that was not adequately tested, and it cost us lives.

Some of my comrades saw that afternoon on Operation Arizona as evidence that the country didn't really care about us. As for myself, I'd already begun to lose trust in the South Vietnamese. Now my faith in my own country was challenged. My world was getting smaller and smaller. It seemed the only people I knew I could depend on were the guys in my squad.

Chapter 46

Shadows

The Marines on the Point prepared for a counterattack. There was no place to dig in on the mound of hard coral, so they set up positions using rocks and trees felled by the pre-landing bombardment. K Company had lost all of their machine guns during the landing at the beach, but they were able to set up a Japanese machine gun that they had captured. They found ammunition in some of the Japanese bunkers—in fact, they had more ammo for the Japanese gun than for many of their own weapons. The batteries for the radio were starting to fade, so Captain Hunt used it while it still worked and made an urgent request for more ammo, water and reinforcements.

They were separated from the rest of the division and low on ammo, not to mention personnel. Everyone began to realize the predicament they would be in if darkness fell before they were resupplied.

Chapter 47

Separated Once Again

We got mortared every night on Operation Arizona. We often would appear to be digging in for the night, only to get up and move again at dusk and dig in all over again, hoping to mislead the VC. They would then come up and probe our lines, and once they had established where we were, they would start dropping mortar shells on us. One night I dug my hole as usual but went to sleep on a nearby grave (up above the level ground). I was very tired and ended up sleeping through the inevitable mortar attack. The guys in my squad told me that they were yelling and trying to wake me but to no avail. I remember dreaming that I was in an artillery attack. When I awoke, the place was covered in smoke. Since I wasn't wounded, they rest of my squad thought it pretty funny that I slept right through a mortar attack.

That same night, the radioman for the executive officer (XO) was hit when a mortar round landed near the area where the command group was quartered for the night. Several people were hit, and I heard that they had a hard time even finding a wound on one of the men who was killed. The corpsman eventually found a tiny hole at the base of his spine. That was one of those weird things that happens. Some guys were blown into pieces, losing multiple limbs, and yet still survived. At the same time, this guy dies from an almost unnoticeable hole that didn't even bleed.

The morning following that attack, Lieutenant Felong came over and talked to Ramsey. I was sitting on the edge of my hole, eating my luscious breakfast of C-rats. A moment later, Ramsey called me over, and the lieutenant spoke to me.

"Catherall, we lost the XO's radioman last night and he needs somebody to carry his radio. You're good on the radio, so I'm afraid you're it. Get your gear together and go report to the XO."

That was it, no discussion.

I definitely did not want to be separated from my squad and be a radioman! But, of course, I was not given a choice. So I put on my pack and went and found Lieutenant Erickson, the XO. I told him who I was and that I was going to pack his radio.

He shook my hand, which was not your typical greeting from an officer to a PFC. "Glad to know you, Catherall." He looked over my shoulder at my pack and said, "I think our first problem is going to be figuring out how to add the radio to all that gear you're packing."

Then he helped me to repack my gear on top of the radio. We made it all work, but it weighed a ton. I had to carry a couple of extra batteries in addition to the radio itself. All told, it added about 35 pounds to what I was already carrying. Once we got it all packed together, he suggested I put it on and try standing in it. I sat down, slipped into it, and discovered I couldn't stand up.

Lieutenant Erickson laughed, "You gotta think like a turtle. Get over on your hands and knees first, then you'll be able to stand up."

And that's how I got to my feet for the rest of the operation. Once I could stand, I didn't want to sit down. If we stopped walking, I would just lean against something when I could. Sitting down just wasn't worth the trouble unless I was going to be down for a while. Walking was interesting too. I learned to lean forward as I walked, so that the weight balanced on my back in just the right way. I was kind of amazed to find that I could walk all day long like that. Of course, the first time I stood up with that pack on, I thought I would collapse any moment.

Lieutenant Erickson was a nice guy, competent and easy going. We spent a lot of time talking about all kinds of stuff, and it made being away from the squad more bearable. It was interesting too, because I got to do more advanced things with the radio, like passing along the info for fire missions when Lieutenant Erickson directed counter-mortar fire.

One night, Lieutenant Erickson and I laid our ponchos down to sleep and then stayed up late talking. He was interested in the fact that I had some education—two years of college—and he was encouraging me to go back to school after I got out of the Marine Corps. Then we heard a sound at the perimeter, and a Marine yelled something.

Lieutenant Erickson said, "You hear that? They're probing our lines."

I said, "Usually they just start dropping the mortars."

He stood up, "That's next. Come on, let's go get ready to

fire counter-mortar fire. Maybe we can get a leg up on them."

So instead of waiting for the attack, we got up and headed over to where we had set up a position to direct our 60mm mortars. We had taken about ten steps when, sure enough, the first mortar round landed—and it came down close behind us. One of the Marines from the mortar crew was standing a few feet in front of me when the shell landed behind me, and I saw his face as a piece of shrapnel went through his cheek. Lieutenant Erickson and I were given a push by the blast. This was the second time in about three weeks that I was close enough to a mortar blast to feel the concussion yet didn't get hit by any shrapnel.

After the mortar barrage was over, we returned to our ponchos where we'd been lying before the attack. Lieutenant Erickson lifted his poncho and said, "Check this out."

His poncho was riddled with holes.

I took a closer look at mine; it had a bunch of holes in it as well. I blew my breath out in a low whistle, "Holy shit, Lieutenant, if we'd been laying there, we'd have been creamed."

He nodded, "Yeah, and think about it, Catherall. I bet this was that first round that hit behind us. If we hadn't stayed up talking…"

I swallowed, "Yes sir, I see what you mean." If we hadn't stayed up talking, it's unlikely we would have gotten up as quickly as we did, and that first round would have been right on top of us.

Lieutenant Erickson gave his ruined poncho a shake and said, "Well, let's hope it doesn't rain."

It took us both a while to fall asleep.

Stories of close calls like that seem astounding, but most everyone who's been in combat has some of these stories. You're in the midst of a lot of flying metal; often the only reason you don't get hit is because you happen to go left instead of right. One night I sleep through mortars landing all around me and I don't get touched; another night I get up when normally I would still be asleep, and that leads to my not getting hit. A guy who's further away from the blast gets hit when I don't, and one guy dies from a nearly invisible wound while another lives when he looks like a train wreck.

Some guys obsessed over those seemingly insignificant decisions that made all the difference. They talked about fate, or luck, or they got religion. However, most guys just shrugged it off.

Chapter 48

Shadows

During the afternoon, a tractor known as an alligator came rumbling down the beach to the Point. It brought ammo, grenades, and water to the men of K Company. The crew even removed the machine guns from their vehicle and gave these to the Marines who were stranded on the strategic mound of coral. My father was part of a line of men who passed the supplies up to the top of the mound.

He watched the alligator as it drove back down the beach across the area that was not held by the Marines. The Japanese fired several mortar rounds at it and he saw the blasts spouting up all around the slow vehicle. But none hit it and it ambled on down the beach unscathed.

Unfortunately, it was not possible to send any reinforcements, but at least the Marines on the mound were now well armed and had water. The water was particularly needed;

virtually every man had finished off the water he brought ashore in his canteens. But when they tapped into the water brought to them, it was almost undrinkable. It had been placed in barrels that previously were used to carry petroleum. Some of the Marines threw up after trying to drink it.

Some resourceful Marines went down to the base of the Point and collected the canteens of the dead Japanese soldiers. They counted 110 dead Japs around the Point.

Chapter 49

A Thirsty Man is a Dangerous Man

By the final day of the operation, we were really dragging our tails as we approached the same river we'd initially crossed to get into the territory. Everyone was baking in the heat. When we reached the river, people started dropping their gear as they walked, and they just kept going right out into the water. I always thought scenes of that sort of thing in the desert movies were exaggerations, but now I know otherwise. The scary part was that no one bothered to set up proper security. We were lucky the NVA didn't anticipate where we would reach the river. They'd have had us at their mercy.

I dropped my pack and radio, my web gear, and my rifle, and I just walked out into the river and sank down into the cool water. It was an amazingly powerful experience. All the heat leeched right out of my body and, within seconds, I felt refreshed, transformed, reborn.

Extreme thirst, or unbearable heat, can lead one to give up all good judgment. On one of those terribly hot days in the Arizona Territory, I found an urn filled with what appeared to be rainwater. It was located behind some peasant's hooch, so I figured the local people must be using it. The water was cloudy—I couldn't see half an inch into it—and it obviously needed to be purified, which meant I would have to fill my canteen, drop in halizone tablets and wait 15 minutes. That felt like forever at that moment; I was so thirsty that I wasn't thinking straight. Instead, I leaned over and drank right off the surface of the water. I was hoping it would be less contaminated on the surface, but like I said, I wasn't thinking straight. If it had been a puddle, it would have been okay—just dirty. But water sitting in an urn probably had time to breed some nasty stuff.

I paid the price for my weakness. When we left the field from the operation, we went on duty briefly to Hoi An and spent the night at a base that had electricity, outdoor movies, and a milk machine in the mess hall. This was a golden opportunity; we were in the lap of luxury. We never got to drink anything cold, much less milk. So as soon as they turned us loose in the mess hall, I excitedly went to the milk machine and filled my canteen cup. But as soon as I held the milk in front of my nose, my stomach started churning. I was nauseated by the smell of it and went outside and got sick to my stomach. From that point on, I threw up for days and couldn't keep anything down. I threw up so much that I had trouble keeping the pills down that the corpsman gave me.

They told me that I had the worms—parasites that live in water. I surely acquired them when I drank the water from that urn. So I never got to drink any milk, and I was too sick to go to the movie at Hoi An.

I did, however, learn to rely on my halizone tablets and not take the quality of water for granted. There may not be anything on this planet more valuable than good, clean water.

Chapter 50

Shadows

After they were resupplied, my father and the other Marines on the Point actually had about 45 minutes in which they took off their shirts and relaxed. They smoked cigarettes and talked about the battle to capture the mound. The men who arrived in the amtrac closest to the mound told of how they had exited their amtrac and charged the Japanese positions so quickly that some of the enemy riflemen were still leaving their protected positions and crawling back to the fighting positions that surrounded the pillboxes. They laughed about catching the Japs with their pants down.

Even though the water they'd received was barely drinkable, the resupply buoyed everyone's spirits. The supply vehicle drove right down the beach to them, so they didn't feel as distant from the rest of the Marine line. And because the high ground gave the K Company Marines the advantage of a better angle of vision, the Japanese had retreated further back and were not firing on them. For a few moments that afternoon, those Marines felt like they had the Japs on the run.

Then the Japanese snipers started shooting.

Few Marines had any moments of being freed up from the fighting that first day on Pelilu. Those few men from K Company who had taken the high ground may have been the only ones. The rest of the First Division was heavily engaged with the enemy all up and down its line.

It is ironic that it was these Marines who had a few moments of relief and a sense of greater optimism about how the battle was going. They were cut off from the main body and sitting on the piece of real estate that the Japanese most wanted to recover.

Chapter 51

Hawaiian Interlude

I went on my first R&R in July. It was quite unexpected. I was suddenly told that I could go if I wanted, and so off I went to Hawaii. It was a very strange experience. Within hours, I was transported to a world where I could have anything I wanted to eat or drink, and I was perfectly safe and comfortable all the time.

It felt unreal.

I arrived in Hawaii and was processed through by some civilian clerks. I had to deal with a young woman who seemed curious.

"So what do you do in Vietnam?"

Something about her question irritated me. "Well, what do you think I do? I'm not there on a scholarship."

She said, "I mean, like, what's your job? I know you're a Marine, but are you like a clerk or something?"

I swelled out my chest, "Hell no, I'm a grunt."

She gave me a look of surprise. "You're in the infantry, huh. You don't look like a grunt."

I responded defensively, "Yeah, well, I am." I looked down and was quiet for a moment. Then I looked up at her and asked, "So what does a grunt look like?"

She shrugged, "I don't know. You just don't seem the type, but I guess there's all kinds of people over there."

I nodded. I knew what she saw—a mild-mannered, skinny boy with geeky, military glasses. I didn't look like Sergeant Rock from the comic books.

I finished processing through and they turned me loose. I had come with a planeload of people but I was the only one from Echo Company, and I hadn't known anyone else on the plane. When they turned me loose, I was on my own—I didn't have any buddies there with me.

The first thing I did was to get a room at a small hotel near Waikiki. I had brought some civilian clothes but I didn't have much to wear and it all seemed too heavy and hot to wear in that climate. The second thing I did was to go and buy a pair of shorts, tennis shoes, socks, and a Hawaiian shirt. And the third thing I did was to find a hamburger and a chocolate malt. I took the hamburger and malt back to my room and sat there and ate it. Once I was done eating, I called home.

My mom answered the phone.

"Hi, Mom. How are you?"

"Don, is that you?"

"Yeah, it's me; can you believe it?"

"Where are you? What, I mean, is everything, I mean, you know, is—"

I laughed. "Everything's fine. I'm in Hawaii on R and R."

Her voice suddenly sounded really happy. "You're in Hawaii? Oh my gosh. When did you get there? How long do you get to stay?"

"I'm here for five days. I got a room right near Waikiki in Honolulu."

We talked for a few minutes. She got my phone number and said they would call back later after my dad got home. That cheered me up, so I determined to go out on the town. I heard stories about guys on R&R who picked up women, gambled, and caroused all night at bars. I was twenty years old, and supposedly too young to drink, but I had heard that most bars would make an exception for guys on R and R from Nam.

So I went out and found a place that served drinks and nervously went in and sat at the bar. It was lunchtime. The bartender stared at me like he knew I was underage, but he still asked me what I wanted and he served me a whiskey sour. It was the only drink I knew by name. I thought I liked whiskey sours, but when I tasted it, I didn't really much care for it. I thought about ordering a beer, I knew I would like that better than the whiskey sour. But I was reluctant to order a beer after a mixed drink, I figured that would mark me as a novice for sure. So I left half the drink and departed the bar.

I spent the afternoon walking around the stores near Waikiki. For some reason, I couldn't identify anything that I wanted to do. The truth was that I really didn't know what to do with my freedom. It was intimidating to be alone in paradise with no clear idea of what to do with myself. Prior to entering the Marines, I had spent very little time out in the world on my own. About the only thing I accomplished that afternoon was to buy a cheap camera, an Instamatic.

After a couple of hours, I wandered back to my little hotel room and took a long, hot shower. I played with the camera a bit, but I felt lost, lonely and, believe it or not, I almost wished I was back with my squad, going on patrol and sitting hole watch. Almost. This certainly was not what I had imagined R&R would be like.

Then the phone rang.

Both my mom and my dad were on at the same time, and they both sounded very excited. After a minute of checking in with my dad, my mom spoke kind of tentatively and asked, "So what kind of plans do you have for your time there in Hawaii?"

"I don't know, nothing in particular. I guess I'll go surfing and out to some nice restaurants."

Then my dad spoke up, "Well, how would you like to have some company?"

"What do you mean?"

"Well, we were thinking of coming out there and seeing you."

My mom added, "Unless you'd rather we didn't."

My dad chimed in, "Yeah, only if you wouldn't mind

having some company."

I was flabbergasted. "Oh yeah, I'd love to see you guys. You mean you'd fly out here?"

My dad said, "Well, as a matter of fact, we can be on a flight that arrives tomorrow afternoon at 2:00 your time."

It was settled, and my state of mind instantly improved. I would have loved to have been a cool dude, hitting the bars and picking up women. But the truth was I didn't really have any idea how to go about such a thing. I was lonely, and there was no one I would rather see than my folks. I didn't know squat about how to have a good time on my own or how to fit into this strange environment. Now I had something to look forward to.

I met their plane at the airport the next day, and my Hawaiian experience changed from the moment they stepped onto the tarmac. They'd been drinking on the flight over, and my dad was feeling no pain. They were both wearing flower leis and laughing and saying goodbye to the people they'd met on the plane. Everyone on the plane seemed to know my dad; apparently he'd been the life of the party on the flight over. My mom was in a playful mood, even laughing at my dad's jokes, regardless how many times she'd heard them. She was a good sport about everything we did for the next four days, and we did all kinds of things.

We went to Waikiki, and I tried surfing. We rented a jeep with a fringe on top, and drove all over the island. We went to a pineapple plantation and ate fresh spears of pineapple with salt. We drove through the clouds at the top of the mountains and found remote bays away from Honolulu. We drank exotic liquors in the afternoon. We went to Duke Kuhanemoka's club, and my dad and I danced with Hawaiian girls in hula skirts while my mom cheered us on. Basically, we had a whole lot of fun.

My parents knew how to have a good time.

One day, we went to Pearl Harbor and took the tour boat out to the memorial that sits over the Battleship Arizona and paid our respects to the men who died there. It was not lost on me that I had recently seen more American lives lost on another Arizona. It gave me a chilling feeling, what my mother always referred to as "having a rabbit run over your grave".

All too soon, it was time for me to go back to the war. Somehow, I'd managed to forget what would happen when R&R

was over, and I think my parents were in the same state of denial. It didn't really hit me until the last few hours. We hadn't talked about Vietnam; I had told them virtually nothing of what I had been through. When the topic of my going back came up, I reassured my mom that I would be fine. But when it came time to catch my plane, I discovered that going back from R&R felt scarier than going to Nam in the first place. The eight months that I had remaining in my tour seemed impossibly long. After all the fighting I saw in June, I couldn't imagine that I would survive eight more months.

At the airport, I got my dad off to the side and we had a short talk.

"Daddy, we haven't talked about what I've been doing over there, but I think you need to know that it's been pretty scary. A lot of guys are getting killed."

My dad nodded, "Yeah, I figured."

"I'm not so sure that I'll make it. If things keep up like they've been for the last month, it just doesn't seem like my chances are too good."

My dad just nodded again.

"So, maybe you need to prepare Mother." I paused and shrugged, "I may not make it home."

My dad put his hand on my shoulder and said, "Don't worry, Son, I'll take care of things on my end. You just do what you can to stay alive. Remember, let someone else be the hero that jumps on the grenade."

I said "Thanks" and found that our short talk really did help. I didn't worry about my mom after that. My dad was very much in control; his composure helped me to hold it together myself.

My mom cried as she always did at separations. I kissed her and hugged my dad, and I flew back to the war. It was a blessing that my mom cried so much when we said goodbye—I was so busy reassuring her that it helped me hold back my own tears. They were in my eyes but they didn't escape.

The return flight carried the same group of guys who'd made the flight five days earlier. The trip from Nam to Hawaii had been crowded and noisy; everyone was in a rowdy mood. It was a very quiet trip back, and there were some empty seats.

Chapter 52

Shadows

Once the Japanese snipers started shooting at the men on the Point, they never stopped. Sniping was not going to retake the mound, but it put an end to the Marines sitting around laughing and telling stories. It also put an end to the feeling that the worst was over.

Darkness was coming and my father and his comrades were certain that the Japanese would try to retake the Point. What they knew—and the Japs did not—was how few men were actually defending the small mound of coral.

Chapter 53

The Short Coffin

When I returned from R&R, my platoon was on temporary assignment south of Danang, near Hoi An. We were covering for a platoon from some other company that was out on an operation. My squad was situated away from the rest of the platoon—guarding a bridge. I didn't even spend a night at the hill when I walked in from R&R. The platoon sergeant told me to grab my gear and I could "catch a ride out to Ramsey's bridge." Ramsey's bridge?

Actually, it was the remains of a bridge, which the VC had blown up. Engineers came out during the day and worked on the rebuild, and then we covered it at night.. This was the first time our small squad had been given so much responsibility. Certainly, we always patrolled on our own, but here we were spending ten days living in an area with just our squad leader, Corporal Ramsey, in charge—no platoon sergeant or platoon commander.

I guess it didn't go unnoticed that Ramsey kept us in good shape through some nasty shit in June. The officers treated Ramsey with greater respect, and I agreed. I was still grateful about how he came out and found me when I got separated from the squad on Union II.

Guarding the bridge was light duty, we had little to do during the day; our main task was manning the positions at night. We only did minimal patrolling of the area, which was unusual, however, I still had difficulty relaxing. We were not hit in the week or so that we were there, but I was always on the lookout. After our experience in June, I no longer felt safe just because nothing was going on.

One afternoon, Mike Watson and I were looking across the river, and we saw half a dozen Vietnamese walking along and carrying something. I ran over and told Ramsey, and he came down to our position with a pair of binoculars.

Ramsey looked through the binoculars for a moment, then said, "It looks like a coffin."

Cowardin said, "That'd be a perfect way to transport

weapons without getting caught. You could carry a machine gun all over the countryside like that."

Ramsey nodded. "Yeah, we better check it out." He looked around for a moment. There was no bridge, so the only way across the river was by boat.

"Okay, Catherall, you and Watson go across on the gook boat and investigate."

Great, Mike and I had each made lance corporal but we were still at the bottom of the hierarchy. Well, this one didn't look too difficult, plus I might have been a little proud that Ramsey felt Mike and I could handle it on our own.

So Mike Watson and I went over to the dropped bridge. Some local Vietnamese had a small flat-bottomed boat which they were using to aid the engineers building the bridge. The Vietnamese rowed us to the other side of the river, and we hiked over and intercepted the coffin squad. There were about six very old men, and the coffin was awfully short. That seemed a little suspicious in itself.

None of the old men spoke English. They made the usual show of chattering away and gesturing a lot, which only bewildered us. We indicated for them to put the coffin down. Then we tugged at the lid of the coffin but it was nailed on, and I was reluctant to take my bayonet and pry the thing open. So instead, we directed them to carry the coffin back to the river. When we got to the river, I yelled across to Ramsey and put the problem in his lap.

"Whattaya want us to do with this thing?"

Ramsey yelled back, "What's in it?"

"I don't know; it's nailed shut."

Ramsey thought about it for a moment, then yelled across, "Then bring it over here, and we'll have a look at it."

I continued to push him to make all the decisions. "How are we going to get it over there? It's too big for the boat."

He yelled, "Just balance it on the fucking boat, and have the gooks row it across."

So the coffin was laid sideways on this little boat and the entire group of old men—the pallbearers—were required to board the boat. When they all got aboard, the boat was heavily overloaded, and there was no room for me and Mike.

Ramsey saw what was happening and yelled again,

"Catherall, you come with them. Don't let them come across unescorted."

Great, I had to ride across with them while Mike waited on the side of the river. I would have been more than happy to wait with him. But someone had to accompany the coffin party; we couldn't take the chance that this group of little old men was going to whip out machine guns and mow us all down.

When I tried to get into the boat, it was clear that there was no room for me. I couldn't fit anywhere down into the boat where the little old men were. The only place where I could sit was on top of the coffin, so I climbed on top of it, feeling as conspicuous as a whore in church. The boat was not very stable with me balanced high atop the coffin, so I did not dare to move around. The little old men were cramped into the boat below me, pressing close on both sides of the coffin. I felt extraordinarily awkward and self-conscious. It was a more exaggerated form of how I often felt around the South Vietnamese peasants. Here I was—six feet tall and covered with weapons, and here they were—a bunch of unarmed old men in sandals, not a one of whom stood higher than my armpit. I was swaying above them as I straddled their coffin, and they were smiling and nodding up at me as though we were out for a picnic together.

The trip across seemed to take a long time though it couldn't have lasted more than a couple of minutes. We unloaded the coffin and popped the lid with a bayonet. Sure enough, there was a child inside, about four years old. The old men smiled at us when we looked inside. I guess they were pleased to be shown to be telling the truth. Of course, they could have been telling me it was their dirty laundry for all I knew. They returned to their side of the river without me. And we returned to being a bunch of adolescent Marines.

For a few moments there, we were prepared to exercise the power of life and death over those old men. When I sat on top of that coffin, covered with weapons of destruction, my power over those tiny old men was embarrassingly obvious. These old men were the elders of their community, attending to the burial of a child—and I was a young man commanding all that power in their home.

Something wrong with that picture.

Chapter 54

Shadows

I grew up in Dallas, right across the street from a lake, and I fished throughout my summers when I was young. My dad taught me the basics of fishing, but he wasn't really into it. He didn't enjoy sitting there waiting for a fish to bite. What he did love was hunting, and he spent many hours teaching me to shoot and hunt. Some of my most treasured times with my dad were when we went hunting.

We hunted some for varmints—which we didn't eat and I sort of felt bad about shooting them—but the majority of the time we hunted for birds, mostly dove and quail. My dad told me about going deer hunting when he was growing up in Minnesota, and I got excited about the idea of going deer hunting. He promised to take me, and I bugged him about it many times. But, for one reason or another, we never went deer hunting.

Chapter 55

Search and Destroy

We went on a search and destroy operation that summer in an area in which everyone was considered to be either VC or VC sympathizer, and we were requiring them to move out of the area altogether. The water buffalo, or water boo, was the main work animal for the farmer, but the Viet Cong also used it like the elephant—to carry supplies. So we had standing orders on this op to shoot all water buffalo. We also were required to burn down some dwellings.

This was so blatantly stupid that, even then, I considered it a brilliant American tactic to aid Viet Cong recruitment. If those peasants didn't hate us before we got there, they sure as hell did after we burned their homes and killed their livestock.

My squad was patrolling an area; Medina was walking point and I was right behind him as we walked through a large field of rice paddies that extended across a series of terraces. We came upon a water buffalo that was standing in a rice paddy slightly below us and only about twenty-five yards away. At first, I just stood there next to Medina, and we sort of looked at each other like, was it really necessary to do this? Then Ramsey came up with the rest of the squad. I don't think he wanted to kill the animal any more than we did, but it was his job to make sure we followed orders.

"All right, you know what you're supposed to do. Go ahead and shoot it."

Medina and I raised our M16s and started shooting. We each emptied a magazine into the water buffalo, but it didn't die. It just stood there. At first, I couldn't even see where my bullets had hit; then I began to see blood. But the damn thing didn't fall; it had just taken forty bullets and just stood there quivering like a leaf, clearly in pain but unable to move.

Ramsey said, "Shit. Come on, everybody shoot it."

I replaced my magazine and all six of us opened up on that poor helpless creature. Incredibly, it still stood there. It was covered in blood and shaking all over but it wouldn't fall down. From our first shots, it never took a single step, but it refused to fall down. The M16 fires a very small slug that doesn't have much knockdown power on a big animal. So that poor water boo had to stand there and bleed to death before it would fall.

It was painful to watch, and as the shooting went on, I began to yell at the animal. "Die, you stupid mother fucker! Don't you know you're dead?" Some of the other guys started to yell things as well.

Somebody fired another magazine into it. Finally, it crumpled over, and it was dead when it hit the ground. There were six of us and two of us had fired a second magazine, all at close range. We hit it over a hundred times before it finally collapsed.

We all just stood there for a moment staring at this senseless example of American foreign policy. Then Ramsey said, "All right, let's move it out. That boo isn't going to get any deader."

As we started walking off, Cowardin yells, "Die, you stupid mother fucker. Don't you know you're dead?" Several guys laughed. A few minutes later, somebody else repeated the line and everyone laughed again. I laughed too but, hey, it didn't sound so stupid when I'd said it.

Chapter 56

Shadows

When I was ten years old, my family vacationed to the town of Monterrey in Mexico. One day, we drove a couple of hours to a resort called Horsetail Falls. It was in the mountains, and we rode burros up a path to the waterfall. We all laughed because my dad was so big that he draped over his burro and nearly dragged his legs on the ground. After our excursion, my parents spent the afternoon in the bar partying, and my dad was pretty loaded by the time we started the long drive back to the hotel.

We came upon an accident in which a school bus had collided with an automobile. The two men from the automobile were lying in the road and local people were crowded around them, but no one was tending to the men. The nearest hospital was more than an hour away, and the people were just passively waiting for an ambulance to come. My dad immediately made his way through the crowd and knelt by the men. Soon he was sending people for blankets, water and materials for bandages. I had to sit in the car for a long time with my mother and sisters, and I was very curious. Somehow, I got out of the car and made my way up to get a look at what my dad was doing.

What I saw never left me. My dad was on his knees, one hand holding a cloth against a man's chest where blood was bubbling out and the other hand was gesturing as he tried to get a nearby woman to tear another piece of cloth into long strips. His hands were covered with blood. To his left lay a second man who was breathing, but his face was bloody and one eyeball was hanging out of the socket.

My dad was clearly in charge, and he was stone cold sober.

My parents told this story for years. They thought it was pretty funny because the next day the Mexican papers reported that an American doctor had saved the two men on the highway. But, of course, the truth is that it was better than a doctor, it was an American Marine combat veteran. When disaster strikes, the average civilian stands around with his thumb up his ass and waits for someone else to do something. If I'm ever lying on that highway, I hope a Marine finds me.

As for my experience that day, I continued to see that man's face with the displaced eyeball every time I closed my eyes for many years afterward.

Chapter 57

Ramsey

When I first joined the squad, Ramsey was off in the hospital because he'd gotten shot in the ass. When he rejoined the squad, I got to know him. We spent some time playing chess and shooting the shit during free time. He was an easy going guy with a wry sense of humor—always making fun of everything military. When the platoon sergeant would come give us a brief talk—or on rare occasion, the lieutenant—Ramsey would make comments under his breath.

One day after we set up on Hill 60, the platoon sergeant stuck his head in our tent and said, "Corporal Feller, your squad is going to move the machine gun bunker on the Northwest side of the hill. The lieutenant wants you to rebuild it on the corner of the hill where the bulldozers graded it flat."

Feller says, "Shit. Why do we have to move it?"

Ramsey mutters to me, "So the lieutenant can have an

unobstructed view from the shitter when he's taking a crap."

The platoon sergeant says, "So we'll have a better field of fire from the corner."

Ramsey mutters, "Which the captain forgot to notice when we laid out the first bunker."

Feller says, "How come us? We get every shit job that comes up."

Ramsey mutters, "Sounds to me like it was the lieutenant that got the shit job from the captain."

The platoon sergeant says, "First and second squads are going to get their turns too; everybody's going to get their hands dirty rebuilding the hill."

Ramsey mutters, "Only time the lieutenant gets his hands dirty is when he tries to wipe his ass and misses."

This is the way Ramsey was before he became squad leader. He kept us entertained with his constant dialogue about the inanity of it all. Nothing was sacred and everything was fair game. But all that changed after he took over the squad. Ramsey did a great job that night in the hot LZ on Union II, and I am forever grateful for the way he found me and put me back into the action without saying a thing about my getting separated from everybody. Still, I couldn't forget that disturbing sense of excitement radiating from him when he told me about the five dead guys in the next hole.

At the time, it almost felt like he was getting off on the deaths, but I now realize it was just how physiologically aroused he was during the firefight. He didn't stay in his hole like the rest of us. Instead, he was moving up and down the line checking on his troops—including sweeping up the one he lost—and doing everything the Marine Corps expects from those in positions of command. His aroused state came across as a kind of fearlessness, a toughness that you find among some guys that seem to have been there forever.

In the weeks after that intense night on Union II, our squad was in a lot of action—mortar attacks, ambushes and some big, open firefights. Several times, I saw that excitement in Ramsey's eyes. He was one of the best squad leaders in the company, but I began to feel uncomfortable around him when we weren't in the field. He was no longer the same loose, easy-going guy with the wry sense of humor. He didn't laugh at the same things any more.

He stopped making fun of the platoon sergeant and the Marine Corps bureaucracy. His laugh changed; it seemed to me a cruel laugh, a sadistic laugh—not the kind of laugh that made you feel there was anything funny. And he was intense!

After we came back from guarding the bridge near Hoi An, there was intelligence that VC in our area were going to attack a local village. Once more, our squad was given independent responsibility, a sign of how much the officers had come to respect Ramsey's ability to get things done. We were assigned to stay in the ville for a few days to reinforce the local Vietnamese Popular Forces (PF's). Just like at the bridge, this meant that Ramsey would be in charge. So we spent about five days living in this little village and manning their perimeter at night. It was not bad duty— providing we didn't get overrun by NVA some dark night—as we got to hang out with the villagers and were generally left on our own during the day.

We had our own intel too; we soon discovered that there were some prostitutes in the village and some of us started planning how to take advantage of that.

The afternoon of the third day, Ramsey came to me and

said we were going to clean up the PFs' M60 machine gun. Of course, that was a royal "we"—what he meant was that I was going to clean it up. He knew my MOS was machine guns.

The little compound had several bunkers in it, one at each of the four corners plus a couple of others. Ramsey had me sit in one of the enclosed bunkers and disassemble the machine gun there, clean all the parts and then put it back together. I worked on it for a long time, soaking the bolt and the receiver in a pan of cleaning fluid and then cleaning them with the wire brush that screws onto the end of the cleaning rod used to clean the inside of the barrel. The machine gun was caked with black grime; it looked like it had never been properly cleaned.

I didn't have a lot of light in the bunker, and it was getting on toward dark. But I took pride in getting the gun back into top condition and so I took my time, trying to clean the grunge out of every nook and cranny. Finally, I was wiping all the parts with an oiled rag and beginning to hurry so that I could get the gun reassembled before dark—it had to be in position for the night—when Ramsey showed up in the doorway. He sat down across from me—blocking my light.

He said, "I know you guys are thinking about these whores."

I looked up and said, "Yeah, well, we did notice 'em. But don't worry, we'll be…", I paused and gave him a knowing look, "discreet."

Ramsey said, "You stay away from 'em. Hear me? I don't want any of you going near 'em."

I shrugged and started trying to slide the bolt into the assembled stock. I thought we were playing a game, and he was supposed to go on record as having told us to leave the prostitutes alone.

Ramsey leaned into my face and said in a loud whisper, "Anybody goes near those whores, I'll kill him. You hear me? I'll kill him."

I didn't know what to say, so I focused on what I was doing. But the bolt wouldn't slide into place like it was supposed to. It had been over six months since I had assembled a machine gun and, to tell the truth, I couldn't quite recall how it worked. I pulled back on it but it was stuck. I pulled back and forth trying to unstick it. Finally, I looked up at Ramsey.

He was still in my face. "You tell the others."

I opened my mouth but no words came out. Ramsey just stared at me for a moment, then he got up and walked out.

I tried to return to my stuck bolt but now my mind was stuck as well. I believed Ramsey. I believed he would kill us if we disobeyed him. There was an utter honesty to the way he spoke those words, and it left a cold, empty feeling in my stomach.

Ramsey had reached the point where he would do whatever he considered necessary to accomplish his mission. The rules didn't matter any more; he made his own rules. For my money, he was the best squad leader in the company. If anyone could keep us alive in the field, it was Ramsey. But he was no longer any fun to hang out with. It seemed like overnight he became like so many of the lifers in the Marine Corps—guys who are smart and competent and hard as nails. Those guys take to combat and the responsibility of command like ducks to water, and a lot of half-assed civilian types like myself made it home because of guys like Ramsey.

Many of those guys pay an enormous price for that competence.

One of the hardest things about combat doesn't occur until

after it's finished—you have to find a way to recover your humanity when you get back with the people you love. Some guys never do recover their humanity. The way I see it, they're casualties as much as the guys in the hospital wards—but no one gets a Purple Heart for that kind of wound.

We left the ville a few days later. The NVA never attacked, and nobody messed around with the prostitutes.

Chapter 58

Shadows

"Take all you want but eat all you take." That sign hangs in every Marine mess hall. Of course, I learned it much earlier—I was in elementary school when my dad and I first started getting into it over his insistence that I eat everything on my plate. Not only did he quote the Marine slogan, but then he turned around and violated it. In the Marines you're responsible for eating what you take, but you at least get to choose what you take. If you choose not to take something, that's your business. I wasn't given that kind of choice about what was on my plate. My dad would load stuff onto my plate that I hated.

What I hated the most was beans. The only times I even tried to eat them, they had been on my plate all evening and become cold. Then I would gag when I tried to swallow those nasty, cold beans. Of course, I tried all the usual tricks—stirring them around on my plate to look like I had eaten some, or slipping them into my napkin so I could throw them away. The tricks didn't work, and many times my dad made me sit at the table until I cleaned my plate.

The dinner table was the field of battle between my father and me. It was a battle of wills—he tried to make me eat, and I stubbornly resisted. Many nights, I sat at the dinner table until very late, long past my bedtime, before I would grudgingly be sent to bed, usually with beans still on my plate. I showed him that he couldn't make me eat those beans, but he showed me the price for defying him.

Chapter 59

Running in the Jungle

One morning late in July, Ramsey stormed into our tent and said, "Saddle up! We're going out to rescue a bunch of Green Berets."

"Bring plenty of ammo, extra bandoliers for everybody, but leave your packs here. We're just going to fly in and come right back out with the Green Beanies. They just want us to set up security for the LZ. The choppers are going to be here any minute, so get moving. Let's go."

We grabbed our stuff and raced out to the LZ where the choppers did indeed arrive very quickly.

Apparently, a Special Forces team was under siege on top of a mountain out west of our combat base. They wanted our platoon to help extract them. We didn't need our packs because all we were going to do was just jump out of the choppers and establish a perimeter around the LZ. The folks on the mountain were supposed to come down and meet us at the LZ. So the plan was: (a) the choppers would drop us off, (b) we would form a perimeter around the LZ, (c) the Special Forces team would join us, and then (d) the choppers would come right back and pick us all up. In and out in less than thirty minutes. Just our one platoon, enough to secure the landing zone and not require more helicopters. Neat and simple.

Naturally, nothing went as planned.

The whole deal went to pieces as soon as we arrived. The field we landed in was filled with greenery, leading whoever planned the extraction to assume that the choppers could set down in this field near to the mountain where the team was located. But it turned out that the field was about three feet deep in water. We discovered that as the choppers started to touch down, and we ended up having to jump off the ramps while they hovered. Since the choppers couldn't set down, it wasn't going to work to bring them back in to that same location. On top of that, the LZ was hot, and we were taking small arms fire while we were trying to run around in waist-deep water.

What a mess!

I tried to follow Mike Watson's dictum to make myself a small target, but I was standing in water, and it wasn't all that easy. The entire platoon moved to the side of the swampy area that bordered the mountain where the Green Beret team was supposed to be meeting us. Someone continued to shoot at us occasionally, but it seemed to be coming from a long distance. So we tried to blend in with the vegetation while the lieutenant talked on the radio to the Special Forces team. Eventually, he announced that the Green Berets were going to go somewhere else, and we were just going to boogie out of there.

Fine, but which way is out of here?

The lieutenant and the platoon sergeant made up their minds and we struck off in a direction that seemed to me to be going (a) further West (rather than toward our valley which was back East) and (b) directly toward the area from which we'd been taking the incoming fire. This made no sense to me, but I later learned that at that point they still thought there were dry fields across the way where we could get the choppers back in to extract us. All afternoon, we walked in water that varied from calf deep to waist deep. As darkness approached, it was pretty obvious that we were not getting a ride home and would not be able to stop for the night until we reached dry ground. Nor were we walking in a straight line. Somewhere along the way, we began to swing around back East toward our valley, but I had no idea how far it was to our own operational area. It hadn't taken very long to fly to where we were, but walking back was a different story.

It ended up taking us three days to find our way out of the jungle, and we moved rapidly because we believed the VC were following us. It was a typical trip through the jungle with two exceptions—being without packs allowed us to move faster than usual, and we had nothing to eat. We were dressed the way we dressed for day patrols, which is a lot easier than lugging a heavy pack on top of all the other gear. Of course, we still had a lot of gear—helmets, flak jackets, weapons, web g ear, loaded magazines, grenades, canteens, etc. The helmet alone weighed in the neighborhood of ten pounds. However, going without food was the biggest factor.

I had been forced to stretch my food before. There were times in the field, especially when we were operating in the jungle, when we were unable to get resupplied and had to make do with what we had. That usually meant eating less often and being a bit hungry while we went about our business—but I'd never been stuck out in the boonies with no pack before.

The first day was kind of frantic. We quickly tried to put some distance between us and the LZ, so we were sloshing through the water and eventually moving through the jungle as fast as we could. As soon as we could do so, we started traveling off the trails and spent a lot of time walking down the middle of streams.

Meanwhile, we started getting hungry.

At the end of the first day, when we finally set up for the night, it became apparent that we were not entirely without food. Practically every guy had some food stashed away in some of those big pockets on our jungle utilities. Everything from candy bars to cans of C-rats. I guess we had all gotten used to carrying some extra food around with us. It wasn't so much that we didn't trust the Marine Corps to get us back to our mess tent when they sent us out without packs; we had simply learned to be less dependent on the mess tent in the first place. Even back at our firebase, guys often would just eat C-rats in their hooches rather than go to the mess tent, which was not especially renowned for its cuisine. I remember when someone tried to convince me that Kool-Aid flavored water on corn flakes wasn't as bad as it sounds and you could get used to it. He was wrong, of course, it was just as bad as it sounds.

So we weren't totally starving, but we were plenty hungry! And our stashes of candy bars didn't last long.

The second day, we were walking down a stream and we passed a big cobra coiled up on the bank. It had its head up and its hood flared out as it watched each of us walk by. I was near the front of the file; we each quietly moved over to the far side of the stream as we walked around it. A moment later, I heard a loud shot from behind me. Our platoon sergeant had shot the snake with his shotgun. When we found a place to stop, he distributed pieces of snake that he had cut from the carcass. I knew you could eat raw snake pretty safely, but I was still repulsed at the thought of eating it. However, I was really hungry, and my body needed fuel. I gagged some eating it, but I got some snake meat down, as did several other guys. I saw one guy throw it all back up.

The odd part was that we could safely shoot the snake in enemy territory but we couldn't make a fire and cook it. The smell of meat cooking would provide a trail right to us while the sound of gunfire was harder to track, especially when we were on the move. However, eating snake meat was not nearly as significant as something else I ate that night.

Someone gave me a can of beans. I hated beans. My dad tried to teach me to eat beans by forcing them on me, and I never learned to eat them. But, of course, I was never really hungry when I sat at my parents' dinner table. Not really hungry, the kind of hungry that makes you relish anything edible.

When I got hold of that can of beans, I ate every single one, and I licked out the sides of the can for every drop of juice. They were cold, of course, and delicious—I savored every bite.

I've had no trouble eating beans—or most anything else—since. I guess I finally learned what my dad was trying to teach me.

Chapter 60

Shadows

My dad told me one of those things that you hear from all soldiers of all wars. Once you're in combat, you're no longer fighting for your ideals—you're fighting for your survival and the survival of your comrades. Nothing really matters beyond that.

Chapter 61

Mike's Car

Mike Watson and I pulled so many hole watches together that it felt like we were married. We usually spent those nights sitting up on top of a bunker, quietly talking while we peered into the darkness. The great danger of hole watch is falling asleep, so Mike and I were always seeking interesting new ways to keep ourselves awake. One thing we did to pass the time was to make up games, and one of our favorites was playing out a fantasy about life after we made it back to "the world". In the fantasy, we had both returned from Nam in one piece, been discharged from the Marine Corps, and were going to school in a small college town that was full of girls. Our fantasy was usually just driving around town in Mike's Corvette, looking for girls and opportunities to have fun.

I would sit on the right side of the bunker and Mike would sit on the left—where he provided all the appropriate sounds and actions attendant to driving. I was usually on girl watch, and our dialogue would go something like this.

"Hey, Mike, check out those girls in that Mustang."

"Yeah, hey, that looks like that girl that dresses so sexy in my English lit class."

"Yeah, and I think the other one is a cheerleader. Look, she's waving at us. I think she digs your Corvette."

"Whoa, they just made an illegal turn."

"Don't let them get away, Mike, turn around."

Mike would downshift and whip the wheel around as we made a U turn, then we would go roaring off after the girls in the Mustang. Believe it or not, we could entertain ourselves for hours with that fantasy.

After I left the squad, Mike told me about how he had shared hole watch with one of the new guys, a young one, and had introduced him to our fantasy. A few nights later, Mike came up on the bunker quietly and the new guy was already there, sitting on top of the bunker.

He had his hands out in front of him and was making driving sounds and shifting motions. Mike cleared his throat. The new guy stopped suddenly, turned toward Mike, and said with embarrassment, "Oh, sorry, Mike. I was driving your car."

Mike and I had a good laugh when he told me about that. Yet, in some respects, that car was more real than many of the things we were supposedly fighting for. I was no longer convinced that I was fighting for freedom for the South Vietnamese—it was no longer clear to me who was being tyrannized by whom. I had already concluded that if I were Vietnamese, there was a good chance that I would be a Viet Cong, defending my home against the oppressive invaders. But fighting so that my friends and I could survive and drive fancy cars and chase girls—that, at least, still had meaning.

Chapter 62

Shadows

My dad nearly spent the war stateside. He was a successful drill instructor and had settled in with his family on Coronado Island outside San Diego. But the longer he performed that job, and the more he watched his recruits ship out for the war, the more disgruntled he became. In the Marine Corps, serving in combat is the pinnacle of a Marine's service. As crazy as it sounds, many Marines chafe at the assignments that keep them out of combat—the same assignments that other men will sell their souls to obtain.

In 1944, the war had been going on for two and a half years, and my dad was finally getting his chance at combat. My mother and my sister moved back to Dallas, and Daddy shipped out for the First Marine Division which was bivouacked on the island of Pavuvu. He was still a PFC, though he had been a drill instructor for nearly a year. In many respects, he would be starting all over in a combat unit.

Chapter 63

Packing the Radio

When I was new to the squad, I had to carry the radio on patrols—a job I hated. New guys always had to pack the radio on patrols and ambushes. No one arrived in-country knowing anything about how to talk on the radio, so we each had our turn at following the patrol leader around like a little puppy. The patrol leader did all the talking over the radio, so being the radioman was about the equivalent of being a pack mule.

On Operation Arizona, I carried Lieutenant Erickson's radio after his radioman was evacuated. Lieutenant Felong said he volunteered me for that job because I was good on the radio, but since the only qualification for carrying a radio was a strong back, I figured he was just stroking me while he handed me a shit job. It was sort of like being the smallest kid on the team and having the coach assure you that handing out the towels is really important. Not that what I felt about my job assignment mattered; this was the

Marine Corps. It's not like I could turn down the assignment and wait for a better offer.

My longstanding aversion to carrying the machine gun was based on my feeling that it limited my mobility. It weighed twenty-five pounds, and then you had to carry all that ammo. The radio also weighed twenty-five pounds, and you had to carry extra batteries. So it seemed to me that the radio would limit my mobility as much as a machine gun. However, when I carried the radio on Operation Arizona, I discovered that being a radioman, especially being the XO's radioman, brought an expected reward—a kind of mobility I had never envisioned.

The XO had more freedom to move around than anyone in the company. The platoon commanders had to stay with their platoons and the company commander generally remained with his command group in the center of things. Only the Executive Officer moved about freely and took a closer look at anything he wanted to know more about. He was a roving troubleshooter, and being with him put me on a different plane of existence. When the rest of the company was required to walk online, the XO and I would move to where we could get the best view.

It was like exchanging the versatility of a pawn on a chessboard for that of a queen.

Not only was I more mobile, but now I knew what was going on. I listened in on every important conversation. As the lowliest member of 3rd squad of 3rd platoon, I never had any idea what was going on. When my squad was deployed as part of the company on operations, we were spread over huge areas, sometimes operating as independent platoons and sometimes as one long line of people. We often heard firing from another area, but we wouldn't know whether our guys had cornered a sniper or run into a battalion. Well, I suppose we might be able to tell if they had run into a battalion, and often we could discern the difference between M16's and AK47's, but we seldom knew what was coming up next for us. It was disconcerting, but I was used to it.

All that changed when I picked up Lieutenant Erickson's radio. Suddenly, I was acutely aware of what was going on. It was like gaining a missing sense, being able to see or hear when previously I could not.

Lieutenant Erickson was perfect for the role of Executive Officer. He sort of strolled through heavy combat with a keen sense of curiosity that outweighed any fear. Whenever anything went down, he wanted to find out what was going on. If any part of the company encountered resistance, Lieutenant Erickson would go to a vantage point and check it out. We were constantly roaming around to the most interesting sites. My experience with him on that operation changed my view of what it meant to be a radioman.

However, I still was glad to return to my squad and business as usual after we got back from the operation. Then one afternoon about six weeks later, Ramsey told me that the lieutenant wanted to see me. I reported to Lieutenant Felong.

He said, "Catherall, the XO needs a new radioman, and he said he'd like to have you if you're willing."

I was aghast. "Do you mean it's my choice, sir?"

The lieutenant nodded. "Yep, you don't have to go if you don't want to. You'd be leaving the platoon and becoming part of the command group."

I frowned, "I'm not sure, sir. I like my squad."

He nodded again and said, "Go think about it. You can let me know later." Then he smiled and added, "Just don't take too long making up your mind. I don't imagine they're going to keep the offer open for long."

I was in a dilemma, similar to when I first arrived and thought I might escape combat by being a clerk. This time, it didn't mean getting out of combat but it was still a tough choice. I felt very secure with my squad, but when I was the XO's radioman I had thoroughly enjoyed the greater freedom of movement and the knowledge about what was going on.

I went back and told my squadmates what the lieutenant had wanted to see me about. Everyone pretty much felt I would be a fool not to take the job and get in on the high living of the command group. But I was still reluctant and said something about not wanting to leave them. Cowardin was about to rotate home. He laughed at me and said, "Yeah, that's why I'm just itching to extend—so I can look at you ugly fucks for six more months."

It seemed clear that accepting the offer would be the smart thing to do, but I didn't find that easy. Ramsey didn't say much in either direction, stay or leave. He just shrugged and left it up to me. The thing that finally helped me make up my mind was talking to Mike Watson. I was the closest to him; we'd spent many long nights together on hole watch, talking about everything in the universe.

Mike said, "Look at it this way, bro. You'll never fill another sandbag for as long as you're in Vietnam."

Boy, did Mike know the right thing to say! I hated filling sand bags and sitting hole watch. I didn't mind the patrols and night ambushes; it was the work details and hole watch that I despised. The radiomen sat watch in the radio shack at night, a luxury compared to sitting in the dark on top of a sandbag bunker.

That settled it; I made the decision to leave my squad and become a radioman. Once more, I got to choose my billet, a very rare event in the Marine Corps. The first time, I'd been able to dodge my machine gunner MOS and carry a rifle instead. This time I added a radio.

Chapter 64

Shadows

I was always fascinated to watch my dad around other men. He stood out of almost every crowd he was in. Not only was he taller than most other men, but he stood straighter and emanated pride—he still had the bearing of the indomitable drill instructor. It was more than his stature, however. When other men learned that my dad was a former Marine and a veteran of the island fighting in the South Pacific, they seemed to treat him differently. They recognized that he had survived hell.

Chapter 65

New Base, New Job, New Family

I accepted the position of XO's radioman in large part because of my experience with Lieutenant Erickson. I figured he would be easy to work with.

So I was taken by surprise when Lieutenant Erickson rotated out of the field a few days after I accepted the job of being his radioman. I only saw him a time or two before he was gone. Then I learned we were moving to a new base. Now I was separated from my squad, waiting for a new Executive Officer and about to move to a new area of operation.

I felt that yucky feeling in my stomach. What had I gotten myself into now?

At Hill 60, I knew the surrounding area like the back of my hand. I had patrolled it back and forth, up and down, day and night. I started working in the radio shack shortly before we left Hill 60. When I checked in with the people out on ambush sites, I could look at the map and know exactly where they were and what they were seeing. Now we were moving to a whole new area. As a member of the command group, I would not be going out on patrols so I would not have that familiarity with the area. I felt at a disadvantage. Was I going to be trapped inside the firebase while everyone else got to know the area?

We made the move and the new base was different from any place I'd been or seen before. It was an old French fortification right on Highway One on the North side of Danang harbor, where Esso had a small plant for loading and unloading tankers. We had our usual tents but there were also old French bunkers with concrete walls two feet thick. These old structures stayed cool in the heat and could take a direct hit from a mortar round. However, as cool as the French bunkers were, it was the location of the base that made it really different. Instead of being at the end of a dirt road out in the middle of nowhere, this base was on the one paved highway that ran from North to South in Vietnam. We were at the point where the road began to climb up from the low-lying valley area and wind its way over the mountain that borders the North side of Danang harbor. On a clear day, we could see some of the buildings in Danang across the bay.

Every day, civilian trucks and military convoys would pass by our base and start their trek over the mountain. Our primary job was to keep the road open—meanng the road over the mountain where it climbed a long series of switchbacks to reach the pass at the top, Hai Van Pass. Once the road went over the pass, it led down another series of switchbacks on the North side of the mountain. There was a small ville in the saddle at the top of the pass. I eventually realized that this was the ville where I'd cheered when the pretty young Vietnamese woman was hit in the head by a bottle. The ville was often covered in clouds, and it had some kind of romantic name that referred to its being in the clouds. There was also a missile defense/radar station manned by a garrison of Marines up on the Eastern peak (the South China Sea side). The Western peak just continued straight into the heart of the mountainous jungle—no villages or anything.

Because of the mountainous terrain, the NVA could travel unhindered from the deepest reaches of the jungle all the way up to Highway One without encountering anyone. Thus, the stretch of highway that went over the mountain was a prime spot for them to ambush convoys, blow up bridges, and harass the engineers who kept rebuilding the bridges and roadwork. It was an ideal setting for ambushes because the vehicles had to slow down to a crawl as they climbed uphill and made the sharp turns through the switchbacks. The ambushers always set up so that they were situated uphill from the road, usually arrayed in an L shape where the road came into a sharp turn—allowing the ambushers to hit the vehicles from both the front and the side. In the four months we were located at the Esso plant, I was to see many, many ambushes along that road, including several in which I was the target.

About the same time that we made the move, a new first lieutenant arrived to assume the duties of Executive Officer. His name was Lyle Johnson. I had been worried that the new XO might not be an easy-going guy like Lieutenant Erickson. But from the first moment I met him, I found Lieutenant Johnson to be one of the finest human beings I've ever known. He always had a smile on his face, and it was not a phony smile just planted on the surface. He was a truly upbeat person.

I met him when Gunny Malave came into the radio shack

and yelled at me—the gunny only had two vocal ranges, loud and louder—to come out here and meet the new lieutenant. I went outside and here was this fresh-faced lieutenant with red cheeks and a big smile on his face. He was a little on the plump side and didn't have that lean, muscular look that is typical of Marine junior officers. He definitely looked like a new guy, with his clean jungle utilities and pale complexion. However, he didn't have that scared "I don't know what the fuck I'm doing here" look that I'd come to recognize among new guys.

That was one of the striking things about Lieutenant Johnson. He was indeed as green as anyone who just arrived, but he never seemed to be in the least intimidated by it. He freely admitted what he didn't know and yet remained unquestioningly in charge. When I first looked at him, I wondered how he had gotten through OCS. But I soon came to appreciate the inner strength of this mild-mannered man. He never complained or seemed to struggle with what he had to do. He took everything that came his way and dealt with it like there was nothing in the whole world that he would rather be doing. Being Lieutenant Johnson's radioman wasn't just good duty; it was a pleasure.

The hardest part about becoming a radioman was leaving my squad. I'd grown comfortable with those guys—they were my family. Now I was the new guy in the group all over again. But there was a difference, I was no longer new to Vietnam. I'd been in enough combat that I felt that I understood what to do, even in a new job with new requirements. That made a considerable difference.

I got to know the two other radiomen in the command group, a corporal and a lance corporal. Mike Bolton was an older guy (late 20's) who had served in the Marine Corps when he was younger, finished his hitch, got discharged and then, for some reason, rejoined and came to Vietnam. He was not actually a member of Echo Company because he was on assignment from Battalion HQ. Mike was the Battalion radio operator. When we were in the field, his radio stayed tuned to the battalion net so that he could provide the company commander with direct access to the Battalion commander. This meant he could quickly get permission for things like medevacs and air support. Bolton was a good guy, but the other radio operator and I gave him a lot of shit because he was of a different generation.

This other radio operator was the company radioman. In a Marine rifle company, the company commander's radioman is referred to as the company radioman. The company radioman is the head of all the radiomen, which includes the platoon radiomen and the radiomen for the company gunnery sergeant (the company gunny) and the XO. Because of the close working relationship with the company commander, the company radioman often knows what the CO thinks—or would think—better than almost anyone else in the company.

The company radioman's name was Bill Rees, and Bill and I became fast friends. Bill had held the position of company radioman for only a few months—since right after the previous company radioman was hit on Operation Arizona in June. At first, our relationship was sort of educational. Bill and Mike spent a fair amount of time teaching me about proper radio procedure. They both knew a lot more about such things than I did.

The first thing I learned was the phonetic alphabet—alpha, bravo, charlie, delta, echo, foxtrot, and so forth. Whenever there was any chance that a word might be misunderstood over the radio, we spelled it out in the phonetic alphabet. And we often practiced by spelling things out to each other. When the platoon commander for First Platoon came looking for batteries for the prick twenty-five (the PRC-25 radio we carried) Bill called to me and said, "Hey, Don, get your alpha sierra sierra in here, the lieutenant wants to know who took all the fresh batteries and we don't want to say it was lance corporal charlie alpha tango hotel echo romeo alpha lima lima."

Mike and Bill taught me many little tricks for talking over the radio. As I noted earlier, I had been keying my handset on ambushes in response to the inquiry, "Sit rep, over", but I hadn't known that they were requesting a situation report.

The most meaningful aspect of my new job was my relationship with Bill Rees. We quickly grew into really tight friends. He had a sense of humor that was a bit like Ramsey's (back when Ramsey still had a sense of humor), and we spent practically all our free time hanging out together and shooting the shit. We could talk for hours on end, which was a good thing because we had a lot of time on our hands monitoring the radio twenty-four hours per day. We worked shifts at night, including the platoon radiomen, but during the day, it was pretty much up to

Bill, Mike, me and the artillery forward observer's radioman. Most of the time, it fell to Mike. He only went out in the field on major operations, and the rest of the time he monitored everything from the radio shack. Bill and I each went out in the field whenever the C.O. or the X.O. went out. We made fun of Mike for never leaving the radio shack. He literally slept in the radio shack, and often ate his meals there.

We called him the mole man.

When Mike came outside the radio shack one day, I was smoking a cigarette up by my tent and Bill yelled to me, "Kate, come check it out; the mole man has emerged from his burrow. Hurry, he may spontaneously ignite out in the sunlight."

Mike took our teasing in stride, but he didn't care for it. "Fuck you guys." was his usual comeback.

I, of course, was immediately ready to pick on Mike. "Hey, watch and see if he sees his shadow. Could be six more weeks of monsoon."

My nickname had become Kate or Cathy because we couldn't say people's names in the open over the air. Thus, I could be referred to as Kate but not Catherall.

Mike was only about eight years older than us, but that put him in a different generation since a few years can make such a large difference at that age. Whereas Bill and I were grunts who learned to talk over the radio, Mike was a trained radio operator with the appropriate MOS.

During his time between his two periods of service in the Marine Corps, Mike had worked as a fire jumper out west. He had some good stories to tell. He also had some unusual talents. Probably his most famous one was that he could touch the end of his nose with the tip of his tongue. Also, he could wiggle his ears and he could raise one eyebrow at a time. These were valuable talents when nothing was going on and we were bored to tears.

But it was with Bill that I had so much in common. We had each made a bit of a mess of our lives before entering the Corps. Of course, that probably applies to about 90% of the guys in the Marine Corps. Bill was from Anamosa, Iowa, where his father was a judge and, for whatever reason, Bill had made a lot of trouble for his dad. Like the time he got a wild hair up his ass and decided to ride his motorcycle across the state without bothering to stop when a highway patrolmen tried to pull him over. We talked about what was going on with him when he did that.

Bill said, "It really didn't have anything to do with my dad. I wasn't trying to stick it to him or anything. It was just that he was a judge," he shrugged, "so if I got in trouble, he got stung by it."

I asked, "Yeah, but why such flagrant trouble? It sure sounds like you were trying to stick it to somebody. I mean, why wouldn't you pull over when the cops got behind you?"

He shrugged again, "To tell the truth, I don't really know. When the first cop got on my tail, I just speeded up. I just felt like it that day. After that, it sort of took on a life of its own. I wasn't gonna stop until they stopped me."

They finally stopped him with a roadblock at a bridge. I asked if he had been on some kind of death wish.

"No, I don't think so. But I guess I was trying to run away from my life. I remember wondering how far I could go. Like all the way to the West Coast or something."

"It must have really pissed off your old man."

Bill nodded, "Yeah, well, I feel bad about it now. I feel bad about all the trouble I made for him." He paused and added, "When I get home, my life will be really different from all that.

I've grown up a lot since then."

"I reckon we all have," I commented.

Bill grinned and said, "Yeah, I haven't shot any little girls in months." When Bill was in his platoon, back before I first met him, he'd accidentally hit a girl in the arm when he shot at some geese and the bullet ricocheted off the surface of the water. We didn't give him much grief about that, but he sometimes made jokes about it himself. He was still embarrassed about it.

Bill and I usually combined our late night radio watches so we could shoot the shit through the wee hours. Combining our watches effectively doubled the time we had to be up but it passed a lot quicker when we spent it together. Between hanging out with Bill back at the base and going outside the wire with Lieutenant Johnson during the day, I found that sense of family once more. In fact, this was turning into the best situation I could imagine. I liked the people I was with, and my time in-country was passing more easily. The decision to leave my squad had worked out better than I could have hoped.

Throughout high school, my best friend Carl and I had been inseparable. In Vietnam, Bill Rees and I came to have that same kind of connection. We hung out together and talked endlessly about practically everything. We even looked alike; we were both tall and thin, fair haired, and wore glasses. Bill had a deeper voice than me so at least you could tell us apart on the radio.

Despite the fact that Bill was senior to me, circumstances had placed me in more combat than him. He had missed Operation Arizona and my squad was the only group in the company to see action on Union II. Bill still had that powerful craving for combat that you find among young Marines. During this period at the Esso plant, we weren't going out on operations, and the CO mostly remained on the firebase when the company was not on an op. So Bill was rarely getting outside the wire. Meanwhile, Lieutenant Johnson and I were getting shot at practically every day as we responded to all the crisis situations on the road over Hai Van Pass.

Bill felt he was missing out, and he groused about it a lot.

One day, I came in after Lieutenant Johnson and I had spent the afternoon squatting behind a truck while a sniper kept an engineer crew pinned down. We eventually called in a gunship strike and, for the first time, Lieutenant Johnson let me handle the whole thing, from tossing the smoke grenades that marked our position to recommending to the gunship commander which direction they come in from. I did all the talking to the gunship commander. It was the first time I had really done all of that, and I was excited. I came in buzzing about it to Bill and Mike.

"One of the engineers thought he'd spotted the sniper's position, so we all busted some caps. Lieutenant Johnson even fired off a magazine. Course, a minute after we did all that firing, the sniper took another shot." I laughed, "You can never hit those guys when they're up in the rocks. So then Lieutenant Johnson told me to call in the gunships, and he didn't say another word. Told me to take care of the whole thing. Man, you should have seen it. The gunships were firing directly over us when they flew over. Empty cartridges were raining all over us."

I was kind of excited and so I didn't really notice Bill's expression until he spoke up. "Shit, man, I should be out there. I've never even talked to a gunship. I'm the company radioman; I should be out there doing that shit."

We all got quiet, and I looked over at Mike. He raised one eyebrow and made a grim expression. Bill generally took everything in stride—I rarely saw him get upset—but it was hard for him to sit back in the radio shack when so much was going on. Getting shot at may not sound like some kind of fun adventure, but that's the way Bill and I tended to view it. Especially Bill, he had missed a lot of the action that others were in, and yet he got the top job. Maybe he felt like he should be doing more to show he deserved it.

Chapter 66

Shadows

My dad didn't set out to be in the Marines. When the war first started, he tried to join the Navy to be a pilot. He already knew how to fly and actually had a biplane. My mother's brother, my Uncle Bob, was his mechanic. He and Uncle Bob went to the Naval recruiter together to join up. They took Uncle Bob because he had had two years of college, but they didn't want my dad because he hadn't finished high school—even though my dad knew how to fly and Uncle Bob didn't.

In the Marine Corps, officers are senior to all enlisted men and have the ultimate power. The officers we respected the most were the mustangs—enlisted men who went on to become officers. My dad was discharged as a corporal. He admitted to me that he might have stayed in the Corps if he'd been an officer, but he didn't want to go to OCS—he wanted to be awarded a battlefield commission.

So my Uncle Bob went on to become a career officer in the Navy and my dad exited the service after the war.

Chapter 67

A Visit to the Clouds

One day in September, Bill and I got to go up to the missile battery on top of Hai Van Pass to see a sort of mini-USO show. This missile battery was hidden away off the road at the top of the pass, often covered in clouds. The job of the missile battery was to fire missiles if the North Vietnamese should ever dare to send jets to bomb Danang. Since the North Vietnamese were not foolish enough to try that, the guys at the missile battery didn't have much to do. From a grunt's perspective, they were living in the lap of luxury up there in the clouds. They didn't send out patrols or have to do anything other than man their lines. Instead, they watched their radar screens and did whatever it was that people who fire missiles do when they're not firing missiles.

I got my picture taken with one of the women from the show. That was the second time that I had seen a Western woman since I'd been in Vietnam. The first time, my squad was walking down a dirt road returning from patrol near Hill 60 when a passenger car drove by with a "round-eyed" woman in it. Seeing an automobile was a major shock in itself, seeing a Caucasian woman in it was simply astounding.

    The guys at the missile battery had their own bar, and Bill and I ended up staying the night and drinking beer. The next day, we borrowed their radio and called back to our company and got them to send a vehicle for us. We thought we were hot stuff being able to call for a vehicle like that, a perk of being the two senior radiomen. The company driver came up with the PC and drove us back to the base. We had resumed our beer drinking early in the morning, and we were feeling no pain. I was normally extremely vigilant on that road, but that morning Bill and I sat with our legs hanging off the back of the PC and shot at objects along the road as we were chauffeured home. It was by far the wildest thing I did during my tour.

    September was a great month. I'd grown comfortable in my new job, and I really liked the people I was working with, especially Bill and Lieutenant Johnson. Because Lieutenant Johnson and I were out attending to every ambush on Highway

One, I saw action on an almost daily basis. But I didn't have that same sense of foreboding that I felt after all the action in June, and I think a big part of that was due to hanging out with Lieutenant Johnson. It was hard to imagine not making it with him around. Nothing fazed him.

The best part was that I was with people I loved; I had gotten closer to Bill Rees than to anyone I knew in the Marine Corps. I would pack Lieutenant Johnson's radio to the ends of the earth, and he'd still be smiling. Life was good—that September at the Esso plant was my happiest time in Viet Nam.

Chapter 68

Shadows

When it grew dark that first night on Peleliu, the men of K Company disappeared into a land of shadows. They were hidden in little depressions, perched behind outcroppings and bent down behind piles of wood and stone on the uneven surface of the coral mound. My father could barely see the man in the next position. And the area of K Company's perimeter was pitifully small. Did the Japanese have any idea how vulnerable the Marines' foothold on the mound really was?

As soon as it was dark, they began to hear movement. Captain Hunt used his waning battery power for the radio to call for flares. He knew that the Japs would be able to walk right up to the base of the mound, just thirty feet below, if the Marines didn't light up the sky.

Chapter 69

Mail Run on Highway One

I settled in as a full-time radioman at the Esso plant. Life with the command group was very different from life in a squad, and life at the Esso plant was very different from life at all the other firebases. We could drive from the Esso plant to the PX in Danang, although I think I only made it there one time, and we had decent quarters to live in. We eventually got a portable generator and had electricity running to some of our quarters. The ocean was down at the bottom of the hillside and we even had a company beer bust there one day. So this looked to be the lap of luxury.

We had elements of one of our platoons stationed down the road toward Danang in the flat valley area. They were at the bridge outside the village of Nam O. The VC had blown the bridge and our engineers had built a little temporary bridge next to this big old iron bridge that they were rebuilding. Our job was to guard it by doing things like dropping grenades into the water all night to discourage enemy frogmen. That never proved to be very effective—whenever the bridge was about finished, the VC would come drop it again.

We also had a full platoon stationed at a village up north of the mountain toward Phu Bai and Hue. Lieutenant Johnson and I made periodic runs over Hai Van Pass to visit that platoon. I also often rode shotgun on the mail run with the company driver in the Mighty Mite (a sort of half-assed jeep). He couldn't drive it alone and had to have someone in the front seat with a weapon at the ready. That was always a little creepy because of the ambushes and snipers along the road. There was one little stretch on the lower end of the North side of the mountain where we practically always took some sniper fire when we drove through it. The creepy part was it being just the two of us in a little jeep. We always drove through that one little section as fast as the vehicle could take us.

On one mail run we took automatic weapons fire from at least two shooters on the way to the ville. We were going downhill and got through the area quickly, but after we dropped off the mail, we were going to have to turn around and drive back through the same stretch. This time, we would be going uphill—much slower.

Once we were on the road, I brought up my concern. "I'm not looking forward to driving back up through that stretch where we took the automatic weapons fire."

The driver agreed, "Yeah, me either. They've shot at me in that final stretch more than anywhere else on the mountain. I always feel uptight when I'm getting close to that part, especially when it's just us alone."

I said, "Yeah, well, I been thinking about that. We're going to be going even slower going back up the mountain."

"Oh yeah, it's always worse going uphill."

"And that was two automatic weapons, man. I mean, we're pushing our luck to be going right back through there."

He shrugged.

I said, "So I've been thinking. Why don't we just park down here in a safe place where we can see around us and wait for a convoy. Then we can just tag along behind them."

He looked at me and nodded, "There you go thinking again, Cathy. And that's actually a good idea." He frowned, "But what if nobody comes along?"

I shrugged, "Well, we'd still have to go over alone. But it

wouldn't be any worse than going ahead right now. And the longer we wait, maybe the more likely the snipers will be gone."

He nodded again and said, "I got a better idea then. Let's drive up close enough to where we can see any convoys coming from the South, cause they'll be coming down from the top. Then if we see someone coming, we'll take off and drive through that section before the convoy reaches it. The gooks'll probably hold their fire so they can surprise the trucks."

I nodded, "Ooh, good idea. And if anyone comes driving down from up north, we just pull in behind them."

He nodded, "Yeah, that works all right. We just gotta find the right spot to park."

So that's what we did. We parked in the middle of a little straight stretch where we could see the road at the top of the mountain, but where we were still pretty safe from anyone sneaking up on us. We figured we had come up with a brilliant scheme. There usually weren't as many vehicles moving south, but there were always convoys moving north, even if they only amounted to a couple of trucks. We sat there and smoked cigarettes and shot the shit. We figured we had a good plan and it was only a matter of time until some trucks showed up.

Guess what, no convoys. We sat around until late in the afternoon. At first, we thought we were so smart, and we were laughing and just having a good time. Then, when no trucks showed up from either direction, we started getting anxious. It was going to get dark and we sure as hell didn't want to be on that road in the dark. We didn't even want to drive it in the twilight. The whole road became super dangerous when the light began to fade; that's when the ambush teams would be moving in. Basically, the VC owned the road after dark. We finally reached the point where our fear of getting caught in the low light outweighed our fear of going over the mountain alone. Worse yet, we were in an area where I couldn't reach anyone on the radio (I always carried a radio on those mail runs). We finally decided we better go for it or we were going to be going over the mountain in the dark. I tried to find the bright side.

"It's been about four hours since we went through there. I bet those snipers have gone home for dinner by now anyway."

Davis snorted, "Or else they're pissed that no more targets have come through, and they're going to take it out on us."

I said, "Great. Just keep your speed up."

"Don't worry, we'll be going as fast as this thing can go."

The snipers were not gone; I guess they were waiting for a convoy just like we were. We got shot at by at least two people with automatic weapons while we were going up the north side of the mountain. It was in the same area as earlier that day. We had just come out of a very tight turn and then had a short piece of straightaway before the next turn and then another little straight stretch. They fired on us through both straight stretches but not when we were deep in the turns. That meant they were too far up the hillside to have the angle to shoot down into the turns. That was encouraging. Still, we couldn't get our speed up any faster than about 25 miles per hour. They may not have been very close, but we were an awfully easy target.

I laid out a bunch of loaded magazines in preparation and fired off four of them as fast as I could while we went through that area. Of course, I had no idea what I was shooting at because I couldn't see the snipers. I just aimed at the general areas where the fire was coming from. I only hoped to make them keep their heads down enough to interfere with their aim at us. We made it through without a scratch—no bullet holes in the jeep or anything—so the threat may not have been as bad as we feared, but it was a scary ride; the light was already flat when we came down the South side of the mountain.

Actually, the ambushes on the South side of the mountain, where our base was located, were much more deadly than those on the North side. The ambushes on our side of the mountain permitted a quicker escape into the mountains; it seemed the ambushers on the north side were forced to just fade into the surrounding territory. The big ambushes, involving large numbers of attackers, were always on our side of the mountain. We figured well-armed NVA manned the ambushes on our side of the mountain while it was more often just local VC on the north side. Of course, any time you started thinking you know where the ambushes are not going to occur, you're asking for trouble. In any case, after that day, we made our mail runs as early in the day as possible.

Chapter 70

Shadows

In the darkness, the Marine positions had become invisible and my father struggled to remember the layout of the mound and the terrain in front of him. They had been on this island for hours; the Japanese had lived there for years. He was well aware that the enemy knew all the little trails up the mound far better than he or the men around him. Even before the first flare went off, he could hear people moving around the base of the mound. He had a large pile of hand grenades in his hole, and he pulled the pin and tossed one down the mound in front of him. He heard a man cry out after the explosion. It was somewhat reassuring to know that he only had to toss a grenade a few yards and he could strike at the enemy down at the base of the mound, but the night had only just begun.

Suddenly, the pile of grenades didn't seem large at all. If he had to keep throwing grenades, the pile would be gone in no time.

When the first flare was fired by the Marine mortars, it lit up the area in front of the mound. The flares hung from small parachutes and swung back and forth as they slowly fell from the sky. No image remained stationary in the shifting and flickering light they emitted. My father stared into a world of moving shadows, the ever-changing scene filtering through his personal lens of fear. What he saw looked like hundreds of soldiers moving through a moonscape of jagged shadows. But that just couldn't be.

Chapter 71

More Fun on Highway One

The Executive Officer's job was usually pretty quiet when the company was not out on an operation. The grunts on the patrols and ambushes saw all the action. But there was one exception, that was when there was an emergency requiring us to throw together a quick response team—a reactionary—and the XO would lead that emergency group as we raced out to help someone in trouble. Reactionaries were rare—except at the Esso Plant where we had local emergencies on a near daily basis. For once, the Executive Officer was seeing more action than anyone else in the company—except his radioman, of course.

Whenever there was any action on Highway One, Lieutenant Johnson and I went to deal with it. I had feared that I wouldn't get to know the area at this new base because I didn't go out on patrols any more, but the reality turned out to be just the opposite. Virtually everything that was happening at this base occurred on the road, and Lieutenant Johnson and I showed up every time. Instead of being insulated from what the grunts were encountering in the area, Lieutenant Johnson and I were privy to all of it.

Mostly, that was about ambushes. Between my frequent mail runs and going out on reactionaries with Lieutenant Johnson, I was ambushed in vehicles several times and sniped at regularly along that road. I usually think of sniping as a shot or two designed to take out an individual, while an ambush was a concerted, surprise attack intended to destroy the vehicle(s) and everyone in it. However, the snipers along the road would often fire off bursts from automatic weapons, as when the driver and I got caught on the north side of Hai Van Pass. They still weren't in a position to really destroy us the way a well-conducted ambush would, so I categorize them as snipers. The most effective snipers were still the single-shot variety. Many times, a lone sniper would completely stop the engineers from doing their work to rebuild the road, and the sniper would often inflict significant casualties in the process. These snipers were different from the people who would fire off burst of automatic weapons fire at passing vehicles; these were guys with scoped rifles who knew how to shoot.

Since Lieutenant Johnson and I always responded to the enemy attacks on the road, I saw the aftermath of dozens of ambushes. We sometimes arrived while the VC were still present, and I got a lot of practice conducting medevacs and gunship strikes. Afterward, Lieutenant Johnson and I would examine the ambush sites and reconstruct how the ambush was conducted. We learned their routines and tactics for these ambushes. They had several favored sites and often set up in the same positions. It didn't matter that the sites had been used before, it worked for them—they kept surprising our vehicles. Since this was the only road that went from Danang to the Northern provinces, the VC and NVA were rewarded with a continuing stream of drivers who didn't know the routines, the favored sites, or the magnitude of the danger.

Highway One was the central focus of our activities while we worked out of the Esso plant. It connected us to a whole world of places that I had never visited as a simple grunt in a squad—the PX, the hospital at Danang, the Naval base on the harbor, the missile battery at the top of the pass, as well as every bridge, switchback and ambush site between Danang and Dong Ha. I came to know that road like my tongue knows the inside of my mouth. And driving over the mountain was always an adventure

Chapter 72

Shadows

The Japanese attempted to infiltrate the Point throughout the night. Sure enough, my dad and his comrades were using up their grenades, so they tried to use them as infrequently as possible. They started throwing rocks punctuated by an occasional real grenade to keep the Japanese soldiers uncertain about what was coming down from above.

Early in the night, the Japanese mortared the Marines for over an hour. The shells exploded all over the top of the coral mound. Since the Marines were unable to dig proper foxholes in the coral, they were highly exposed to the mortar bursts and several more Marines were injured and killed. The cloudy night had been completely dark. After the mortars landed, smoke clung to the rocks for hours. My dad feared the Japs would mount a counterattack during that period as the Marines were effectively blinded. But no counterattack materialized—only the steady stream of attempts to sneak into the Marine lines.

Some of the enemy soldiers made it to the top of the mound, but none lived long once they got there.

Chapter 73

Harassing the South Vietnamese

One day that fall, one of our platoon commanders was up on the road conducting some kind of roadblock operation. The lieutenant had staked his people out near where the road starts to get steep as it begins the climb up the mountain. They were stopping vehicles and checking the papers of the South Vietnamese. I was riding shotgun on the mail run to the north side of the mountain. When we came up in a jeep, the lieutenant stopped me with a gleeful look on his face.

"Hey, Catherall, you want to see something funny?"

"What's that, Sir?" I responded.

He gave me a sly look and said, "Park yourselves over there for a few minutes. Watch the fun." So we hung out there for a while and watched.

The trucks operated by the Vietnamese civilians were old and decrepit. When they came to a stop on a steep incline, most of them would start to roll backwards. So each truck carried a young boy who rode standing on the running board and holding on to the outside of the truck. The boy held a triangular shaped piece of wood with a piece of rope attached to it. The boy's job was to hop down whenever the truck stopped and quickly wedge the block of wood behind one of the rear wheels to prevent the truck from rolling back down the mountainside. When the truck was about to move forward again, the boy would station himself near the wheel holding the rope attached to the block of wood. As soon as the truck pulled out, the boy would snatch out the block of wood and run to his station on the outside of the truck.

The lieutenant's 'fun' was to finish his inspection and let the truck go, and then stop the boy from catching the truck—under the pretext of taking a second look at the boy's papers. The boys would fidget terribly—like someone being prevented from taking a badly needed leak. Meanwhile, the truck would be driving off, the driver oblivious to having lost his wheel blocker, while the boy frantically looked back and forth between the departing truck and the American officer holding his papers. The lieutenant had perfected his timing; he would detain the boy just long enough to put the boy far behind his truck yet keep his hopes alive that he could catch the truck if he ran fast enough. When released, the boy would go charging up the road carrying his block of wood and trying to get the attention of the truck driver.

The lieutenant and his men would then laugh at their great fun. When the lieutenant performed this little charade for my benefit, he winked at me when he began to scrutinize the boy's papers. I was supposed to appreciate how humorous it was. I had been in-country about half a year at that point and my sensitivity to the South Vietnamese people had declined radically. I'd already come close to murdering a civilian, but I still didn't find anything funny about putting innocent people in such a bind. I smiled politely for the lieutenant and continued on my way.

I saw a similar sort of sadistic harassment when we had a VC prisoner on Operation Arizona. We were walking through sand so hot that I could feel the heat through my boot soles. The prisoner had lost his shoes, and his feet were getting burned. So he pulled a big leaf off a banana tree and would stand on his leaf whenever we stopped walking. The guys guarding him thought it funny to take his leaf and tear it into smaller and smaller pieces as the day wore on. Again, everyone seemed to get a kick out of watching this guy fidget as he tried to stand on less and less leaf.

Perhaps this harassment was a lesser equivalent of my impulse to kill the old woman. All of us seemed to have come to resent these people for whom we were risking our lives. But I didn't like what it had done to me. We had become exactly what the enemy accused us of being—hostile, arrogant invaders. We were no longer fighting to liberate these people, we were just fighting because their enemy had become our enemy.

Chapter 74

Shadows

The morning after that first night on the coral mound, everyone was red-eyed, unshaven and dirty. Most of the men had not slept at all during that long night. They started the morning by carrying the wounded and dead Marines down to the tiny stretch of beach where the mound reached the water. But shortly after they had moved the wounded, a huge volume of fire opened up on them and everyone raced to their positions.

Now they saw what the Japanese soldiers had accomplished during the night.

There was a gully running parallel to the beach about 30 yards inland from the base of the Point. The gully was too deep for the Marines to be able to direct their fire into it. The Japs had moved all kinds of personnel and weaponry into the gully during the night. They had also moved snipers into the trees, behind rocks and bushes, and virtually everywhere a marksman might have a line of fire at the top of the coral mound. Now all the snipers opened up, machine guns fired from the gully and from further back in the trees, and mortars started shelling them from close range. My dad realized that there was a 60 mm mortar tube firing from right out in the ditch in front of them, and a larger 82 mm mortar was firing from further out. The volume of fire was intense, and Marines were being hit all around the mound.

The Marines were returning fire and rapidly eliminating those Japanese soldiers who were exposed in the bushes and trees. But the volume of the enemy fire far outweighed what the Marines could produce, and Captain Hunt saw that they could not hold out for long against such odds. He was unable to reach anyone by radio, so he sent a runner down the beach to seek reinforcements.

The Japanese did not charge the mound. Instead, individual soldiers dodged from boulder to boulder as they pressed ever closer. The men of K Company still had the advantage of the higher ground and bodies began to accumulate among the boulders as Marine marksmanship took its toll on the enemy. But even with that advantage, their numbers were diminishing, especially as the mortar shells fell among them.

It looked like the Marines of K Company were about to be overwhelmed. Then one of the Marine marksmen announced that he could tell where the large Japanese mortar was firing from—only about 100 yards away—and he fired a rifle grenade at it. The mortar immediately quit firing. Someone yelled for everyone to throw their remaining grenades into the gully and suddenly every Marine was heaving hand grenades as far as they could throw. The gully started exploding with grenades, and dozens of Japanese soldiers boiled out of the far side and ran for cover.

Amazingly, the small force of Marines had turned the battle into a rout.

Moments later, an Alligator came rumbling up the beach. The runner had rounded up 15 additional Marines, as well as more water, grenades and bandages. They quickly unloaded the tractor and placed the more seriously wounded Marines aboard it.

Captain Hunt had been close to pulling his troops back to a smaller perimeter, which would have allowed the Japanese to climb the coral mound and be on a level with the Marines. It would have been the beginning of the end. But fifteen additional Marines made all the difference. Now the perimeter was adequately manned once more.

My father was still alive and untouched, and now it felt like they had a fighting chance. Once L Company reached them, they would be part of a long line held by the First Marine Division. That was a consoling thought.

Chapter 75

Suffering on Highway One

My failure to be touched by the suffering of the Vietnamese reached its apex that fall.

Most of the ambushes on the road over Hai Van Pass were perpetrated on American vehicles but not all. I saw both Americans and Vietnamese wounded and killed in these ambushes but usually not at the same time. One day, I would see Americans, the next day Vietnamese, and the next day Americans again. I got a cold, heavy feeling in my stomach every time I saw Americans hurt; no matter how many times I saw it happen. But I discovered I had a curious lack of feeling when the victims were Vietnamese. The grisly scenes piled up in my memory banks, but they had no feeling attached to them.

One day, the VC exploded a mine beside the road when a Marine truck, a 6x6, passed. The six-by was only minimally damaged and no troops were injured, but a laborer, an old man working on the road, was killed. I saw his body lying on the side of the road, with his brains extruding from his skull. I found myself looking at his broken skull and the exposed brain with curiosity, no other feeling. The mine was embedded in the rocky hillside next to the road; it was not detonated by the truck striking it—it was command-detonated by someone hiding up higher in the rocks. He must have known that there were workers on the roadway, though perhaps he couldn't see over the edge enough to know that one of them was standing near the mine. But it may be that he just didn't care enough to wait for another vehicle.

 Lieutenant Johnson and I were traveling up the road one day when we heard firing. We hurried ahead and found a contingent of ARVN (Army of Republic of Viet Nam) soldiers exchanging fire with someone located above the road. At the highest point up the road, a jeep was on fire, and a man's body was seated in the passenger seat. Lieutenant Johnson wanted to get up to the jeep, so he and I darted from cover to cover until we got close to the burning jeep.

 Some VC were still shooting from the hillside, though they didn't seem to be hitting anyone down on the roadway. But their firing was enough to keep everyone's heads down, so we didn't do anything about the burning jeep. I was crouched behind some rocks out in front of the vehicle and had a perfect view of this man's body sitting upright in the passenger seat. It continued to burn for a long time. The combustible parts of the vehicle burned up, and the fire went out, but the body continued to smolder.

An ARVN soldier kept running around trying to throw dirt on the smoldering body. The snipers were firing at him, and we yelled at him to get his ass behind cover. But he either didn't understand or didn't care, and when the firing finally stopped, he was still out there covering the body in a pile of dirt.

We learned that the burning body was an ARVN colonel, and the guy trying to put out the fire was his driver, I guess his loyal driver. He nearly got himself killed trying to throw dirt on the colonel's body before the VC had withdrawn. The colonel was long past being saved at that point but I guess this man couldn't stand by and watch his colonel's body continue to cook.

I felt nothing when I saw dead Vietnamese in situations like this, but I didn't give it much thought at the time. I just felt I'd become accustomed to death. Then one day an ARVN truck was hit by a mine like the one that killed the old laborer. The mine was embedded in the side of the road on an outer turn, which differed from the usual pattern of setting up ambushes on the inner turns where the vehicle had to slow down right in front of the ambushers. On the outer turn, however, there is a greater chance that the vehicle will lose control and go over the side of the mountain, and that is exactly what happened in this case. The truck went over the side, and it was loaded with troops.

The mountainside was not a total dropoff, but it was impossibly steep, and the truck went bounding down the side of the mountain, smashing against huge outcroppings of rock that littered the slope. The men in the rear of the truck bounced out and landed on those huge rocks. Seven ARVN soldiers had broken backs, and some of their bodies had split open when they hit the rocks. The wounded were spread across the side of the mountain, and it took a long time just to get all those casualties back up to the roadway.

As our guys kept carrying casualties up, we laid them out on the roadway, and I helped the corpsmen take care of these wounded men while we waited for the medevac choppers to arrive.

Two of those men died while I was tending to them. One

was literally in my arms—I was carrying him to the chopper, holding him in my arms like a small child, when his grip tightened around my neck and he kind of froze. I knew he had just died. The other died while I was tending his wounds. He had no pants on, and so I saw his genitals as he died. He sucked in his last breath and then ejaculated at the moment of death.

I had no idea such a thing could occur.

I was curious, but in a detached way. I was curious about the man ejaculating as he died, but I didn't have much feeling about the death itself. It was a curiosity. By this point in my tour, I had become completely numb to the suffering and death of the Vietnamese. I didn't find any pleasure in harassing them, but I could watch them die with no feeling. I'd reached the point where I no longer viewed them as fellow human beings. Indeed, I have experienced greater concern seeing animals suffer.

I wrote my sister that night and told her about all the ARVNs that were hurt and killed and how I'd had no feeling about it. It disturbed me. I recognized that something was very wrong that I could watch these people suffer and have no feeling about it.

There didn't seem to be much I could do; I saw the same thing happen to pretty much every Marine around me sooner or later. On the other hand, my feelings about the suffering of Americans did not disappear. I never viewed Marine casualties without having that heavy feeling. I learned to numb out when I dealt with their wounds and their pain, but the feelings were still there and often popped up later. It was different with the South Vietnamese—I was numb to their suffering and nothing ever popped up after the emergency was past.

This must be the same dehumanizing process that underlies genocide and, perhaps to a lesser degree, bigotry. It was a very ugly thing to find within myself. Here I was in the midst of my tour—what a term, it sounds like I was a tourist—and I had stopped seeing our allies as human beings.

Would I ever recover my humanity?

Chapter 76

Shadows

Throughout the second day, tractors ferried more men and supplies to the K Company Marines on the Point. Sporadic sniper fire and even an occasional mortar shell landed on the Point, but the Japanese did not mount another attack like the one in the morning. My father and the other men on the Point were feeling optimistic. They had received seven machine guns and thirty additional troops. The tractors had also brought word that the Point would now be covered by artillery and mortar fire. Everyone felt sure that it was only a matter of time before the rest of the division linked up with them.

However, there continued to be a significant gap between the Point and L Company's lines. The regimental command finally accepted that L Company was too heavily pinned down to move, so they sent a company-sized force down to fill the gap and reinforce K Company. But the Marine detachment came under heavy fire as soon as they entered the no man's zone and they were unable to establish a foothold. Somehow, several tractors were able to drive down the beach to the Point, and more than one individual Marine successfully ran across the undefended area, but whenever a significant body of troops tried to enter the gap, they were mortared and machine gunned relentlessly. The Marines of K Company had been resupplied and reinforced, but they remained isolated. And another night was approaching.

Chapter 77

Peacenik

One evening that fall, a very strange thing happened. An American civilian came walking down the road right up to our lines. Fortunately, our sentries didn't shoot him; they just took him to the company commander. He spent the night with us and was transported to Danang the next day.

It turned out that he was part of a peace mission that was sailing in a yacht to North Vietnam. He'd been put ashore by his comrades and had climbed the mountainside until he came upon Highway One, then he walked down it until he came to our lines. The group may have been transporting medical supplies to the North Vietnamese, but whatever their purpose, it was totally bizarre to have an American civilian come walking out of nowhere in the darkness!

This was the period in which the peace movement was gathering momentum back in the states, though we were mostly oblivious to it. Personally, all I ever saw about the anti-war movement were some articles in Time magazine. So this guy was just an oddity to me. I don't recall anyone being particularly angry at him; we were just amazed that anyone would do something as stupid as walk down that road in the dark, unarmed. I never spoke to the guy myself, but I wished him luck if he was doing something to try to end the war. However, mostly I just figured he was crazy.

Chapter 78

Shadows

After my father died in 1987, my uncle (my mother's brother) gave me some letters that my father had written to my mother's father from the South Pacific. In them, he acknowledged some of the mistakes he'd made with his life. However, he did not regard his service in the Marine Corps as one of those mistakes. In fact, he spoke of it as the turning point; he felt he was a changed man, and he wanted his father-in-law to know that he would be a better husband if he made it home.

Those letters could be ads for the Marine Corps. It wasn't about the fighting, the honor of serving one's country, or even the appreciation of life that comes from facing death. It was about finding one's competence.

Chapter 79

On Highway One with Lieutenant Johnson

Lieutenant Lyle Johnson was a very secure, mild-mannered man from Missoula, Montana. He was a rare breed of man—always upbeat, smiling and enjoying himself. In all the time I spent with him, I never heard Lieutenant Johnson say a harsh word to anyone. He was a genuinely kind man—not your usual Marine officer. No offense to Marine officers, but being warm and accepting is not one of their most prized values.

Lieutenant Johnson was new to combat; he was a first lieutenant and had not served in Vietnam as a second lieutenant. But he slipped right into the routine with no problem. He told me that Captain Higgins had recommended he consult me if we got into any difficult situations and he had questions. So he did exactly that, which helped me recognize that I had something useful to offer. And we got a lot of opportunities to deal with difficult situations since he went out every time someone was hit on the road over the mountain. I always accompanied him—both on the reactionaries and any other times that he went outside the wire.

Emergencies were pretty much a daily event for several months. Either a convoy would get ambushed or an engineering crew would get pinned down by sniper fire. We would get the call for help, and Lieutenant Johnson and I would call for people to join us. Then whoever was in the area would climb into a truck or the PC (personnel carrier, like a long bed pickup truck) and we would go zooming off to the site of the action. Sometimes, Lieutenant Johnson and I would be up the road already in a jeep (actually a Mighty Mite), and I would pick up a distress call on the radio and off we would go.

The VC, or probably NVA, running the ambushes never had enough time to clear completely out of the area after an ambush, but they usually withdrew up the hillside and hid in caves, tunnels, and rock formations. These hiding spots were extremely difficult to find, you had to walk right up to them in order to see them—which required our troops to climb a very steep hillside and expose themselves with nowhere to take cover. Meanwhile, the VC remain hidden in well-protected positions from which they could pick off our guys. A single sniper could control an area of roadway for hours with this advantage.

Our one advantage was firepower; we could bring in helicopter gunships and spray bullets all over the hillside. Unfortunately, this seldom really made much impact, the enemy positions were largely bulletproof unless the chopper could target a specific hiding spot and hit it with a rocket. Otherwise, the choppers just sprayed machine gun fire over whatever area we told them to hit. It was different, though, when we reached the ambush site quickly enough to prevent the VC from escaping to their hiding spots. Then we had a clear target.

Some of these situations were terrifying and people were hurt and killed, but sometimes it didn't feel all that dangerous, especially if the problem was a sniper who was not really hitting anybody but simply preventing the engineers from getting the road repaired. When we arrived, Lieutenant Johnson had to decide what action to take.

This is where I got the most from the experience. Lieutenant Johnson would turn to me and ask, "Lance Corporal Catherall, what's the usual response in a situation like this?"

If it was, for example, a sniper up the hillside, I would say something like, "Well, sir, if we try to climb the hill and find him, we're just giving him a chance to shoot some of our guys. If we call in gunships and let them strafe the shit out of the hillside, they might get him and they might not, but we won't be risking any of our guys, and it'll at least interfere with his shooting at people."

Lieutenant Johnson would then say, "Sounds good. Do it." And I would take it from there.

When there were casualties, he would always ask me where I thought it would be best to bring in the choppers, then he would put me in charge of calling them, guiding them into the LZ, etc. When the gunships and medevacs arrived, he just let me do all the talking over the radio, directing the firing of the gunships and the landing of the medevac choppers. He conveyed total confidence in my ability to get the job done, and I responded by doing everything possible to live up to that.

I discovered that being a radioman was much more than being a pack animal. That fall, I did things I would never have had the opportunity to do in a squad. I became proficient at directing fire from artillery, jet aircraft and helicopter gunships, and I coordinated the landings of helicopters, especially medevacs. Lieutenant Johnson turned over the direction of medevacs and gunship strikes to me. If he needed something done over the radio, he didn't ask for the handset; he would just tell me what needed doing, and I would take care of it.

One day, Lieutenant Johnson and I were going to drive over Hai Van Pass to go visit the platoon that was stationed North of the mountain. We were just a few minutes out of the Esso plant when I got a call from Bill.

"Echo Five Mobile, this is Echo Six, over."

"Echo Six, this is Echo Five, over."

"Five, this is Six. We just got a call from Battalion. There's an ambush in progress up the road in front of you and they're asking for help, over." Apparently the people being ambushed had called someone on their own frequency and notice had reached Battalion Headquarters, who notified us.

I told Lieutenant Johnson. He said, "Find out where they are and how big their convoy is."

"Six, this is Five. Can you find out where they're located

and also how big is the convoy?"

Bill was one step ahead of me. He already had the answers to both questions. "It's a small convoy, just two trucks. They've already got a Whiskey India Alpha and are going to need a medevac. They say they're right at the bottom of where the steep switchbacks start, over."

I told Lieutenant Johnson, "It's just two trucks, Sir. And they're not far ahead, Bill says they're right where the switchbacks start."

Lieutenant Johnson told the driver to step on it and told me to tell Bill to send a reactionary to join us. Meanwhile, we hurried to where the group was in trouble.

I called Bill, "Echo Six, this is Echo Five Mobile, over."

"Go ahead, Five, over."

"Five Actual says to send a reactionary. We are enroute."

"Roger that, we're already getting a truck loaded down here. They should be on their way in another minute. Anything else, over?"

"You might see if you can line up that medevac, over."

"Roger, we're already on that too; Mole Man is talking to

battalion. I'll let you know when we hear something. Six out."

We reached the part of the road that puts you on the face of the mountain and we could hear automatic weapons firing. It was unusual for an ambush to be set up this far down the mountain—usually, the VC preferred the higher reaches where it was too steep for us to reach them without exposing ourselves.

We came around a long gradual bend in the road, where the uphill side on the left sloped down to the road at a gentle angle. The firing was only about a quarter mile further ahead.

Suddenly, a machine gun opened up on us from a little way up the slope. I thought I saw where it was set up behind a pair of boulders a short distance up the slope, and I fired off a magazine, but, of course, my rounds were spraying wildly from the fast moving jeep.

The machine gunner kept firing as we were exposed for a long stretch. He fired a lot of rounds, and he was more accurate than I was. I was seated in the back of the open jeep, and I felt really exposed. The bullets were hitting around us, and then—wham, wham—I heard rounds slamming into the jeep. The driver nearly lost control and ground to a sudden halt off to the right side of the road (where the dropoff was). The bullets had hit the left rear tire and had not only flattened the tire but had sheared off a lug and the tire was canted at a bad angle.

Lieutenant Johnson didn't hesitate. He jumped out of the jeep and said, "Let's go," and he started running up the road. I was changing magazines, being the only one of the three of us to get off any rounds at the machine gun, and I sure didn't want to be without a loaded weapon. I think Lieutenant Johnson feared I had some thought of shooting it out with the machine gunner because he yelled back at me, "Forget them, Cath, let's get to the guys in trouble."

I started running after Lieutenant Johnson and the driver. We were quickly out of sight of the machine gun, but we still had to run a quarter mile uphill.

Lieutenant Johnson yelled back to me again. "Warn the reactionary about that machine gun!"

I was wearing a twenty-five pound radio on my back, and I was huffing and puffing trying to keep up with Lieutenant Johnson and the driver. Now I had to make a radio call as well, and I didn't feel like I could stop running to make it.

"Echo Six, this is Echo Five, over."

"Five, this is Six, over."

"Six, this is Five. Tell the reactionary that there's a machine gun set up to hit whoever's coming to help." I was gasping and having difficulty getting all the words out.

"Roger that, Five. Are you okay? And where is it?"

"Uh, it's on a big curve." I paused, trying to get my breath. "We're okay, we're running up the road to the ambush, over."

"Oh, that's very helpful. I'll tell them to watch out for the curves." Bill's sarcastic reply would have been funny if I'd had the breath to laugh. Needless to say, the road was nothing but curves.

I was finding it damn near impossible to talk on the radio and run at the same time, so I slowed my pace. "I can't really tell you which curve. But it's soon after the road stops paralleling the coast and turns up the mountain. The gooks are set up on a much less steep slope than they usually use. The road curves around to the left and you're exposed for a long ways. They hit the Mighty Mite, it's in the road toward the end of the curve."

"Okay, I'll make sure they know. Watch your ass, over." Bill could hear the firing at that point.

"Roger out."

Another voice came on the radio; it was whoever was carrying the radio for the reactionary. "Six, this is Echo Romeo Mobile. I followed all that, and I have a pretty good idea where he's talking about."

"Echo Romeo Mobile, this is Echo Six. Roger that, out."

I had now dropped back so that I was almost fifty yards behind Lieutenant Johnson and the driver. I tried to pick up the pace again. I could see the two trucks in the road and we were getting close now. Lieutenant Johnson stopped running and I was finally able to catch up.

He pointed towards the trucks. "They're still up in the rocks. Do you know where you'll want to do the medevac?"

We were at the beginning of the last curve into where the trucks were. At this point, the curve went into the side of the mountain and back out to the right, then it went into a deep switchback. That's where they hit them. I looked around me. "We probably ought to go back down the road to where it widens," I paused, "or else right there in the middle of this curve" I indicated the area right in front of us. "But that's not such a good spot if the gooks are still up there."

Lieutenant Johnson nodded. "I think we'll call in some gunships, but that may take some time. If we can get our six-by up there, we can take the casualties back to whatever spot you want." He pointed back down the road with his thumb. "Go ahead and request a gunship strike. But if our truck can get these guys out, you go with them and do the medevac. I'll handle the gunships. Catherall, your job is to make sure that medevac gets off. Got it?"

"Yes, sir."

"Okay, let's go. Stay close to the mountain when you run across that open stretch. They may not be able to shoot there," he grinned, "or maybe not."

We jogged down into the curve and then ran across the open area. Then we climbed up around the switchback and called to the Marines behind the second truck. They had a man on the ground. They said that they had two casualties and that the ambushers were spread fairly wide, including over the stretch we just sprinted through. About then, I got a call from the reactionary.

"Five Mobile, this is Romeo Mobile, over."

"Romeo, this is Five, over."

"What's your situation, over?"

"We're with the convoy. They've got two Whiskey India Alphas that need medevac, over."

"Roger, we hear a lot of shooting, over."

"Affirmative, the gooks are still in the rocks above the road. What about you, did you find that machine gun, over?"

"Negative, they must have cleared out. We saw your vehicle, and we're down the road from you right now, over."

I looked back and saw one of our six-bys parked on the road a few hundred meters back from where we had stopped before we ran across the open area. There were Marines coming down the road toward that area now. I called to Lieutenant Johnson, who was now on the verge of running over to join the people behind the truck. "Sir, the reactionary's here. Do you want me to have them bring the six-by up?"

"Negative, they have too good an angle of fire on the roadway. We're going to have to carry them up close to the mountain—same way we came up here. Get four men up here to help us carry the casualties. Have some stay down there and get some kind of perimeter on that area where you said we could land the choppers. And go ahead and request gunships, then you go take care of that medevac."

"Aye, aye, Sir."

First I called Echo Romeo and requested that they send four men to carry casualties and try to secure the area where the road turned down in the corner. It seemed to be the hardest to hit from the rocks above us. Then I called Bill again.

"Echo Six, Echo Six, this is Echo Five, over."

"Echo Five, this is Six, over."

"Six, this is Five. Request a gunship strike, over."

There was a pause, then I recognized Captain Higgins voice. "Echo Five, this is Echo Six Actual. What's the situation there, over?"

"Six Actual, this is Echo Five. We have two Whiskey India Alphas that need medevac. The November Victor Alphas are still in contact, so we are trying to move the casualties to an area where we can get the chopper in, over."

"Roger, let me speak to Five Actual."

I looked up and saw that Lieutenant Johnson had indeed run over to join the people behind the truck, and I was pretty sure he didn't want me coming over there. On the other hand, I didn't exactly like having to tell the C.O. that I was separated from Lieutenant Johnson. I didn't think he would like it, but more than that, I didn't like it. Even though Lieutenant Johnson was only about twenty-five yards away right then, I was uncomfortable. I felt it was my job to look after him—I considered myself his bodyguard as much as his radioman. I stayed close and looked out for him, then he could attend to things like looking at maps and getting the big picture.

"Echo Six, this is Echo Five. Five Actual is going to use the convoy radio to direct the gunship strike. He's sent me to handle the medevac, over."

That seemed to satisfy Captain Higgins. "Roger, Echo Five. Sounds like you've got your hands full. We'll get those gunships for you, and have them contact Five Actual through the convoy's net. Anything else, over?"

"Echo Six, this is Echo Five. Any news on the medevac, over?"

"Negative, we'll let you know as soon as we hear something. Six out."

A group of four Marines and a corpsman arrived, and I directed them to where Lieutenant Johnson was located. He now had two casualties laid out next to him. I watched them place the wounded men on ponchos and the corpsman tended to them for a moment. Then each of the Marines picked up an end of the ponchos and they sprinted back to my location as quickly as they could while carrying wounded men. That wasn't terribly fast, and someone fired a burst of automatic fire at them as they crossed the open area. I saw bullets hit the roadway right under one of the ponchos, but no one was hit.

I said, "Come on," and led the way back down alongside where the mountain met the roadway. We hustled up to the bend in the road, which was relatively protected compared to the rest of the area. If we tried to go beyond it toward where the truck was parked, we would be out in the open again and for a long distance. A sergeant from one of the platoons was in charge of the reactionary. I found him and said we wanted to bring the medevac chopper into the protected area deep in the curve. He was a little skeptical.

"You bring a chopper in here and you're going to draw

their fire for sure."

"Lieutenant Johnson's going to call in gunships. It should be okay after that."

He nodded and asked, "What kind of shape are these guys in?"

I didn't know, so I turned to the corpsman who was working on them. "Doc, how bad are these guys hurt?"

He looked up at me and shook his head, "Bad. They're both hurt bad, but this guy has lost a whole lot of blood. He needs to be medevaced as soon as possible."

The sergeant said, "Let's hope they can get those gunships in here ricky-tic. What's the word on your medevac?"

I was a little flustered. Without Lieutenant Johnson there, I felt like I was expected to make some decisions, and I really wasn't sure what to do. So I called Lieutenant Johnson, sort of.

"Echo Six, this is Echo Five, over."

Bill's voice came back immediately, "Go ahead, Five, this is Six."

"Do you have any word on the medevac, over?"

"Negative, they said they were working on it, over."

"How about the gunships, over?"

"That's even less sure than the medevac. You're getting the medevac chopper for sure, we just don't know when yet. Gunships are busy today, I guess. They couldn't promise us anything, over." This only made the prospect of running the medevac more dicey.

"Six, are you in contact with Five Actual, over?"

"Affirmative, we've got the convoy's net up and running, over." Well, that was good news, at least. I could have gotten the frequency and called Lieutenant Johnson directly, but I didn't want to leave my frequency in case the medevac showed.

"Would you tell Five Actual that we are in position and ask if we should proceed with the medevac if it arrives before the gunships? Tell him the doc says these guys need to be medevaced as soon as possible, over."

"Roger, wait one." There was a break of a minute or two, then Bill called again.

"Echo Five, this is Echo Six, over."

"Six, this is Five, over."

"Five, this is Six. Affirmative on your last. Proceed with the medevac. Five Actual said they will lay down covering fire when the chopper comes in, over."

"Six, this is Five. Thanks much, out."

I told the sergeant and he just nodded. Then he had some of his men climb a short ways up the hillside to be in a better position to provide covering fire.

A moment later, I got the call that we had a medevac arriving in five minutes. I told Bill I was leaving the net, and then I tuned my radio to the medevac frequency. Bill had told me the name of the medevac chopper was Yellow Ambulance.

"Yellow Ambulance, Yellow Ambulance, this is Castillian Echo Five, over." No response.

"Yellow Ambulance, Yellow Ambulance, this is Castillian Echo Five. Do you read me, over?"

The response was the usual garbled transmission we always had when we talked to aircraft, especially at a distance.

"Castillian Echo Five, this is Yellow Ambulance. I read you. We are crossing the water right now. Can you describe your LZ, over?"

"Roger, Yellow Ambulance. We are right on Highway One, pretty low on the mountain, down where the road just begins to climb. We're in a spot where the road curves in toward the mountain. I will pop yellow smoke, over."

"Roger, yellow smoke. Is your LZ secure, over?"

"Negative, Yellow Ambulance. We still have enemy in the area. Also, we have some friendlies along the road and in the rocks just above the LZ. We are a ways away from the enemy, but you may draw their fire, over."

"Roger, Echo Five. Go ahead and pop a smoke, over." I pulled the pin on a yellow smoke grenade and tossed it down on the surface of the road. I looked out and could see the chopper, a CH-34, still up pretty high.

"Yellow Ambulance, this is Echo Five. I have popped a smoke and I have you in sight, over."

"Roger, Echo Five, we have you. Any significant wind down there?"

"Not that I can tell, Yellow Ambulance. Recommend you come in over the road as though you were driving uphill, and then turn around and leave in the same direction. The enemy are clustered in the rocks above the two trucks up the road from us."

"Roger, Echo Five. Looks like a tight fit. Keep your people

off the roadway and get ready to load fast, over."

"Roger, Yellow Ambulance. I will guide you in."

"Roger, Echo Five."

I yelled to everyone to get ready. We had both casualties off to the side of the road with the corpsman and the four guys who carried them down from the trucks. Everyone else was spread around in a perimeter. I could hear firing so I knew our guys were laying down the covering fire. I stood out in the middle of the road waving my arms to guide the chopper. He came in fast. When he was centered over the area with the widest expanse, I closed my fists and crossed my arms. He dropped down and our guys quickly got the two casualties aboard. One of the Marines gave me a thumbs up, and I gave the same to the chopper pilot. He picked up into the air, wheeled around and started back down the road, almost like a car running about twenty feet above the road surface. Then he suddenly rose higher and sailed away.

I went back on the radio long enough to thank Yellow Ambulance, then I switched my radio back to the company net. I reported to Bill that the medevac was completed. Then I walked over and sat down on the edge of the road that faced out from the mountain. It was the first time I'd sat down since we jumped out of the jeep. The sergeant came over and said, "You probably don't want to sit there."

I gave him a stupid look and he said, "We took some incoming. In fact, they were shooting at you when you were standing out there just before the chopper landed. So why don't you go sit under those rocks on the other side of the road?"

I got up and moved. I had no idea that we'd taken incoming fire, much less that anyone had been shooting at me.

It was another hour before the gunships arrived. By then, the firing had stopped and the NVA clearly had gone to ground. I rejoined Lieutenant Johnson and we had the Hueys do a strafing run, but we didn't think it was doing much good. After that, we made arrangements for getting the damaged truck back to Danang and having the Mighty Mite picked up. The remaining personnel from the convoy went back in the second truck.

It was late in the day when Lieutenant Johnson and I returned to the Esso plant. We never did make it over the mountain that day.

I walked into the radio shack and both Mike and Bill were there. Bill had saved some supper for me and Lieutenant Johnson. I sat down and ate, and the three of us talked about the day. I thanked them for handling everything at their end. As usual, Bill and Mike were on top of everything and made it all come off smoothly.

I talked about getting ambushed in the Mighty Mite and how they virtually shot the wheel off.

Bill said, "Yeah, when I talked to you right after that, you were breathing so hard, I thought you'd been hit."

I laughed, "That was the hardest part of the day—that run. Man, that nearly killed me."

Mike said, "Sounds like you were closer to getting killed when you were landing the medevac chopper; you just didn't know it."

I shrugged, "Yeah, but since I didn't know they were shooting at me, it was never scary. It was a lot closer in the Mighty Mite; the rounds were hitting all around us. Of course, the closest I saw rounds come today was when they shot at the guys carrying the casualties away from the truck. I saw bullets hitting right under the guy they were carrying. That was the closest call today."

Mike grumbled, "Yeah, except for the guys getting carried."

I nodded, "Yeah, that's true. They were both in the front of the lead truck, and they got pretty fucked up."

Bill frowned and said, "and as usual, I'm sitting back here missing the whole thing." He gave me a forlorn look, "You know, sometimes I wish I was the X.O.'s radioman and you were the company radioman. Then I'd be out having all the fun."

Mike Bolton snorted, "You've got a strange idea of fun, Billy boy."

I shrugged, because I knew exactly what Bill meant. I wouldn't want to be stuck back at the base when so much was happening.

Chapter 80

Shadows

My dad told me that they used to create souvenirs to sell to the Navy guys—they would do things like make a Japanese flag from parachute silk, add bullet holes and some blood, and then sell it to one of the guys on the ships. He said the best souvenir was a Samurai sword—which they couldn't fake—it would get you a bottle of liquor every time. He laughed at the thought that somewhere there were Navy veterans who were displaying captured Japanese flags in their basements, and those flags were actually pieces of parachute.

Another thing he told me was about their attempts to make liquor on Pavuvu. They mixed up the ingredients and then left the concoction in a can to ferment in the sun. He said they had to set them away from the people because most of the cans blew up. The resulting brew was called jungle juice. If the can didn't blow up, the surviving liquid was supposed to be some potent stuff.

Chapter 81

A Boat Ride

Lieutenant Johnson and I got to run around much more than anyone else in the company. We drove over Hai Van Pass regularly, and we went to a bunch of different places in Danang: the PX, the Naval hospital, and other operational headquarters, including the headquarters for the Naval outfit that patrolled the coastline.

The Navy people that patrolled the coast used to talk to us on the radio all the time. They often notified us of activity along the coastline, and we would send detachments out to investigate. Most of these missions were on the peninsula that extended out from Hai Van Pass into the South China Sea. This was the area my platoon was choppered to months earlier when we were still at Hill 60. That was the day I saw the girl get hit by the bottle.

We developed an ongoing relationship with the Navy, and Lieutenant Johnson was our primary representative. One day, he came into the radio shack early and told me to make sure I had a fresh battery in my radio because we were going on a trip, but he was mysterious about where. Then we drove to Danang to the headquarters area of the coastal patrol. They had a sweet setup on the harbor. Their buildings were air conditioned, and they had a great mess hall. Lieutenant Johnson and I ate in their mess hall, and then he popped his surprise on me.

"I hope you don't get seasick, Catherall."

"I don't think I do, Sir, but I've never been out on the ocean so I don't really know."

"Well, then you're about to find out."

He had a sly look on his face. I asked, "What do you mean, Sir?"

He grinned, "We're going for a boat ride today." And that's what we did.

We rode in one of the small, fast boats that the Navy used to patrol the coast. We crossed the harbor in it and went toward the Esso plant, then followed the coastline around the peninsula and north toward where second platoon was stationed in a coastal village south of Phu Bai. We passed the beach area where my platoon had inserted months earlier on the day we climbed the pass. We saw places where the mountainside had separated and created hidden little harbors and huge stony islets that stood near shore. It was incredibly beautiful! Lieutenant Johnson was interested in seeing the peninsula from the sea and the Navy guys made sure that we saw it from every possible angle. All day, we were oohing and aahing at the sights. Basically, it was a lot like Big Sur in California, a mountain that descends thousands of feet right down to the ocean.

We ended the day back at their headquarters and had another fine meal. Lieutenant Johnson spent time negotiating with the Navy guys and ended up arranging for us to get some building supplies—lumber and corrugated roofing—that we were unable to obtain through the usual Marine Corps channels. By the time we left the Esso plant, we had it fixed up better than any firebase you ever saw.

Even though our little trip had a tactical purpose, for me it was like a vacation. It was a fun day. I felt like a kid being taken on a special trip to a special place. It was awesome to see the beauty that most everyone else never gets to see. It didn't feel like there was any danger, even though the Navy guys warned us about taking fire when we were close to shore. I just felt the exhilaration associated with being on the ocean in a boat. We never got very far out to sea but there were plenty of waves and spray. And I never got seasick.

Chapter 82

Shadows

The Marines of the First Division had been led to believe that the invasion of Peleliu would be quick and relatively easy—they expected resistance, of course, and they knew there would be casualties, but no one expected the kind of fierce resistance they encountered. The officers planning the invasions had predicted the Marines would be in control of the island within 48 hours of the landing. The reality proved to be very different. What was supposed to be a rapid assault that would quickly overwhelm the enemy turned into one of the deadliest fights in the history of the Marine Corps.

Chapter 85

"The CO's Been Ambushed"

The first week of October Captain Higgins went on R&R. During his absence, Lieutenant Johnson became acting CO and, as Captain Higgins was due to rotate out of the field when he returned from R&R, Lieutenant Johnson would then become the official new company commander. Thus, being acting CO was preparatory to taking over the job. The morning of October 5th, Lieutenant Johnson was both XO and CO—he still felt compelled to be on top of everything and decided to take a drive over Hai Van Pass to check on the platoon that was stationed at the ville north of the mountain.

When he came into the radio shack looking for me, I was in my tent about fifty yards away. Normally, he would have just stuck his head out the door and hollered at me to come get my radio, but Bill Rees was there and pleaded with Lieutenant Johnson to take him instead. Mike Bolton told me of their conversation.

Bill said, "I should go with you because I'm the company radioman."

Lieutenant Johnson smiled and said, "But I'm still the XO as well, and Catherall's my radioman."

"But Lieutenant Johnson, when you become CO, I'll be your radioman and Catherall will be assigned to the new XO."

Lieutenant Johnson nodded, "Yeah, I guess that's right."

Bill said, "So while you're acting CO, you may have two radiomen, but I'm going to be your radioman as soon as Captain Higgins rotates."

Lieutenant Johnson succumbed to the logic of Bill's argument. "Okay, Rees, I guess you've talked me into it, but you know Catherall's not going to like it." The two of them, along with three men and the driver, got into the PC and headed up the road toward Hai Van Pass.

I wandered into the radio shack a few minutes after they pulled out. Mike looked up when I came in and said, "You're not going to like this."

"What?"

"Lieutenant Johnson just left in the PC to go over the pass.

He took Bill to carry his radio."

"What the fuck! Why didn't you call me? I was right there in my tent."

"Bill argued with him, said Lieutenant Johnson is company commander right now and so he should take the company radioman." He shrugged, "Lieutenant Johnson said okay."

I was pissed. This was the first time he had ever gone out without me, and I didn't even get a chance to argue that I should have been the one to go with him. I went outside for a cigarette.

A couple of minutes later, Mike stuck his head out the door. He looked really serious. "Cath, get in here."

I went in and could hear Mike talking to someone on the radio. The first thing I heard was, "It looks like the company commander's dead. We've still got activity though, and we haven't even gotten to the PC yet, over." I could hear firing in the background.

Mike looked up at me. "The PC was ambushed. Second Platoon was nearby providing security for an engineer crew. They're strung along the road down below it. That was the platoon commander."

I immediately stepped outside the door and yelled, "Reactionary! We need people to the Six-by now. Grab your shit and hurry. Let's go." I stepped back in and found Mike was already checking the battery on a radio backpack. I pulled on my web belt with the big pouch full of magazines and grabbed my M16. Mike held out the radio for me to put on. He said, "Here's some smoke grenades." He handed me a couple of yellow smokes which I clipped on as I raced out the door.

Mike stepped outside the radio shack and yelled, "Just stay on the company net and let me know what you need. I'll coordinate with Battalion."

I climbed up into the rear of the six-by and stationed myself in my usual spot—standing behind the cab. Marines were piling on fast. We never had a unit standing by for the reactionaries. We just yelled that someone was in trouble and people appeared instantly; there was never any lack of volunteers willing to race to someone's aid. One of the reasons you gotta love the Marine Corps.

We went roaring up the road within just a couple minutes of getting the call. While we were driving to the scene of the ambush, I contacted the lieutenant that Mike had been talking to in the radio shack.

"Echo Two, this is Echo Romeo, over."

"Echo Romeo, this is Echo Two Actual."

"Two, this is Romeo. We are enroute with a reactionary force. Do you know any more about the situation, over?"

"Affirmative, Romeo. We've reached the PC and have the enemy engaged. The company commander and his radioman are both dead, and we have several bad casualties that need medevac ASAP. We're still in contact with the enemy and it looks like a fairly large group. I don't think any of them had a chance to withdraw. We got here right after it happened because we were deployed just around the corner. I guess the November Victor Alphas didn't know we were so close by, over."

I was stunned. Lieutenant Johnson and Bill were both dead. That was the first thing I heard, yet I almost immediately filed it away and focused on my job. There were casualties and we were headed into a firefight. I had to stay alert and attend to the task at hand. Somewhere in the back of my mind I knew that I had heard something totally devastating, but I had an amazing ability to put it out of my mind for the moment.

"Roger, Echo Two. We will be at your position in about three minutes. We'll stop down the road from you and approach on foot, over."

"Roger, out."

The ambush had not been very far up the mountain. We could hear the shooting as we drove up. We stopped just shy of where the road curved around toward the ambush site and jumped out of the truck. Then everyone hustled up the road. I found the lieutenant crouched behind a rock outcropping on the side of the road. He recognized me and came back to speak to me.

"The company commander and two others are dead, but we got four WIA's that are all hurt bad and need to be medevaced. There's about a dozen gooks up there behind those rocks." He indicated where his men were firing toward the rocks. "We got them to keep their heads down mostly now, but they fired on my people when we tried to move the bodies. We have the wounded men out of the fire; they're in the middle of the big turn over there, but we haven't been able to move them back here yet."

He looked me in the eye and said, "I know you've done this a lot, so you just do what you would normally do. You got something you want done, just tell me."

I said, "It sounds like we could use some Hueys in here to pin 'em down while we move those casualties." I pointed back down the road, "There's a wide place in the road back there where we could bring in the medevac. I've used it before."

The lieutenant nodded and said, "Just tell me where you want my men."

I nodded, "Okay, sir. If you could put some men down around the bend to make sure the LZ is secure, I'll call in some gunships. As soon as we get the casualties around this bend, we'll medevac them. I'll call for the medevac, and I'll take care of directing the gunships."

He said, "Fine. Let me know if there's anything else you want my people to do."

I said, "Aye aye, sir."

The lieutenant seemed about to go, but then he held my eyes a moment longer. "You're Lieutenant Johnson's radioman, aren't you?"

"Yes, sir."

"I thought that was you up there." He nodded toward the

ambush site.

I didn't know what to say to that so I just stood there. The lieutenant turned and walked off.

I contacted Mike Bolton and explained what we needed. He took care of requesting the medevac and gunship strike, since that had to be done over different radio frequencies. Meanwhile, I started running from cover to cover and working my way up to the PC, which was sitting in the middle of the road.

When I reached the PC, I could see the bodies lying on the road next to it. They had gotten Lieutenant Johnson's body out of the cab, but then left it on the roadway alongside the others.

I focused on the VC.

The next couple of hours were very busy. Since our platoon showed up so quickly, the VC on the hillside were forced to change their usual pattern and remain in position and keep shooting. Consequently, the bodies remained on the roadway for a long time. We had moved the live casualties out of the open area, but we still needed to get them to a staging area where we would bring the medevac. And since we had the VC pinned away from their hidey holes, it was a good time to call in gunships.

A pair of Huey gunships arrived quickly. I talked to them on the radio, telling them where the VC were located and where our troops were. Basically, none of our troops were above the roadway. I ran up to the forward most point where our troops were and popped a yellow smoke there, told the gunships that was our forward most position and that our troops were along the road behind that point. Then the gunships swept in and strafed and rocketed the VC positions. They actually had some targets and cranked out a lot of firepower.

As soon as the gunships started their work, the lieutenant's men carried the four casualties down the road to the medevac point. I was very busy—directing the gunships from the ground and changing channels to talk with Mike Bolton back at the base, as he arranged the medevac. Half the time I couldn't speak over the radio because of the automatic weapons fire and the noise of the gunships flying over our heads and shooting their guns and rockets.

I passed the bodies of Bill and Lieutenant Johnson on the roadway when I ran up to mark our lines with smoke grenades, and I passed them again on the way back. The whole time I was directing the gunship strike, I was in the vicinity of the PC and their bodies were near me. Yet I never took a good look at them—instead I focused on what I was doing.

After the wounded were moved to the medevac point, the lieutenant's men moved the bodies of the KIA's. I managed to finish the gunship strike and move down the road to set up for the medevac before the chopper arrived. I got through the medevac the same way I did with the gunship strike—by focusing on my job; it kept me numb and preoccupied. I eventually learned how badly their bodies were damaged—Lieutenant Johnson, who had been sitting in the front seat, was shot eighteen times, and Bill, who was seated in the rear of the truck, was hit in the torso by a B-40 rocket. I still didn't look closely at their bodies.

While we waited for the medevac chopper to arrive, I helped the corpsmen tend to the casualties. One Marine was still alive but very badly wounded—his arm was blown off at the shoulder. I've always believed he was sitting next to Bill in the rear of the truck when the B-40 hit, though I've never really known for sure. The corpsman and I were very busy trying to control the bleeding. The Marine was in a terrible state of emotional pain; he kept trying to turn his head and look at his shattered shoulder where there was nothing but broken bones sticking out, and blood seeping out of his exposed lung tissue.

He kept saying, "Oh God, oh God."

I tried to keep him from looking at his injury. I didn't want to physically restrain his head, so I tried to talk to him and get him to focus on me. "Look here. Pay attention. Just hang on. Try not to turn your head. We're going to get the bleeding to stop. Just lay still." I was trying to keep his focus away from his shattered shoulder, but then his words changed and he began pleading with us to put him out of his misery. "Please, man, just kill me. Make it fast. Doc, kill me. Please, doc, do it now. Please." He was extremely agitated when he said these things, but then the corpsman gave him a shot of morphine and he calmed and got quiet. He died shortly before the medevac arrived.

After he died, the corpsman looked at me and said, "It's a miracle he stayed alive as long as he did."

The whole time we were working on him, the bodies of Bill and Lieutenant Johnson were only a few feet away. I oversaw the handling of their bodies as they were loaded aboard the choppers. I saw Bill's body begin to come apart when they lifted it to put it in the medevac chopper. Lieutenant Johnson's body was a bloody mess. Yet, despite noticing these things, I never really looked at them. My eyes looked in the direction of their bodies but never fully focused.

Once all the casualties were medevaced, I boarded the truck to return to the Esso plant. I felt like a zombie.

Chapter 86

Shadows

Throughout the second day on Peleliu, the Marines of K Company waited for the rest of the division to cross the gap and close ranks with them. The men of K Company could not abandon the Point; they could only wait for the rest of the division to reach across to them. Meanwhile, the entire division had its hands full. As darkness approached, my father and his comrades began to accept that they were about to deal with another night cut off from the rest of the division.

The Marines of K Company were on their own.

The Japanese too seemed to have realized that the men on the Point were on their own. As darkness was approaching, voices began to call out in English to the Marines, promising that no one was coming to help them and that no Marine would survive this night.

Chapter 87

Survivor

The numbness broke as I rode back to the base. I stood against the railing of the truck and my eyes stared at the mountain, but I saw only what had occurred over the past few hours. The idea of survivor guilt was certainly unknown to me at that time, yet I remember repeatedly saying to myself, "I am not going to feel guilty about this"—as though I could convince myself that the guilt was irrational and I didn't need to feel it.

But in my heart I knew I should have been there.

When I got back to the base, the tears finally broke through. I leaned against the wall outside the radio shack and sobbed and sobbed. Never in my life had I experienced a sadness as intense as this. Gunny Malave, the company gunnery sergeant, came up and put his arm around my shoulders while I was crying my eyes out.

He said, "Hey, I know how much it hurts. People die in

war, that's just how it is. No matter what we do, people gonna die."

It's hard to convey how much comfort I took from his words. The gunny was a gruff old guy that never had anything sensitive to say to anyone. He was the senior enlisted man in the company in the field (Top was the most senior, but he remained back at the company office in the rear), and Gunny Malave spent the majority of his time yelling at people. When you hear something caring from someone that gruff, it just means that much more. Fleeting moments of tenderness from men like the gunny are a big part of what leads so many to regard the Marine Corps as family.

I've spent countless hours thinking about that ambush. As far as I could tell, they were taken completely by surprise. Bill and the others in the rear of the truck were apparently sitting down and had no warning. The ambush probably was set off with the B-40, so the guys in the rear of the truck never even saw it coming. The angle of fire made it clear that the enemy positions were spread around the curve in the road, such that some of the ambushers were firing straight into the front of the truck while others were firing from the side at the men in the rear of the truck. No one had time to voluntarily exit from the truck; the driver and Lieutenant Johnson never left their seats. There were three survivors, the driver and two of the guys in the rear, at least one of whom was blown out of the truck. Nobody was in any condition to talk when we medevaced them. I know the driver survived because his wife wrote a few months later and reported that he'd had seven operations at that point but was doing okay. I'm not sure how it happened but the NVA apparently got a grenade into the cab, and it went off in his lap. His genitals were blown off and he was unconscious when we arrived. It was a miracle that he survived.

 I cannot help but think that the entire ambush might have gone differently if I had been there. I had a very different level of awareness than the people who were on the PC that day. The ambush site was one that the NVA had used before; I knew it was a danger area. I never sat down when I rode in the PC with Lieutenant Johnson. I always stood behind the cab with my rifle and scanned for ambushes. I knew the likely areas. I knew how the NVA liked to set their ambushes off with something explosive, like an RPG or a bomb buried next to the road, followed by a hail of automatic weapons. The explosion tended to confuse the troops in the vehicle long enough for the rifle fire to do its job. Your best defense against these ambushes, far and away, is to spot the ambush and set it off prematurely. The NVA would wait until you drove into the kill zone, so if you started firing before reaching it, the explosives would be less effective and the rifle fire less accurate.

    I automatically assumed the post of lookout whenever we travelled in the PC or the six-by. Lieutenant Johnson and the driver were always sitting down low in the cab, so it was my job to watch from above the cab, and to do so with my weapon locked and loaded. Whenever we went over Hai Van Pass, I scanned every rock, constantly searching for ambushers positioned above those tight turns. I knew we were a big fat target, and I knew that you get a moment's notice at most. If they fire a rocket, you may see it in the air because the missile travels so slowly. I've heard of guys jumping out of the way in time because they saw a rocket propelled grenade coming at them. Moreover, I was especially watchful when the PC was unescorted and loaded with personnel.

That's the kind of big fat target the VC prefered; they could get a bunch of kills and be able to escape without being impeded.

When Lieutenant Johnson and I traveled in the PC with a load of other Marines, I was often the only one paying such close attention. Most guys felt a false sense of security because driving along scenic Highway One overlooking Danang Bay was more like being in Big Sur than the rice paddies and jungle of Vietnam. They felt like they were in the rear. They were used to being highly vigilant out in the field, but sitting in a truck was a time to smoke cigarettes and let someone else do the work.

It was different for me. I'd seen the aftermath of too many ambushes along that small stretch of road. I could never relax in the PC when we were unescorted; I know I'd have been watching. Hence, the question that plagued me was whether I might have been able to set the ambush off prematurely if I'd been along. But I wasn't along, and I'd probably have been killed if I had been.

I became company radioman that day and remained in that position until I rotated home five months later. It was an extraordinary position to have, and it brought many new opportunities. I liked the job and did well at it, but I got the position because Bill went in my place and got himself killed, and I wasn't there to help protect Lieutenant Johnson and, try as I might, I couldn't help but feel guilty about both of those things. It may seem odd that I felt responsible for taking care of Lieutenant Johnson, inasmuch as I also saw him as a father figure whose approval meant so much to me. But those two dimensions of our relationship never felt inconsistent to me. Part of my job was being his bodyguard, I looked out for him so that he could focus on doing his job.

It was another turning point in my life. I had left the security of familiar relationships in my squad to work in the command group. That move turned out better than I ever expected—not only did I find a new niche but I found a new family. And then, once more, I lost that source of security. This time, I stayed and the family left.

Chapter 88

Shadows

My dad said he didn't realize how isolated he had felt until late in the afternoon of the second day. They heard heavy machine gun fire and mortars exploding off to their right—in the direction of the division lines. They had pretty much given up hope of linking with the division before another long night. L Company was pinned down and unable to expand into the breach. Twice that day Regimental command had sent company-sized forces to attempt to take the Japanese held territory between L Company and the K Company Marines on the Point. Each time, they were repelled. Now the sounds of heavy fighting told my father and his comrades that their fellow Marines were trying yet another time to reach across to them.

Shortly before nightfall, a pair of Marines appeared and announced that I Company had successfully assaulted the gap and established a line that came right up to the mound. Thirty hours after the landing, K Company was finally connected to the rest of the division. I Company didn't add any troops to the Point itself, but they provided a line of communication so that Captain Hunt could call for artillery support. More importantly, they covered K Company's right flank; it was no longer possible for the Japanese to completely surround the Point.

Knowing that they were now connected to a line of Marine companies that spanned the beach was a tremendous relief for my father and the other Marines on the Point. They were part of a division, and that felt a lot more powerful than a company alone and surrounded. They were about to face another night on the Point, and everyone expected the Japanese troops would attack more aggressively, but the Marines of K Company were no longer alone. They had more men, machine guns, mortars, and hand grenades. They still faced hundreds of enemy soldiers, but it felt hugely different from the lonely feeling of the previous night and the massive battle of that morning.

That night, the Japanese attacked with a vengeance; they probably knew this was their last chance to retake the Point and push the Marines off the island. There were at least three separate attacks that night, but the men of K Company repelled each attack. The Marines' firepower was much greater than they had been able to produce that morning. The Japanese soldiers kept at them all night long, but it only resulted in bigger piles of bodies in front of the Marine positions. Several times, enemy soldiers made it into the Marine perimeter and there was hand to hand fighting, but the Marines were never overwhelmed. My father, who had instructed hand to hand combat in San Diego, said he fired at some soldiers who entered the perimeter but he never engaged anyone in hand to hand combat himself.

Shortly before dawn, the Japanese made a final desperate effort to capture the Point—by encircling it from the sea. Dozens of Japanese soldiers entered the water and attempted to slip up on the Marines from the unguarded seaside while their comrades kept the Marines busy on the inland side. However, Captain Hunt had anticipated the possibility of an encircling maneuver from the sea and stationed two Marines to keep watch. Those Marines alerted the rest of the company and Captain Hunt dispatched a machine gun to the ocean side of the Point. The Marines set the machine gun up on the beach and killed many of the attackers in the water.

The others made it to the niches in the cliff of the Point. The only way the Marines could reach those men was with thermite grenades, which produce tremendous heat. It was an awful scene of men bursting out of the hidden positions, some in flames with the ammunition in their belts exploding as they ran for the water. None of the Japanese that attacked from the water survived.

No one knows why the Japanese did not attempt this maneuver the previous night. If they had done so, there would have been no troops to spare to watch the seaward side, and the attackers in the water might have succeeded in overwhelming the small group of Marines defending the Point. Instead, they died without inflicting any casualties on the Marines.

Chapter 89

Life Goes On

I think losing close friends in war is a unique kind of experience, very different from other losses in life. There is no time to mourn your loss; you have to keep on going like it never happened. You're often so busy when it happens that you can't even take the time to consider the implications. So then it catches up to you at some later point when you finally lower your guard. One moment you're relaxing with friends, the next you're a blithering idiot. Maybe that's where the idea of crying in one's beer comes from. And when it does finally catch up with you, there's all that's occurred since then. Life just kept on going, and now it feels like the loss was a long time ago because so much has occurred since it happened. So the feelings don't seem to make so much sense anymore, and it's hard to feel them the way you know you should.

The other thing about losing friends in war is that you keep getting replacements. It's all organized for you—you turn around and someone else is sleeping in your friend's bed and doing your friend's job. Or you're doing it yourself, and someone else is doing your job. So the loss of your friends is kind of invisible…but you don't get as close to the replacements.

Mike Bolton and I were both sad about Bill's death, and I was sad about Lieutenant Johnson—I probably knew him better than anyone else in the company. I didn't get as close to anyone else as I had been to Bill, but I continued to make new friends. Amazingly, I continued to have fun and to laugh when there was something worth laughing over. We had a Battalion Scout living in our tent for a while, named Andy Pinckney. He was from back East, had one of those East coast accents, and told some hilarious stories. We also had an artillery FO, a corporal named Shelburne, who had been in the Marines for several years and was another born entertainer.

Shel had been a sergeant but he got busted for dealing on the black market while stationed in Italy. He either had played baseball or should have played baseball because he had an incredible pitching arm. One day we had a little competition with a bunch of dud grenades to see who could throw one the farthest uphill at one end of our perimeter. Everyone gave up after Shel heaved one over the top of the hill.

Shel's most notable ability, however, was his marksmanship with the pistol. Several of us carried .45 automatics; it was standard issue for radiomen, officers and non-coms, among others. However, virtually everyone who rated a pistol still carried a rifle because a pistol was worthless, except for close in-fighting. Excuse me, I should specify worthless to me, because Shel seemed to regard the pistol as his weapon of choice. He'd been on the Marine Corps pistol team and actually thought of the pistol as an offensive weapon. During one firefight, Shel was witnessed standing upright, with his left hand in his pocket and his right arm extended, popping away with his pistol. I guess this was back before they taught people to hold a pistol with two hands, as in the TV police shows. Needless to say, all the sane Marines were lying on the ground and firing from behind cover.

Shel was famous after that. We, of course, gave him shit about it, but he was unabashed. He insisted that he could be as effective as any rifleman. One night, I became a believer.

I was sitting radio watch, and Shel had stayed up with me to shoot the shit. We had a candle burning, and the radio shack was dimly lit. Mike Bolton was asleep on a cot in the middle of the room. Suddenly, I saw movement out of the corner of my eye. I turned, and there on the floor was a big snake, and it was reared up in the air and inspecting Mike from the head of his cot, weaving back and forth, like it was looking in Mike's ears. I signaled Shel as soon as I first saw the snake and was still deciding how to best deal with it when there was a loud explosion behind me and the snake went flying. Shel had shot the snake through the head with his .45 from about eight feet away, perhaps an easy shot in the Westerns, but I was impressed.

Mike came up from that cot with both eyes wide open and a whole new outlook on life.

Shel was wounded during the Tet Offensive, and we never heard what happened to him after he was medevaced.

Chapter 90

Shadows

With the dawn of the Marines' third day on Peleliu, the Japanese effort to retake the Point ended. Only the occasional crack of a sniper's rifle indicated that any enemy soldiers were still around. The main body of the Japanese forces had pulled back deeper into the island. The commanders of the First Division later revealed their concern that the Japanese might take the Point and then sweep down the beach where the Marines were spread so thin. If the Japanese had been able to send a large contingent of troops down the beach, they could have cut the Marines off from their supply line and trapped them between a force on the beach and the forces occupying the rest of the island.

Such a maneuver could have changed the course of events on Peleliu, but the Japanese were unable to take the pivotal piece of high ground—just thirty feet high—that would have opened the way to such an attack. The Marines of K Company, undermanned and low on ammo, withstood everything the Japanese threw at them. After 48 tenuous hours, the First Division had secured the beachhead on Peleliu.

Chapter 91

Another New Lieutenant

A day or so after the ambush, Captain Higgins returned from R&R to discover that Lieutenant Johnson was killed during his absence, and Battalion had already sent out a new company commander for Echo Company. The new guy was First Lieutenant Doug Chamberlain, another green officer who had not been in combat before. This was the guy whose radio I was now going to be packing. Captain Higgins didn't even return to our combat base—I assume they didn't want him to make it harder for the new commander to assume command. Captain Higgins was Echo Company's C.O. through some rough times. He received a Silver Star for his actions the day our rifles jammed on Operation Arizona. Not an easy act to follow.

Normally, company command is a captain's billet, but the reality was that first lieutenants often commanded companies in Vietnam, because there weren't enough captains to go around.

Assuming command of a rifle company in a combat zone is pretty much a guaranteed way to make captain, however, and Lieutenant Chamberlain soon became Captain Chamberlain. Lieutenant Johnson was posthumously promoted and buried as a captain, which pleased me.

Lieutenant Chamberlain had not served as a platoon commander in Vietnam, thus, his first combat command was at the company level. Battalion had him lined up to be X.O. of another company, so that he could follow the same learning path that Lieutenant Johnson was on. But the sudden loss of Echo Company's C.O. forced the Battalion Commander to install the young lieutenant earlier than planned. To make matters even more irregular, the reason Doug Chamberlain didn't serve as a platoon commander was because he was busy playing on the Marine Corps basketball team. Word about this spread rapidly and more than one Marine bemoaned our fate to have a commander who had never commanded.

Most of the Marines in a rifle company know the company commander only from a distance. When I was in a platoon, I never exchanged a single word with the company commander and only very rarely did I speak to my platoon commander. It was amazing how much that had changed in only a few months. I would be at this new C.O.'s right hand whenever anything was going on. More than anyone in the company, I would see exactly how he performed in the field.

I'd been through a similar process with Lieutenant Johnson, but it felt different this time. I was more confident after all I'd learned with Lieutenant Johnson. I felt I had something to offer this new commander. I saw him less as father figure and more as a guy needing all the help he could get to do a very tough, and very important, job.

Today, I look back at that transition as the biggest turning point in my life. It started on Highway One, as Lieutenant Johnson and I dealt with crisis after crisis, and I learned to handle situations beyond the range of most lance corporals. The change culminated with the arrival of our green commander. I saw that I could help him as he learned his new job—in my humble way as his radio operator, of course—and I was no longer intimidated by what might be expected of me. I had achieved that fundamental sense of competence that separates the new guys from the wise veterans.

First, I achieved it as a grunt, now I felt had done the same as a radioman.

Chapter 92

Shadows

On the morning of the third day, I Company moved up onto the Point and relieved K Company. After holding the Point against repeated attacks for two full days, K Company was pulled out of the line and placed in reserve. K Company had hit the beach with a large complement of 235 men. By the third morning, they were down to just 78 men. Over 500 Japanese bodies littered the ground on and around the Point.

To put these numbers in perspective, consider the experience of Easy Company of the 506th Parachute Infantry Regiment, made famous by Stephen Ambrose in his book *Band of Brothers* and the 10-part HBO miniseries of the same name. Easy Company parachuted into Normandy on D-Day, June 6, 1944, with 139 men. They were pulled out of the line on June 29 with 74 men. They lost almost half their numbers—65 men—in 23 days. K Company lost two thirds of their troops—157 men—in 48 hours.

Chapter 93

Elephant Valley

Bill Rees and Lieutenant Johnson were killed in early October of '67 and the Tet Offensive occurred at the end of January of '68. In between those two events, Echo Company made several small-scale operations into an area called Elephant Valley. The valley followed the Song Ca De River, which exited its path through the mountains next to Hill 190 and then crossed an area of flatlands to the village of Nam O where it met the South China Sea not far from the Esso plant. Elephant Valley was out beyond any villes and was occupied only by NVA troops. It was thick jungle where a large force of men could hide easily, and we believed the NVA were staging large units in the area. Thus, we generally went into the valley in either full company strength or at least a couple of platoons.

This was where I first saw Captain Chamberlain perform in the field and, sure enough, he turned out to be an outstanding officer—as though he'd been leading troops through the jungle for years. He turned out to be another one of those steady leaders who was calm and in control no matter how chaotic the situation. He also seemed to always knew where we were and where we were going, which is no mean feat in the jungle. However, he did have one habit that was different from the other company commanders I'd seen. He always wanted to be close up on the action and see things for himself. I don't mean simply checking things out—I mean right up there before anything happened. On a number of occasions, Captain Chamberlain and I walked right behind the point man as the entire company walked single file through the jungle. Normally, the commander walks in the middle of the column, but Captain Chamberlain wanted to see things as the point man was seeing them. This preference of his did not bother me—indeed, it reassured me. This was the kind of leader who was not going to send his men anywhere that he wouldn't go himself. Nor was he rash like some gung ho junior officers known for taking unnecessary risks and putting their men into situations that were beyond their capability.

    These missions up into Elephant Valley were delicate; we

were too large a unit to sneak around off the trails like a recon team but too small to put up much of a fight if we happened into any of the large NVA units which were staged in the area. We were beyond artillery range, in enemy territory, and ensconced in heavy, mountainous jungle where it was often impossible to land helicopters. Thus, we were basically on our own, so it was crucial that our commander know what he was doing.

What we didn't know at the time was that the NVA were shying away from major confrontations because they were preparing for the Tet Offensive. That is retrospective knowledge, however. From our perspective at the time, we were in a hairy situation, and needed to be extremely careful. We became very good at moving through the jungle without making any noise. On several occasions, we actually surprised small units of NVA. That was quite an accomplishment, for a group of sixty to a hundred men to walk through the jungle quietly enough to surprise a group of two to a dozen men. We literally bumped into guys didi-bopping up the trail with their AK47's slung.

This valley went west and a little north until it met up with the Ho Chi Minh Trail, a few clicks south of the A Shau Valley.

We got pretty far out there. One time we walked on a trail that was paved with bricks, really more like a road. That was an eerie feeling—to walk on that paved trail so far out in the middle of the jungle. It was obvious that the enemy was using the trail to transport supplies but it was empty and quiet when we were on it. Sneaking around in territory that was controlled by the NVA was the kind of experience that Recon teams had—it was unusual for the average grunt company.

For the most part, we did not have any large actions take place on those trips up the valley. We never went out without having some encounters with the enemy, but they were usually brief and we had superior firepower. We were ambushed one time while we were sitting on top of amtracs going up the river; that was nasty. And we had a couple of firefights that were prolonged enough to bring in air support. However, most of the activity in Elephant Valley was either encounters with small units or the demands of dealing with the terrain, and sometimes the terrain was the more difficult of the two.

There were thirteen snakes indigenous to Vietnam and

twelve of them were deadly poisonous. These ranged from the big king cobras to tiny little bamboo vipers. The bamboo viper was referred to as the "two-step" snake because of the deadly nature of its venom. It was just a little over a foot long, very thin, light green with a thin red stripe. My only experience with a bamboo viper occurred one morning in Elephant Valley. Captain Chamberlain and I had spent the night in a foxhole that had been dug by some grunt on a previous mission. I was sitting on the edge of the foxhole eating breakfast when the viper came out of a little hole in the side of the pit and started cruising around. It moved fast with its head and the front of its body held up off the ground. I killed it with an entrenching tool. Then I thought about how it had been there all night while we slept in the hole. Snakes don't offer much threat during the cool night so it's no surprise that it didn't do anything, but it was still a chilling thought.

    Just moving around in the jungle and setting up at the end of the day was a major accomplishment. Most of the time, we had leeches on us and were wet and uncomfortable—not to mention tired and hungry. Nothing was more appreciated than the rare opportunity to be dry and have a hot, unhurried meal.

The day after I killed the bamboo viper, we were walking along one of these large trails and we heard voices and smelled food cooking. The skipper and I and a half dozen Marines quietly edged up the trail. We paused there for a long minute just listening to them. It sounded like there was a group of about half a dozen Vietnamese—which meant NVA soldiers—eating breakfast in a campsite off to the side of the trail. They were inside a hedge that made it hard to sneak into a position where we could capture them. They were obviously unaware that we were on the other side of the hedge, only about 10 to 12 feet away from them.

Captain Chamberlain leaned over and whispered, "I want one more fire team up here. Tell everyone else to stay put and stay very quiet."

I nodded and waddled back up the trail a little ways so that I could talk over the radio without making any noise that the NVA could hear. I put my hand over the mouthpiece of the radio handset and whispered into the radio. "Echo Two, this is Echo Six, over."

Echo Two Actual came on the radio (Echo Two was the radioman, Two Actual was the lieutenant.) "This is Echo Two Actual, over."

"Two Actual, this is Echo Six. We've got a group of gooks right off the trail up here. Skipper wants you to send one more fire team up. Tell them to be very quiet about it."

"Roger, Six. Will do."

"Six out."

A moment later we had four more Marines. Captain Chamberlain motioned for everyone to form a semi-circle around the area where the enemy soldiers were. He gave me a grim look and shrugged. I realized his shrug meant he was saying that there was no sense trying to crawl into this hedge and capture these guys. Then he pointed his M16 toward the thick hedge, and everyone knew what we were supposed to do.

When everyone was in place, we opened up on them with our M16s—firing blindly through the hedge. I kept my fire close to the ground and sprayed back and forth as I fired off the magazine. We quickly replaced our empty magazines and went into the campsite. They never had an opportunity to fire back.

One of them was not killed outright; we followed his blood trail and found him a short distance away. Several Marines gathered around and stood over this guy, who was still breathing.

He lay there looking up at us as he died. Then I was surprised to see the corpsman get down on his knees and try to revive this guy with mouth to mouth resuscitation. He was really working hard at it too.

One of the Marines standing near me muttered, "What the fuck, man? We just killed that dude. What the hell does he want to try and save him for?" He shook his head and spoke with a contemptuous tone, "Fucking leave him there to rot, for Christ's sake." Then he turned to walk away, but paused and looked back at the corpsman. This time, he spoke more loudly, "Save your breath for Marines, Doc. We don't need to be dragging no wounded gooks around with us anyway."

It did feel mighty strange to see the corpsman try so hard to save a guy that we had just made every effort to kill. I felt sympathy for the corpsmen; they were forever trying to keep dying guys alive, often an impossible job. Our job as grunts—just killing the enemy—was a lot easier. The corpsmen had a completely different orientation, and they definitely had the tougher job. Killing people was nothing compared to the pain of trying to stop people from dying.

It gave me an eerie feeling to look through the campsite where these guys were sitting around talking and having a nice breakfast. Everything was in place, their half-eaten breakfast still sitting there. What a way to end your life, eating your breakfast and chatting with your friends, and suddenly everyone is being shot to pieces. It was an ugly way to kill them; they never had any chance. But it was the best way to ensure that we got them without any of us getting hurt. We might have taken them prisoner if conditions had made it possible to do so without endangering our own troops. But this was a war of ambushes, and the goal of an ambush is to get the advantage and kill everyone before they can shoot back. By the time of this particular incident, I barely gave much thought to how the enemy died. Indeed, shooting them at breakfast was just fine. It meant another encounter in which no Marines were hurt or killed.

Not that I felt particularly good about it though. There were no feelings of glee or sadistic pleasure in getting the kills—just a slight feeling of relief that we were on the giving end of this particular ambush, and not the receiving end. I've been on both ends, and I know the terror of being the target in an ambush; it's a feeling that can haunt you for a lifetime.

Chapter 94

Shadows

By the time they were relieved, K Company had taken the heaviest casualties of any company in the division. My father and the other men who were having their first exposure to combat had already seen more of their comrades die in that forty-eight hour period than the veterans had seen in all of the fighting on Guadalcanal and New Britain. Many of the men had not slept at all, and everyone was dog-tired. They moved down to a secured area on the beach where they were given coffee, sandwiches, beans, and fresh apples that had just been ferried ashore on an LST. The men of K Company ate the food and drank their fill of clean water. The intensity of their tenure on the Mound was over, and the food and water had an intoxicating effect. Many of them collapsed on the sand and fell asleep in the hot sun.

But things were not going well further inland. The Marines had reached the area where the Japs were dug in, a series of steep ridges named the Umurbrogol Cliffs. The Japanese had taken advantage of the natural terrain to create positions that were extraordinarily difficult to assault. It was not a situation in which the Marine commanders could long afford to leave any troops in reserve. The remaining Marines of K Company were not the only ones who were exhausted after the first 48 hours on Peleliu.

Chapter 95

Short Round

Despite my acquired indifference to the pain of the South Vietnamese, many images of their suffering remain with me. One of the most graphic sights occurred shortly before we left the Esso plant. Whenever a war is occurring around a civilian population, I think about this particular event. For me, it represents the price civilians pay when a war is fought in their homeland.

We received word that an arty short round had landed in a village near our base. A "short round" refers to an artillery shell that did not have sufficient powder and fell short of its intended target. As I understand it, artillerymen can add packets of powder to increase the range of a shell. If they didn't add enough packets, however, then the shell would fall short somewhere along the trajectory path. This was a rare event; the general level of accuracy of the artillery was astonishing. But now and then mistakes will happen, either through human error or faulty materials.

In this case, I accompanied Captain Chamberlain as he went to this ville to ascertain the damage. What we found was that the round had landed on a hooch and killed two infants. The skipper talked with the village chief and gave them a few hundred piasters in compensation. I don't know exactly how much he gave them, but I know it didn't amount to much. And with the small payment, the problem was resolved as much as it was ever going to be. The reimbursement of a paltry sum for innocent human lives did not escape us, but there wasn't much we could do. Most of the people whose children were killed never got anything.

But the image that stayed with me was the sight of the mothers of the two infants. They were seated side-by-side on the ground, rocking back and forth, and wailing with profound grief. Each woman had a swollen breast exposed and was methodically squeezing the milk out to relieve the painful pressure. Though they were mothers of infants, neither looked young. Two grief-stricken, old mothers wailing and squeezing their milk out onto the ground—this is the image that comes to mind when I think of the pain of noncombatants who live in a war zone.

That image has come to me when I encounter stories about

Americans filing enormous lawsuits and demanding compensation over events for which most of the people in the world would never even consider themselves entitled to anything—like the woman who spilled her coffee and burned herself and then sued McDonalds because they made her coffee too hot.

    Boy, do we live in a society that hasn't got a clue.

Chapter 96

Shadows

The Japanese are an enormously disciplined and industrious people. During the first half of the Twentieth Century, those energies were channeled into empire building. For decades, the Japanese conquered their neighbors, building their Greater East Asia Co-Prosperity Sphere. They conquered most of their end of the world, including independent countries like China, Korea and the Philippines, as well as French, Dutch and English colonies like Indochina, Indonesia, Hong Kong and Singapore—not to mention islands throughout the South Pacific. They were conquering those neighbors at an astonishing pace.

The traditional warrior culture of the Samurai, with its intense emphasis on honor and the concomitant avoidance of shame, was used to shape the immensely successful Japanese military machine. That code, combined with their military experience of conquest after conquest, led the Japanese to adopt certain tactics in warfare.

But the war with the Americans changed the course of Japan's expansionism, and eventually changed their tactics as well. Though the early months after Pearl Harbor saw the Japanese continuing to add to their conquests, the Japanese empire entered a new phase the day the Marines invaded Guadalcanal in August of 1942.

The Japanese became the defenders instead of the attackers.

They were not completely inexperienced in the tactics of defense, but they had largely defended in situations where they had the leverage of being ruthless occupation forces in someone else's home. The Japanese occupation of the Phillipines is a perfect example. The Filipino guerillas were superb jungle fighters and could not be defeated. Indeed, no guerilla force can ever be entirely defeated by occupying troops. But the Japanese maintained sufficient control of the guerillas through the use of ruthless reprisals against the civilian populace.

In the South Pacific, the Japanese were the defenders but they had no leverage over the American Marines; there was no population to threaten. Neither country was fighting in their homeland, but the Japanese were defending the land and the Marines were trying to take it away from them. This situation required the Japanese to employ new tactics, and they were slow to make the shift. The Japanese defenders employed some of the jungle fighting and guerilla tactics that they had learned from the Filipinos and the other conquered peoples. But they also continued to employ the tactics that had worked so well for them throughout the expansion of their sphere of influence.

For example, the Japanese had defeated many enemies with their banzai charge, in which fearless Japanese soldiers overwhelmed the enemy positions with a human wave attack or died trying. The banzai charge was a tactic of intimidation, on both a group and individual level. The individual Japanese soldiers were willing to die for their cause; most of them were experienced warriors; and many were personally skilled in the martial arts of close combat. To face a horde of such warriors was truly intimidating.

But the banzai charge was a tactic that worked best when assaulting and taking a position. It was not really a very good defensive tactic. The Marines first encountered the Japanese banzai charge on Guadalcanal. Like the Japanese, the Marines' only choice was to fight or die, so the Marines responded to the Japanese banzai by standing and fighting to the last man. Despite the Japanese soldiers' skill in the martial arts, the Marines fared well in close combat because of their greater size advantage. Most importantly, the Marines excelled in one area beyond all others. Despite the many young Marines who want to think they are Johnny Badass after completing boot camp, the fact is that Marine training focuses on discipline, attitude, and physical conditioning—not on creating the world's greatest close in-fighting martial artists. But there is one skill that the United States Marine Corps teaches better than any other military unit in the world—and that is marksmanship.

It took the Japanese high command half the war to recognize the futility of gathering their troops into a large crowd and charging a group of Marine marksmen.

A major obstacle for the Japanese was the rigidity of their military system. Local commanders were not free to employ new tactics if their superiors told them to do otherwise. Ultimately, the Japanese high command had to make the decision to change tactics. This finally occurred in mid-1944. The high command instituted the kamikaze attack; they put an end to the banzai charge; and they adopted an entirely new strategy for defending the islands.

The defense of Peleliu was the first test of the new strategy. The commander of the Japanese forces, Colonel Kunio Nakagawa, brought in mining engineers to dig tunnels and expand the network of limestone caves that riddled the Umurbrogol Cliffs. They created an underground facility where the entire Japanese force could survive untouched and unseen for weeks or more. Some of the caverns were large enough to hold a thousand men. They built narrow entrances, rolling steel doors, and concrete barriers that could absorb explosives without damaging the personnel deeper in the caverns. Nakagawa's troops stockpiled weapons, ammunition, and supplies throughout the subterranean network. They placed artillery and mortars in concealed sites, protected by heavy steel doors that could be rolled into place. They positioned many of the artillery pieces on the reverse slopes of hills so that attackers would be unable to determine where the fire was coming from. And they covered the Umurbrogol Cliffs with pillboxes and bunkers protected by steel doors, concrete walls and narrow gun ports. There was no clear perimeter that could be taken in an assault. Instead, the Japanese were spread throughout the ridges, their positions connected underground.

The result was that there was virtually nowhere the Marines could go that they were not subjected to enemy fire. Every time they knocked out an enemy position, another one opened up on them a few steps further ahead. When they thought they had secured an area, enemy soldiers would pop out of the ground behind them. Even when they thought they had destroyed some of the cave positions, more enemy troops arrived by tunnel and began firing from the positions once more.

Once the Marines had secured the beachhead, Nakagawa pulled all of his troops back to the Umurbrogol. Now the Marines were in for a fight the like of which none of them had ever seen before.

Chapter 97

The VC in the Spider Trap

Captain Chamberlain did not follow his predecessor's routine of sending the XO to check out the action on the road. Instead, he preferred to go and see for himself. Consequently, I continued to spend a lot of time outside the wire. One day late in November or early December, a convoy was ambushed on Highway One quite a ways north of Hai Van Pass, almost to Phu Bai. This was beyond the mountainous area; the road had descended from the pass and come back down to near sea level. Captain Chamberlain and I were on the North side of the mountain, on our way to visit the platoon stationed there, when I picked up a radio transmission from the convoy.

I said, "Skipper, there's a convoy getting ambushed. They're calling for help."

He said, "Where are they?"

"I don't know, sir. Wait one." I contacted the unknown

convoy and inquired about their location.

"I don't know exactly, Skipper, but they're northbound, already passed over Hai Van, but they haven't reached Phu Bai, so they're somewhere north of us." I asked the operator with the convoy how long ago they passed over the pass.

"Skipper, they reached the flatlands only about twenty minutes ago. They're not very far ahead of us."

Captain Chamberlain told the driver to keep going north, so we continued on past the point where we would get off the main road to see our platoon. I continued to monitor events over the radio. The fighting was still going on—I could hear the firing over the radio. This was a large convoy and an unusually large ambush. Soon, however, I heard that ARVN troops had arrived unexpectedly and routed the ambushers. The Skipper said we would go on and have a look anyway and see if we could help with their casualties.

The NVA soldiers had departed by the time we arrived. The first thing we did was to check in with the convoy commander to see if we could help with his casualties. A medevac was already on the way, and Captain Chamberlain offered my services to direct the landing of the medevac chopper. We got that done quickly; then Captain Chamberlain went over to survey the area where the VC had been set up. As usual, I was right behind him with my radio, shadowing him wherever he went.

The enemy positions had been set up in an area where railroad tracks paralleled the roadway. Some of them had fired from behind the railway while others were spread around in spider traps in front of the railroad tracks. They had hit the convoy with B-40 rockets and automatic weapons. We roamed around for several minutes, finding shell casings and trying to recreate the VC positions. As usual, it was a well set up ambush. Indeed, the VC would have inflicted a lot more damage were it not for the arrival of the ARVN's.

While we looked around, a few ARVN's milled around the area with us. Eventually, Captain Chamberlain and I sat down near the railroad tracks to study the map. We were sitting there side by side when, suddenly, one of the ARVN's started shouting and pointing his rifle at us. I had no idea what he was talking about, of course, but my first thought was that he must have been VC and was about to shoot us (I always assumed some of the

ARVN were VC). He ran up to where we were sitting and started firing at the ground a few feet behind us. Then he reached down, ripped the cover off a spider trap, and proceeded to pull a VC soldier out of the hole. The VC was gushing blood and clutching a rifle, and he only lived a few moments.

It feels strange to think about that guy in the spider trap, still alive and armed, but he had failed to escape with his comrades. Perhaps he was wounded, or perhaps he just didn't have an opportunity to get out. One way or another, there he sat with an American officer and a radioman so close he could just about touch them. He certainly could have killed us, but that would have pretty much guaranteed his own death. So it appears he decided to stay put and hope to go undiscovered, perhaps to fight another day.

Then he got killed anyway.

I wonder what was going through his mind as he sat there listening to us talking. Did he turn over his options, weighing his chance of killing some Americans against his chance of survival? Or was he already in so much pain that it didn't matter?

All I know is that there are many times that I might have died. Sometimes I lived because I made a decision, other times someone else made a decision that I had no control over. Either way, I was just plain lucky.

Chapter 98

Shadows

There were more than ten thousand Japanese soldiers on Peleliu. The vast majority of them retreated into the caves of the Umurbrogol and prepared for a long siege. As terrible as the fighting had been on the Point, the K Company Marines had the decided advantage once they had taken the high ground. It would be a very different story in the fight for the Umurbrogol Cliffs. The Marines were the ones performing the assault and they had to fight for every step they took.

Despite the enormous casualties K Company had taken in the initial assault, my father and the other surviving Marines were recruited into the fighting for the Umurbrogol or, as it came to be known, Bloody Nose Ridge.

Chapter 99

Non-Combat Casualties

My friend Shel was a forward observer for the artillery, and he had his own radioman, a guy named Gilmore, who had two accidental discharges with his .45 pistol. One of those occurred when he was sitting across from me on a cot. He had just finished cleaning his .45 and was replacing the magazine. Opening the breach of the pistol cocks the hammer back. In order to safely lower the hammer and un-cock the pistol, the slide must be returned to the closed position, and the trigger is then pulled on an empty chamber. After all that, you insert the magazine. Gilmore made the mistake of inserting the magazine before he closed the slide, which caused it to chamber a round. When he then pulled the trigger, he shot a bullet right past my ear.

It scared both of us, but me more than him. A few weeks later, we were on an operation in the jungle and packing up to move out in the morning. Gilmore was brushing his teeth and a moment later his .45 goes off, and he's got this look of surprise on his face. Again, no one was hurt, but I sure didn't trust that guy with a weapon after he'd had two accidental discharges.

We had been in thick jungle for several days and were due for resupply, but we were having difficulty finding any place where the choppers could reach us. Finally, Captain Chamberlain decided to climb to the top of one of the hills and use explosives to blow away a bunch of trees and create a hole in the canopy where helicopters could drop or perhaps lower supplies to us. We set up on top of the mountain for the night and, the next morning, we blew down a section of trees with C4 explosive. Then I called for the resupply choppers.

There were three choppers; all were the old single bladed CH-34 choppers. I popped yellow smoke grenades to help them find our little hole in the sea of green treetops. They formed up and took turns hovering over the hole, dropping crates of supplies from 100+ feet in the air. I stood on the edge of the cleared space and directed them over the radio. We didn't want anyone to get hit by a case of C-rats. The first two choppers successfully dropped their loads. Each had very carefully maneuvered into position and allowed me to tell them how near they were to the trees. All was going well. Then it was the third chopper's turn.

As soon as I saw the third chopper moving into view, I knew we had trouble. He was coming much faster than the other two had. Instead of inching his way into position, he tried to dart in and pull up to a stop.

As soon as I saw how fast he was coming in, I started trying to warn him, "You're coming too fast. Pull back and try a second run, over." When a chopper is hovering like that, it stands on a column of air. As I understand it, this guy's abrupt move caused him to slip off his column of air and drop down a little ways. I don't know how much he dropped but I could tell his rotor was in danger of hitting the trees, and I tried to warn him over the radio, "You're too close to the trees. Pull out! I repeat, pull out! You're going to hit the trees."

It was too late; his rotors hit the trees and, all of a sudden, the entire helicopter comes crashing down among us. All the way down, the spinning rotors kept hitting more trees—so pieces of rotor kept breaking off and flying out among all of us on the ground.

The fuselage of the chopper landed on its belly about fifteen feet from where I stood. Aviation fuel spilled, but fortunately didn't ignite. The whole thing happened so fast that I didn't even crouch down or look for a tree to get behind. I just stood there with the radio handset at my ear and watched those rotor blades shredding and flying into Marines. No one in the chopper was badly hurt but we had seven casualties from our company. Three guys had back injuries—two were hit by pieces of rotor and the third was a short machine gunner, named Shorty, who was under the fuselage when it hit. This was a disaster!

The situation only got worse when the pilot followed his crewmen out of the chopper. He was a short guy wearing aviator sunglasses, a pistol in a shoulder holster, and an ascot inside the collar of his flight suit. A fucking ascot! I have no idea what kind of person this pilot actually was but I considered him to be a cocky young shit who'd just gotten a bunch of men badly hurt by trying to be a hotshot and not take reasonable precautions. That may be an unfair assumption but it is pretty much what all of us thought. Now this fancy dude and his crew were going to have to walk out of the jungle with us, and a lot of guys were talking under their breath about another accident happening—this time to the pilot.

Captain Chamberlain picked up on how people were feeling and had a brief meeting with the lieutenants and platoon sergeants. He said, "I don't want this pilot to have any accidents during his stay in the jungle. You understand? Make sure all your men get the word. This guy may be a colossal dickhead, but he's not going to get hurt while I'm responsible for him."

Meanwhile, our situation had become more complicated. We now had seven casualties that needed to be medevaced and we were still in a location where we couldn't get a chopper down to the ground. So this time they sent two Chinook helicopters, the double bladed chopper that we used on our assaults. These two choppers each had a winch mounted outside the door; they took turns hovering and lowering a collar to us for our casualties to hang from while they were winched up. The choppers didn't have a basket, so our casualties had to hang in the air with a collar under their arms, and that's how they were extracted. It sounds insane but three guys with back injuries were hoisted into the air while hanging in a collar.

The pilot and his crew were with us for another three days while we walked out of the jungle. No accidents occurred—everyone steered clear of the pilot, like he was carrying the plague. Taking casualties is an inevitable consequence of combat, but losing people because some guy in an ascot flew his helicopter like a teenager drag racing the family car—that was a bitter pill to swallow.

Chapter 100

Shadows

I have never been able to determine whether K Company remained intact when they were sent in to reinforce other elements of the 1st Marines later that day. There were so few of them left that they may have been broken into fire teams and spread around as needed. I only know that my father ended up in charge of a group of men and was promoted to corporal after they left the island.

He told me that the battle for Bloody Nose Ridge was the worst fighting he encountered in the war. The Marines had to climb across exposed ridges, constantly coming under fire from everything from snipers to machine guns to mortars and artillery. Casualties continued to mount all around; each day they found Japanese soldiers popping up behind them from areas they thought were secured. Almost every day, they spent long hours pinned down, usually trying to destroy a position in which their only target was a tiny slit in a steel or concrete wall. The Marines, of course, provided much better targets for the gunners inside those positions.

Every night, the Japanese were very close to the Marine positions and there was intense combat in the dark. The Marines dug in as best they could, but they were trying to hold ground that was terribly exposed and the Japanese exacted a heavy toll, especially with their mortar and artillery barrages. At one point during the night fighting, my father's section of the line received some replacement troops to reinforce their positions, and several new lieutenants were placed in my father's sector. Within thirty minutes, all the new lieutenants were dead and the non-coms were again in charge.

Bloody Nose Ridge was pure hell.

Chapter 101

Freezing in the Tropics

Throughout the fall, we went on small operations up into Elephant Valley. Each time, the weather was wetter and colder. We didn't have a lot of enemy contact—generally just a few skirmishes each time we went out and even those only occurred when we surprised the enemy. But the weather was a bitch. The wettest and coldest of these excursions was our last outing from the Esso plant in December before we moved further North to our next firebase.

We were out for about 12 days. As soon as we jumped out at the LZ, it started raining, and it didn't let up for more than a few minutes the whole time we were out there. We had to stay at the site of our first bivouac for about three days because we were in a valley and it had flooded from the relentless rain. We set up camp on some slightly higher ground and prepared to stay for awhile. Captain Chamberlain and I stretched our ponchos and some plastic sheeting—I have no idea where that sheeting came from—into a lean-to and dug a trench around it to divert the water. We spent several days huddling under there, trying to stay dry. As always in the monsoon rains, the nights were the most miserable.

Finally, we determined to make our way to higher ground. The mountains were nearby but getting to them was a challenge. When it poured down like that, the small streams turned into raging torrents, and we had a lot of difficulty crossing them. In order to get out of the valley, we had to cross one of those raging streams. It was only about fifteen feet across, but the current was so intense that it took us nearly an hour just to get ropes stretched across the stream and tied to trees on each side.

Getting a first guy across was an interesting challenge. Initially, we tied ropes around several Marines, each of whom tried to get to the other side, but they all ended up getting swept downstream and had to be hauled back out. We finally made a human chain and got a guy over halfway across, and he was able to get to the other bank.

Once we had two ropes stretched across the stream, we crossed on the upstream side of the upstream rope, with the force of the current pushing us against the rope so hard that it left marks. You had to kind of slide your feet along the bottom in order to move against the current. You couldn't hold onto the rope because you had to hold your weapons above the water, but the force of the current kept you tight against the rope. If you lifted your foot more than an inch or two off the bottom, however, it was nearly impossible to get it back down. A number of Marines were swept under the rope and carried downstream where we had the second rope and several Marines set up as catchers. I made it across without getting swept off my feet; probably because I was carrying a ton of gear.

After we got out of the little valley where we'd been bivouacking, we avoided the low country. As usual, we moved during the day and humped to the top of a mountain each night. Humping to the tops of the hills at the end of the day in order to have a secure position on high ground was always a killer, but it was particularly bad during the monsoon. The hillsides were wet and muddy and it was almost impossible to climb up them— especially with seventy plus pounds of gear on my back. Almost impossible, but not quite.

Trying to dig foxholes in the mud was totally ridiculous.

The rain just refused to let up—I was soaking wet for about ten days straight and couldn't do anything to get dry. Along about the seventh or eighth day, I reached the point where I could no longer maintain my body warmth. I started shaking and couldn't stop. I thought I had pneumonia, because I didn't know what hypothermia was at the time—and there was no way I was going to get medevaced. We were in thick jungle where a helicopter couldn't reach the ground. Unless we had a serious enough situation to justify blowing down a bunch of trees so a chopper could hover and winch a man out, we were on our own.

I was miserable. I had nothing dry to wear, and I couldn't stop shaking. Everyone was in the same boat, but I seemed to be the only one who was hypothermic, body fat being another unknown at that time of my life.

We had no tents, of course, but we did try to create rainbreaks with our ponchos at night. One night, we made a circle of ponchos and burned an extra pair of boots that had come with a supply chopper back in the valley. The fire didn't put out much warmth, and it stunk to high heaven, but just sitting before it lifted my spirits.

Toward the end of the op, I was shaking constantly and couldn't stop. My friends tried to help me get warm but they could only do so much; no one had anything dry to offer me. Captain Chamberlain slept spoons with me at night, which helped. The last couple of days, I slept very little and got most of my warmth from the exercise of walking. We just kept walking and walking.

Finally, we reached the edge of the mountains—a steep cliff with a trail going down it in switchbacks. From the top, you could see the South China Sea and our firebase at the Esso plant. We walked all the way down the cliff trail and across the lowlands to our base. I had managed to walk all the way back, and I think the continued walking was the only thing that kept me warm enough to stay alive.

When we got back to the Esso plant it was the day before my twenty-first birthday. All I cared about was getting warm. I went into the dingy old French bunker where I had a cot, and I laid out a big, warm casualty bag—like a big feather and down sleeping bag. The bag had been passed along to me like many other things that stayed in the company and just rotated through owners. (I had a Thompson submachine gun that was given to me and which I then passed on when I left. I never carried it in the field, but it was fun to take on the mail runs.) Since it was close to Christmas, I had some care packages from home, and someone had sent me a big container of talcum powder. I took off all my clothes—I was a total wrinkled raisin—and covered myself with talcum powder from head to foot; then I climbed into the casualty bag and fell into a deep sleep.

I awoke late in the evening of the next day, feeling like a new man. I had slept twenty-six hours. I learned that Captain Chamberlain would not let anyone wake me and had personally taken my radio watch. That may not be in the Marine Corps officer's manual, but it's the kind of thing that distinguishes those officers who command the greatest loyalty.

I'd slept through most of my 21st birthday, but I was warm and dry and thankful to be alive.

Chapter 102

Shadows

On his second day of fighting on Bloody Nose Ridge, my father's unit came under intense artillery fire. They had been trading small arms fire with some Japanese soldiers who were not in a bunker when the incoming artillery grew so thick that everyone—Japanese and American—jumped up and started running for cover. My father was actually near one of the Japanese soldiers, but they were each too busy running to worry about shooting their weapons. Then a shell landed and the Japanese soldier was blown apart. My father was knocked unconscious and wounded by shrapnel from the same shell. He was placed on a litter and carried back to the beach for medical evacuation.

He regained consciousness as he was being carried to the beach. At the beach, he assessed his wounds—several small shrapnel holes—and decided he wasn't hurt badly enough to remain there. So he let the corpsmen clean and dress his wounds, then he found his rifle and hiked back into the island to rejoin his unit.

Chapter 103

The Meaning of Luxury

We had to go beyond normal channels if we wanted to improve our living situation. While at the Esso plant, Captain Chamberlain collected a bunch of chicom grenades and two AK-47 rifles and gave them to the Navy outfit that patrolled the harbor. In return, the Navy sent us two truckloads of building materials, primarily wood and tin roofing. Another time, they gave us copper wire, light sockets and a generator. I'd never had electricity on a combat base, but at the Esso Plant we had a bunch of old French bunkers that we could safely illuminate without making them glowing targets at night. When I finally got hold of some wire and a bulb—after the officers had taken theirs—I electrified the radio shack by attaching my piece of bare copper wire to the live, and also bare, wire strung between two hooches. I only gave myself a couple of jolts in the process.

In December, we left the Esso Plant and moved North to a

more isolated and exposed base—not a place where you dare illuminate anything. So we left the generator for the company that replaced us at the Esso Plant. Then, in January, we moved again, this time to Hill 190, and we had a renewed opportunity to use a generator. For one thing, we could power an arc light that would be mounted on the top of the hill. So one day I accompanied Captain Chamberlain—we called him Skipper, a naval tradition—to Danang in a six-by. The skipper had obtained some kind of standard form for acquisition of materials. We went to this huge fenced parking lot that was covered with generators. While the captain kept the non-com busy, the company driver walked among the generators, found one that looked good and wrote down the serial number. Then we slipped the number to Captain Chamberlain. He informed the supply sergeant that we'd come to pick up generator serial number such and such. We then found the appropriately numbered generator, hitched it to the rear of the truck, and drove off with the supply sergeant clearly dissatisfied but unwilling to defy a captain.

    Our relationship with the Navy outfit that patrolled the coastline and Danang harbor led to other interesting things. They had helped us in various ways—from the building materials to the recon by boat that Lieutenant Johnson and I took in September. So the skipper was happy to help them out when they asked for some assistance entertaining a visiting admiral.

Their headquarters was located across the bay from us. I'm not sure how far it was but I would guess ten or fifteen miles. They could see our base from their headquarters because we were a few hundred feet above sea level at the base of a mountain. We couldn't see them across the bay, but they had a nice setup, including a two-story building with a veranda on the second floor. On this particular evening, they planned to entertain the admiral by taking him out on the veranda where he would be looking across the harbor toward our base.

We were set up at our end with all our troops on the perimeter, and I had a central role in our little play. I fired off a red pop flare, which means "enemy in sight", and everyone on the perimeter fired their weapons. After two minutes of firing, I fired a green pop flare, and the show was over. But in that short two minutes, we fired an amazing amount of ammo. We had machine guns firing, a couple of platoons of riflemen firing their rifles, the

106mm recoilless rifle firing, the mortars firing flares, and our stationary .50 caliber machine gun firing up the mountainside.

A night firefight like we were creating is a like a fireworks display. There are streams of tracers punctuated by lots of individual tracers that go bouncing off at various angles after hitting things. You could pick out the .50 caliber rounds because they seemed to go on forever as they bounced up the mountainside behind us. The mortar and 106 rounds make brief flashes of white light where the explosions occurred and the entire landscape was covered by a murky smoke that was lit up by the canopy of illumination rounds floating in their little parachutes overhead. A pretty eerie sight.

Apparently the plan worked, and the admiral saw Echo Company engaged in a firefight across the harbor. I hope he got a rise out of it and presumably had something to talk about when he went back home. Afterwards, the skipper sat down and estimated what our little display had cost. A single rifle round cost 13 cents and then the costs went up radically as you deal with .50 caliber, .60 and .81 mm mortar, and 106 recoilless rounds. They used to say it was the cost of a new Cadillac every time the battleship New

Jersey fired one of its sixteen-inch guns.

Our little phony two-minute firefight cost tens of thousands of dollars, but that is a mere drop in the bucket of the colossal American military machine, far and away the richest military in the world. We couldn't get the lumber and generator that we needed through proper channels, even though unused generators were crowded into parking lots in Danang. But we could get all the ammo we wanted. So we shot off thousands of dollars worth of ammo, just to help some Navy guys impress an admiral, so they would keep helping us get lumber and other supplies that they could get so easily.

These days, whenever I see the incredible amounts of money that are appropriated to the Department of Defense, I think about that evening. Yet all we did was shoot our weapons for two minutes. Just think about those flyboys that get to play with the multi-million dollar aircraft.

Chapter 104

Shadows

In the first hour after K Company hit the beach at Peleliu—while they were still eliminating some of the positions on the Point—Colonel Ross, a member of Colonel Puller's regimental command group, visited them in person. The colonel had set out with his radioman to get a firsthand look at how each company's zone was faring. His radioman was killed as they moved down the beach, and the colonel continued on his own. He was the first to inform Captain Hunt of the size of the gap between K Company and the rest of the division. After a brief check-in with Captain Hunt, the colonel took off running back down the beach, again crossing the section that was held by the Japanese.

Soon after K Company secured the Point, the Division command group landed further down the beach—long before the Marines had anything beyond a toehold on the island. These high ranking officers risked their lives right along with the men they commanded, because that is how the Marine Corps operates.

Chapter 105

Christmas, 1967

We left the Esso Plant in mid-December, right after my episode with hypothermia. The hill we moved to was remote—just the opposite of the Esso plant. The firebase was located in the mountains southwest of Phu Bai, on a hilltop that was surrounded by other wooded hilltops, which made it an inviting target for snipers. Fortunately, the distance was great enough that sniper fire, though frequent, was seldom accurate. The road to this base was so muddy that it was barely passable and couldn't be depended on in bad weather, such as the wet, cold conditions that prevailed. Our primary connection with the rest of the Americanized world was via helicopter.

On Christmas Day, 1967, a two star general—perhaps the commander of the First Division but I'm not sure—planned to visit our remote firebase. It was a big deal that a general was coming to visit. We had a major 'clean up the base' effort. We put planks of wood down all over the place so the general wouldn't have to walk in the mud. We wore clean utilities and the gunny had a sharply starched cover. We looked amazingly good to be living in such godforsaken conditions.

I had a special job for the general's visit—standing in the LZ with my radio and guiding the chopper in for its landing. Thus, I would be the first person that the general saw from Echo Company, and I was supposed to make a good impression. Well, I was the first person that the general saw from Echo Company. In fact, I was the first, last, and only person that the general saw from Echo Company.

He came in a CH-34 escorted by two Huey gunships. The gunships kept flying circles around us while his personal chopper set down in front of me. The pilot signaled me over as soon as they set down. The rotor was still rotating, so I pulled my antenna down as I stepped up on the wheel and stuck my head in his window. The pilot yelled over the noise of the engine.

"When was the last time you took fire in this LZ?"

I yelled, "Yesterday afternoon, we took some sniper fire."

He nodded and turned his head for a moment. Then he

turned back to me and motioned with his hand for me to step down and move away from the chopper. Without another word, they lifted up into the air and pulled away.

End of visit.

I trudged back up the hill to where the CO and a number of well dressed Marines stood waiting. After I explained what the pilot asked about, everyone was nonplussed. The skipper looked puzzled. The only person who didn't seem surprised was the gunny, who nodded his head like it was what he expected.

I didn't get much of a glimpse of the general but I did get a glimpse at the inside of his helicopter. The walls were covered with some kind of fabric that looked to me like red velvet. It was a strange feeling to be on this remote base in cold monsoon weather, getting our covers starched and making walkways over the mud so this dude could make a symbolic visit in his velvet helicopter.

I remember just standing there and watching the chopper pick up and fly away, one of those unforgettable moments.

Chapter 106

Shadows

When I was seven years old, we were between homes and spent several weeks in a cabin at Lake Texoma. One day, my mother encountered a big King snake near the cabin. King snakes are harmless to humans, but we didn't know that and she was very frightened with her children in the yard. My dad picked up a piece of wood to use as a club and tried to kill the snake with it. The snake literally went up the side of a tree, which I had no idea was possible, and I watched my dad bludgeon the snake to death.

It was the most brutal thing I had ever seen.

Chapter 107

Wild Things

The beginning of January, 1968, we moved to Hill 190, which was located at the edge of the mountains that rise from the flatland west of the village of Nam O. The hill was near the Song Ca De River that wound across the flatland, passed under the Namo bridge and exited into the Bay of Danang. That was the bridge we used to guard when we were at the Esso plant. Hill 190 was next to the point where the river exited the mountainous area, and there were no civilians further inland from us. However, our area of responsibility included thirteen villages in the surrounding valley. We made several excursions into Elephant Valley from Hill 190 both before and after the Tet Offensive that occurred at the end of January. We had limited action on those ops, but we did have some unusual encounters with wildlife.

I had two run-ins with bees during my tour. The first occurred on Highway One on the North side of Hai Van Pass. A detachment from one of the platoons was attacked by bees and called for help over the radio. Captain Chamberlain and I went to help rescue them, and he brought a bunch of high-density smoke grenades, which we used to chase off the bees. Then we took care of the guys who got stung. One of the platoon radiomen was stung the worst. I helped the corpsman pull stingers out of him with a pair of tweezers, and you could tell that he was hurting bad. We finally removed his shirt and found his back to be just covered in stingers! The bees had somehow gotten up under his radio on his back and stung the hell out of him.

After that day, I had a newfound respect for bees.

Months later, during one of our forays from Hill 190, I had my second encounter with bees. We had a Kit Carson Scout guiding us. The Kit Carson Scouts were former VC who had changed sides. We never knew how much we could really trust them, of course, but our understanding was that the VC would kill them as painfully as possible if they were caught. As you can imagine, it was still pretty weird for us, and most grunts were not very friendly toward these guys. The Kit Carson scout was accompanied by a scout from Battalion Headquarters to help interpret.

As we quietly walked through the jungle in single file, we passed a big swarm of bees hanging from a tree limb. We gave them a wide berth, each Marine silently pointing the swarm out to the guy behind him so that no one would disturb them. I was near the front of the line, well past the swarm, when something set the bees off and they attacked us. My previous exposure taught me what those bees were capable of doing, and I knew what I would do if anyone set this bunch off. I wasn't going to outrun those bees, so I quickly got down on the ground, rolled into a ball, and covered myself with my rubber poncho. I received no stings, but several people were stung badly, including the Kit Carson Scout, who went into anaphylactic shock and died. The corpsman tried to revive him but to no avail. Since it was so difficult getting choppers in there, we had to carry his body out.

Later on that same mission, we were walking down the middle of a stream, and Captain Chamberlain and I were up walking right behind the point man. Captain Chamberlain often felt the need to be at the head of the column. I think he wanted to be there this particular time because there was no trail and he wanted to make sure where we were going. We came upon an obstruction across the stream, but there was a spot where we could wade through a deep pool under an overhang and come up on the other side. So the point man went through first, and then Captain Chamberlain followed. When it was my turn I climbed down into this small pool about waist deep, and then I stepped on something that moved under my foot. This bright green lizard about three feet long came scrambling out of the pool and ran between the legs of the point man who was standing there waiting to help me climb out. It scurried across the rocks and into the water on the other side.

Captain Chamberlain, the point man, and I stood there with our mouths open. I think all three of us were scared out of our wits.

I have since learned that the beast was a Bengal Monitor. I saw one at the Lincoln Park Zoo in Chicago. Other times in the jungle, I saw bears, an elephant, stone apes, deer, and a lot of snakes. We also saw the tracks of tigers, and one time one of my squadmates swore that he saw a tiger following our point man when we were on patrol. That seemed unlikely, but we did find a lot of tiger tracks on some of those trails.

There were all kinds of wild things in the jungle, but, of course, it was the human beasts that we feared the most.

Chapter 108

Shadows

A few days after getting knocked out by the artillery round, my dad and his squad found a cave that they wanted to explore. So my dad took a .45 pistol and his comrades lowered him into the cave. He landed on solid ground and when his eyes adjusted, he saw that he was facing a lone Japanese soldier who was sitting cross legged with his rifle across his lap. The man made no effort to shoot. My dad was frightened when he realized he was facing an enemy soldier and killed him with the .45.

This man clearly could have killed my father, but he did not. By this time the outcome of the battle for Peleliu was probably apparent, and this soldier must have known that he was doomed to die. Maybe he had lost the desire to take another's life as well.

Chapter 109

Tet Begins

It would take a whole book to do justice to the Tet Offensive of 1968, and then I'd only be offering one perspective. For me, it all started about 10:30 in the evening. One of our bunkers—maybe one of the ones with a starlight scope—called the radio shack on the land line and reported some strange activity outside our perimeter. They had spotted a flag flying a short distance outside our main gate. At this point in my tour, I slept in the radio shack. One of the platoon radiomen was doing the watch but I was always listening with my third ear. I was so adjusted to my role that I just about always woke up when someone called on the radio and the tone of their voice conveyed trouble. Yet I slept through the normal check-ins.

This call came in over the land line, so I only heard our end of it, but I could tell that something was going on. It was our bunker down near the gate. I went to the Skipper's hooch to tell him what we'd heard.

"Skipper, one of the bunkers just reported that it looks like someone has put up a flag out near the front gate."

Captain Chamberlain snorted, "Great, it's probably a VC flag and they want all the locals to see how secure they are when the sun comes up." He rolled out of his cot. "Come on, let's go check this out."

We walked back to the radio shack, which was near where he slept. He talked to the guys in the bunker on the land line, and then he turned to the company gunny.

"Gunny, put a detail together to go outside the wire and retrieve that flag. Scare up four or five men." He turned to me and said, "Cathy, you're in charge of the detail. Watch out that they haven't booby trapped this thing. They may want us to come out for it, so be careful."

I said, "Aye, aye, Sir" and went to collect up the people the gunny had picked. These were all Marines who didn't have other duties, including one of the truck drivers assigned to the company. I wore my radio so I could stay in communication with the captain, and off we went.

We went outside the wire and found not only this big Viet Cong flag, but also small paper flags mounted on bamboo sticks about three feet long and stuck into the ground right in front of the concertina wire. The paper flags extended most of the way around our perimeter, which meant some individual or individuals had circled our base—walking right out in front of our bunkers—and put up dozens of these little flags, and no one had noticed.

I was reminded of the three captives who so quietly escaped during my first operation.

I called the skipper and notified him. "Echo Six, this is Echo Romeo. We found the big flag, and we also found a bunch of little ones on bamboo poles. They're stuck in front of the wire every ten meters or so. Looks like they may go completely around our perimeter, over."

"Romeo, this is Six Actual. Roger that. Can you get the big one down, over?"

"Six, this is Romeo. Affirmative. It looks like we can get to it, over."

"Okay, get it if you can. And bring me a couple of the small ones, but don't worry about getting the rest of them."

"Six, this is Romeo. Roger, out."

The big flag was mounted on a tall pole that was wrapped with barbed wire. About the time we reached the pole, we started taking fire from a hedgerow about 100 meters further away.

I told everyone to get down and hold their fire. It was dark and hard to see where the incoming fire was coming from, other than the vicinity of the hedgerow. They, of course, would have erected the flag and consequently knew more about our position than we could know about theirs. I figured whoever was shooting wanted us to fire back and give them some muzzle flashes to make us better targets. We'd already been baited out to where they wanted us to be, and I didn't want to help them any further by providing muzzle flashes. Therefore, my plan was simple: grab the flag and get out of there.

"All right, you guys, just hold your fire. They can't really see us very well, they just have an idea where we are. So let's don't help them out with some muzzle flashes. I'm going to shinny up that pole and get the flag, and then we didi mau out of here."

I took off my radio and handed it to someone and got ready to try climbing the flagpole.

Unfortunately, the truck driver couldn't tolerate the strain of being shot at without shooting back. So as I'm about to shinny up the pole, he jumps up and starts making a lot of noise, saying shit like, "Come on, you motherfuckers."

I had to grab him and pull him down. Then I held him down; he was shaking with his urgency to get up and fight.

I was pissed and scared by his behavior.

"Shut the fuck up, Goddamit."

He got louder, saying "I ain't going to stand here and get shot at without fighting back. I ain't afraid of them."

I then did something that I never imagined I would do. I held my M16 in front of his face and shook it. "You shut the fuck up or I'm gonna shut you up for good. You hear me?" I was getting kind of loud myself, even though it was all in a whisper. He scared me more than the incoming fire, and I was enraged because I felt he was endangering all of us.

He shut up.

After a moment, I went back to the flag, now feeling unsafe from both sides, and shinnied up the barbed wire-covered pole and pulled down this VC flag. It was about four by six feet—half red and half blue with a yellow star in the center. The flag was clearly homemade—the yellow star was made of paper, but the rest was cloth.

It only took a few minutes to walk back inside the lines, but I made sure to keep the unstable guy in front of me. Later, I thought about the night that Ramsey threatened to kill anybody who messed around with the whores in the ville. That had seemed way over the edge to me, and I thought Ramsey had lost all control. Yet I'd just threatened another Marine.

Maybe I wasn't as different from Ramsey as I thought.

As for the truck driver, he was medevaced out a few weeks later as a result of a kind of freak situation. We were called out on a reactionary; one of our units was in trouble near a local ville and the skipper sent a reinforced platoon. Reinforced meant that several other extra people went along, including me—in case we needed air support or artillery or had to run any medevacs. The truck driver was along as well.

We were all walking across a field in the dark when something exploded right between me and the truck driver, apparently a booby trap. I was knocked off my feet and disoriented by the blast, but I wasn't hit by any shrapnel. This was the second time that I got knocked down by an explosion without receiving any shrapnel. However, this time I was deafened by the noise of the blast, and it took a long time to get my hearing back. My ears were ringing, and I was unable to use the radio for several hours.

    The truck driver was also disoriented by the blast, but he never came out of it. He was walking around in circles, and we medevaced him, and that was the last I saw of him.

Chapter 110

Shadows

My dad and I used to go out in the woods with the .22 rifle, but about all we could find to shoot were squirrels and rabbits, and we never ate those, so he didn't like for us to keep shooting them. However, when some of his coworkers invited him to join them for some dove hunting, he agreed that dove were good to eat and arranged to take me on my first bird hunting expedition.

I was very excited.

When we arrived, they gave me a .410 gauge shotgun to use, the smallest gauge you can get on a shotgun. I had never fired a shotgun, so one of the men suggested that I should fire it to see what it feels like. Up to that point, I had only fired the .22 rifle, which didn't kick much, so I wasn't prepared for the recoil of a shotgun, even the little .410. I pointed it at something and pulled the trigger, and the next thing I knew, I was flat on my back. The recoil of the shotgun had knocked me completely on my butt, and all of the men roared with laughter. I could see how it was funny to them, but it wasn't funny to me. It hurt, and it scared me.

Plus, it highlighted what a little shrimp I was to be knocked down by a gun that was practically a toy compared to the big 12 gauges they were using.

Fortunately, my dad understood that the reason I got knocked down was because I didn't have the shotgun tight against my shoulder. He showed me how to hold it tighter, and had me fire it again. Sure enough, that made all the difference. In fact, it didn't even hurt when I had it firmly up against my shoulder. So I was more prepared to go forward with the hunting, but I still had a different feeling about this powerful gun. I was a little afraid of it.

It turned out that I didn't do any hunting. I never seemed to be able to get the gun into the air and pointed in the right direction when the birds came in. So, mostly, I just retrieved the birds my dad had shot down. I was still enjoying the afternoon, especially watching my dad. He found a spot that was under a flyway, and he was hitting birds right and left. It pleased me to see how my dad's marksmanship impressed the other men.

Daddy let me sit near him while he was shooting from his

hot spot. This wasn't really dangerous; he had spent a lot of time training me in gun safety. We never crossed a fence without unloading our weapons, he made sure I always knew which way my weapon was pointing, and I had learned to treat every gun as loaded. So when I sat near him, I understood the importance of arranging myself so that I didn't shoot in the wrong direction. But I ended up not shooting that day anyway; I just sat near him and retrieved the birds as he shot them. He wasn't far from the other men, but he was getting all the hits. Late in the afternoon, he shot a bird down that was only wounded. I tried to retrieve it, but whenever I got close to it, it would jump into the air and flap awkwardly for a few yards.

I chased it, but I was timid about grabbing it. The truth is I was afraid to grab a live bird. Hey, it might have pecked me to death with its tiny beak.

Finally, I stopped chasing it and yelled, "Daddy, I can't catch this thing. It keeps flying away from me."

One of the other men was nearer to me. He yelled, "Shoot it a second time; that'll stop it."

So I blasted the poor bird from about six feet away, and it

totally disappeared into a cloud of feathers—pretty much like the glass ashtray my dad had shot at the dump.

My dad and his friends all roared with laughter.

Well, I didn't feel completely ridiculous; it wasn't the same as when the shotgun knocked me down. But it was kind of horrifying to see what that gun did to a living organism at close range. There was literally nothing left but a cloud of feathers.

Chapter 111

Nam O

Our biggest action during Tet took place about five or six days into it. The VC had taken over the village of Nam O, which was a fair-sized village located on the Southern side of the point where the Song Ca De river crosses Highway One. This was the bridge Echo Company guarded back when we were stationed at the Esso plant. The river came out of the mountains next to Hill 190 and ran across the flatlands to Nam O and then into the harbor. Every convoy that went North from Danang passed through Nam O. It was a popular place to stop and buy cokes, baked goods, and the like.

At the beginning of the Tet Offensive, several hundred North Vietnamese and Viet Cong soldiers went into the village of Nam O and took control of it, which effectively stopped all travel north from Danang. Right away, we knew they were there, but we were busy with our own problems. The VC had shut down all our ground supply routes, and vehicles no longer came to our firebase. We were only accessible via helicopter, and those were in high demand, so only people with high priority got helicopters. Before the Offensive was over, the artillery battery ran out of shells, and we lost all artillery support. You had to be practically getting overrun to rate any kind of air support. Meanwhile, the VC were harassing us at night and causing us to use up ammunition, and we weren't getting any more.

So it was five or six days into the siege before we could get it together enough to go after the forces holding Nam O. It needed to be a ground assault because our planes couldn't shoot into the village—the NVA surrounded themselves with groups of civilians whenever planes flew over. The night before we went to retake Nam O, I was talking to Davis, the company driver. We were all a little nervous about what we were in store for the next day. We knew there were a lot of enemy soldiers in Nam O.

Davis said, "I'm not shitting you, man, I had like a premonition tonight. I don't think I'm going to make it tomorrow."

I didn't like the way he was thinking. "That's just bullshit, Davis, so don't even start thinking that way. You go into a firefight convinced you're going to get hit and you're more likely to make some kind of stupid mistake."

"No, man, this isn't just getting nervous. This was different. I've come close too many times, and I just had this really clear feeling that tomorrow's my turn."

"Shit, Davis, stop saying that. You know it's the new guys and the guys that are short that get hit the most. That's because they're in their heads instead of paying attention to what's going on around them. Man, you gotta just focus on what's in front of you."

"Look, Cath, that's how close I came last time." He held up his hand that had one finger that had been shot off. "I think I'm just outta luck. I don't feel scared so much as just I know what's coming."

"You don't know shit, man, you just got yourself convinced is all. You and me, we're short, and short-timers tend to get all superstitious. I'm telling you, you gotta go into tomorrow with an open mind. You start thinking you know what's going to happen and you'll make it happen."

Davis' attitude made me nervous. And knowing we were

almost certain to be in a big firefight the next day didn't help. Usually, these things happened without warning, but this time was different. This was more like traditional wars for land where you attacked the enemy's position—like my dad assaulting a beachhead in WWII.

The next day, we got up early and prepared for a big battle. We took two rifle platoons and left everyone else to guard our hill. There were exactly 60 of us, counting the skipper and myself. Fortunately for us, ARVN Rangers got the job of going in to roust out the NVA. Our job was to provide a blocking force outside the village, where it was assumed the NVA would flee.

We rode in amtraks down the river toward the village and got out of the tracks about a click and a half (1500 meters) from the village. Then we hiked out into the middle of the dried rice paddies and set up our ambush. We laid behind a long rice paddy dike, with the skipper and me in the middle and a platoon extending out on each side of us. The place where we set up seemed arbitrary to me but I was soon to be reminded that Captain Chamberlain knew what he was doing. It was the most bizarre ambush I ever saw. Here we were, broad daylight, sixty marines in helmets and full gear, lying out in the middle of a huge open field with no cover other than the paddy dikes.

Fighting erupted in the ville. We could see smoke and hear the firing. Planes started flying close overhead—the old propeller driven Skyraiders flown by the South Vietnamese Air Force. And then, amazingly, a large group of men came walking directly toward us. As they got closer, I could plainly see their weapons—they were holding their rifles down by their sides to hide their outline from the planes. A large group of these VC walked directly into the center of our ambush. It was hard to believe that they didn't see any of us. I could see all these Marines lying prone with their rifles aimed directly at these guys, and not a one of them saw us. I guess they were preoccupied with the planes flying overhead.

The skipper and I were dead center in the middle of the line, and the platoon commanders, along with their radiomen, were located at each end of the line. The skipper said, "Tell everyone to fire on my command."

I passed the word over the radio. Everyone exercised good fire discipline and held their fire. Then, when the group of VC was about twenty-five yards in front of us, the skipper gave the command to fire, and I relayed it over the radio to the platoon commanders. Our two platoons opened fire and shot down eighteen guys in one volley. None of the VC got a shot off. Neither the skipper nor I fired our weapons at that point because it was obvious we didn't need to.

After that, the VC knew we were out there, and we no longer had the surprise factor. Indeed, it was now our turn to be the targets. We had to make our way across the huge expanse of open field toward where the main body of the VC were positioned, and they were shooting at us every step of the way. We got on line and began moving across the field. The VC were dug in behind a line of paddy dikes on the other side of the field, but they were still separated from the ville by a large flooded ditch that ran behind the ville. We advanced across the field by sprinting from dike to dike. The skipper would wait until everyone was lined up behind a dike, then he would give the signal and we would all get up and charge to the next one, where we would flop down behind the next dike.

When we first started across the field, we could hear the bullets around us but no one was getting hit. We were a long way from their positions, probably eight or nine hundred yards or more. But after we got about halfway across, Marines started going down every time we sprinted toward another dike. We weren't hitting any of them yet because they didn't have to get up and expose themselves the way we did. And we couldn't even stop to tend to our wounded; we kept going and left it to the corpsmen to take care of them.

As we got close to their side of the field, the skipper got stuck in some mud, and I ran back to pull him out. I was in contact with both ends of our line, but no one was reporting casualties in the midst of the assault. So when I ran back to the skipper, I got my first sight behind us, and I was shocked to see how many Marines were down. The corpsmen were busily attending to casualties that seemed spread all over the field. I believe close to a dozen people went down crossing that field! And since everyone else had reached the next dike while I was back helping the skipper, he and I were now the only targets. The VC focused their fire on us, of course, and bullets were snapping through the air and hitting the ground around us.

I felt very exposed, but we made it to cover without getting hit.

For once, there was no lack of targets in a big firefight! I could see every one of the VC—shooting at us as we were shooting at them. We'd reached the point across from the main body of the VC. They were organized into a long line behind a paddy dike, and we were in a similar line facing them maybe a hundred and fifty yards away. I could see every one of them distinctly—perhaps thirty of them—lying there firing at us.

We lay behind the dikes and fired at each other for ten to fifteen minutes. This was the first time that I'd done any serious shooting in months. Since I'd become a radioman, I seldom fired my weapon. Radiomen didn't even have to carry a rifle if they didn't want to, although everyone does. I carried both an M16 and a .45 pistol, but I rarely used either one as a radioman. A few times up on Highway One, I had helped lay down covering fire but that hardly counted as serious shooting because I never had a decent target. This day, however, we needed every weapon to be firing, and the targets were never clearer.

So I laid there and fired off about seven magazines. I was surprised when I fired up the first magazine, because I could see my bullets hitting the dry dirt in front of the enemy positions. I was hitting low and this was frustrating. I am embarrassed to admit that I had allowed my rifle's sighting to get out of whack, a major mistake for an infantryman. I initially tried to compensate with my old machine gunner trick of firing on automatic in three round bursts, but the accuracy was terrible at that range. So I switched to semi-automatic and started firing one round at a time, paying attention to where my shots were hitting.

My accuracy improved, and I adjusted my fire, trying to allow for where my bullets were hitting. I felt very calm and cool once I settled down, and I approached it like I was on the rifle range. I would fire, wait for the bullet to strike, and then adjust my aim. I can't say for certain how many I hit or what kind of damage I did, but I thought I hit several VC once I adjusted my aim.

At one point, while we were laying prone and shooting at each other, an M-79 grenade exploded on the dike right in front of one of the VC. It blew most of his head off and sent his conical hat flying.

Everyone on our line cheered.

That sounds awfully callous, but an aggressive spirit helped us maintain our momentum and overcome our fear. After all, we were running across a big open field toward people with automatic weapons who were trying their damnedest to shoot us. In some respects, the cheering and team spirit were a little like a football game, though we were playing for higher stakes. Many people get insulted when words like 'playing' and 'game' are used in this kind of context, I think they feel it discounts the human life that is involved. But we were just doing what seemed to come naturally when we had to run at them while they were shooting at us.

Within ten minutes or so, their line was pretty shot up and offering little resistance. We got up and assaulted again.

When we reached their positions on the far side of the huge field, they were dug-in a little better. For the first and only time, I killed a VC soldier at close range. He was halfway in a fighting hole and badly shot up, but he was alive and holding a rifle, and we were still under fire and assaulting their positions. This was one of those times when you didn't take prisoners, just as we didn't stop to attend to our wounded as we assaulted across the field. This wounded VC didn't look like much of a threat, but I couldn't just walk past him knowing he was alive enough to squeeze off another round. So I shot him and walked on.

At the end of the afternoon, we had a body count of sixty VC. We had quite a few casualties, though I don't believe any of ours were killed. However, there were KIA's among the CAC unit that was somewhere further behind us. We established a small perimeter near the river, and I called for medevacs. Teams of Marines were bringing in the guys that were spread over the field from the assault. That's when I found Davis, my friend who'd had the premonition the night before. He hadn't been killed, but he'd been shot in the foot, and it was one of those really painful wounds. I tried to say something comforting to him, but he was hurting too much for conversation.

I directed the medevac and sent him on his way and, of course, never saw him again.

The following day, we went into the village of Nam O and searched house to house. My only moment of excitement that day occurred in the back yard of one house. The yard was basically a corral, and it had a water buffalo in it. The big animal was spooked, first by the firing and now by people coming into its quarters. I was following the skipper with my radio on, and I was carrying my .45 pistol in my hand since we were in close quarters. Suddenly, this water buffalo charged through the group of Marines and came straight at me. After seeing one take a hundred bullets the previous summer, I knew the futility of trying to stop a water buffalo by shooting it, so I didn't even try. Instead, I emptied my .45 into the dirt in front of me, and the water buffalo veered around me and ran out of the enclosure.

Everyone laughed at my firing at the ground, but I knew it made more sense than firing at the buffalo and possibly annoying him.

The fight at Nam O was the most killing I saw during my entire tour. More people may have died at other times, but I had not witnessed it directly as I did that day at Nam O. I saw almost every one of those VC as he was hit and went down. By that point in my tour, I could find no energy to expend on feeling bad about the VC who died. It is only now, many years later, that I mourn all the people who died that day. It's no longer about us versus them; it's just death, lots of violent death.

Chapter 112

Shadows

Despite his impressive physical presence and his combat-honed vigilance, not to mention his temper, I never saw my father threaten another person. He was always polite and respectful to others, even when I might question whether they deserved it. He was a deacon and then an elder at the church, and worked on Sunday mornings as superintendent of the Sunday school and later as a greeter at the front door. When he disagreed with someone, he didn't raise his voice or speak abusively. He tolerated others' views and never mistreated or took advantage of people.

Mind you, my mother and sisters and I saw another side of him at home. We saw his temper, his pain, and his stubbornness. At times, I could see a simmering pain in him, a flame that burned low but never went out entirely. I could see not only pain but guilt and rage and a cynical ugliness. He had more than one side to his nature, of course, because his public self was real too. I even saw moments of peace and genuine contentment, especially in his later years, but those moments were rare.

Chapter 113

Siege

After we had rousted the NVA out of Nam O, we returned to our firebase. We had won a decisive victory, but we were getting short on supplies. The Tet Offensive was going strong all over Vietnam. Suddenly, everyone had their hands full. The siege of Khe Sanh and the battle for the city of Hue were being waged further north of us, and these battles were draining the few resources available. My company was basically stranded out on our firebase. The road to our firebase was shut down—held by the VC—and no vehicles could get through to us. Meanwhile, the resources continued to diminish. After a few days, the artillery battery notified us that they were out of ammunition and were no longer available for fire missions. We got one or two ammo resupply drops by helicopter, and then those stopped. Captain Chamberlain got on the radio and told battalion that we were running low on supplies and needed resupply.

Battalion responded that we would have to get by on what we had.

It took a while for the seriousness of the situation to sink in. One afternoon, Captain Chamberlain let me sit in on a meeting with the platoon commanders and the platoon sergeants. He started by announcing that he had asked the gunny and the XO to inventory the ammo in the ammo bunker. He held up a sheet of paper.

"This is what we're down to."

One of the platoon commanders took the list and whistled. The XO said, "That's right. We're almost completely out of mortar ammo and we're close to the end of the M16 and M60 ammo."

Captain Chamberlain said, "I've decided to distribute everything that's left."

The gunny said, "All of it?"

The captain said, "Everything. Make sure every bunker on the perimeter gets its share of Claymores and pop flares. That stuff will just stay in the bunkers. We'll divide up all the M16 ammo and the grenades among the rifle platoons. The gun teams will take all the machine gun ammo, of course, and they've already been assigned to permanent bunkers. Do the same with everyone on the hill. I want every man on this base—the cooks, the drivers, everyone—to know exactly where he goes when we get hit."

One of the lieutenants asked, "Don't we want to have some central supply depot that people can go to? What if we get hit on one side of the perimeter and use up our ammo on that side?"

Captain Chamberlain said, "If that happens, we'll be shifting personnel from the other sides, and they'll have to carry their ammo with them. No, there's no sense leaving anything in the ammo bunker. From here on out, everyone has got to make what they have last, because that's all they're going to get."

Word was passed. "Don't fire up your ammo needlessly." This was serious. We began to prepare for the possibility that we would reach the limit of our capacity to defend ourselves and be overrun. The skipper also passed the word to burn anything you didn't want the enemy to get their hands on. The gunny organized work parties to fill several fifty gallon drums with diesel fuel, then set them afire at different points around the hill.

I asked the gunny what I should burn. He said, "Burn anything you got that could help the enemy. Like those little notepads that you carry, anything that's got radio frequencies or call signs. Don't leave nothin' they could use."

I said, "Okay, Gunny, but what about personal stuff? People are burning all kinds of stuff."

He gave me that look of his and said, "You want your parents to get a letter saying someone saw you rape a child? I wouldn't leave them nothin' that could identify you."

I shuddered at the thought of someone using my personal stuff for propaganda purposes. So I threw in all my letters, photos, and a diary I'd kept through most of my tour. I also got ready for the possibility that our command center would be overrun. I rearranged the radio shack so that I could have some cover in the rear of it and be able to shoot at the doorway. I placed thermite grenades on top of all the radios, so that all I had to do was pull the pins, and the grenades would burn down through the radios and destroy them. I loaded and placed the Thompson and a grease gun at hand. Both were old-fashioned submachine guns. I also put extra M-16 magazines and some frag grenades in handy places.

Then we waited.

The waiting lasted a few days. We were probed every

night, but there were no concerted attacks. Usually, our guys would fire a bunch of ammunition up when they were probed, but now they held back. The whole situation ended abruptly when a truck unexpectedly appeared one day. Apparently, the road had been cleared, and we didn't even know it. So the whole thing ended with a whimper instead of a bang. But here is the interesting part. For those few days, the Marines on that hill were the calmest and quietest I ever saw them be.

    I remember going into the mess tent—we were eating some pretty nasty stuff by then—and noticing how quiet it was. Everyone on the hill seemed to be in a sort of contemplative state of mind, I know I was. In many respects, I'd never felt more at peace. The anxiety that I normally lived with was about the possibility of dying. When I no longer considered it to be just a possibility, when instead I accepted it as just about certain, then I stopped worrying about it. It was a time to appreciate the hours I still had rather than worry about whether I might die. In a way, it removed me from the short-timer state of mind and returned me to the way I felt during the middle of my tour, when I couldn't imagine anything beyond the immediate moment.

Of course, once the siege was over, I returned to my normal state of anxiety, which was building daily as I neared the end of my tour.

Chapter 114

Shadows

On Easter Sunday, April 1, 1945, the First Marine Division made their final amphibious assault of World War II. They were part of a combined Army-Marine force that landed on the beaches of Okinawa. The landing was not resisted, but the three-month-long campaign to conquer the forces on the island produced the greatest casualties of the war in the Pacific.

The American forces pushed their way across the island, and the fighting was focused on the advancing line held by the American forces. One evening, my father was in charge of a section of the line, including a machine gun position. A group of native women approached his position, and he yelled the phrase they'd been told to use in order to get the civilians to halt. But the group of women would not stop; they just kept walking toward the machine gun. Finally, my dad ordered the gunner to open fire on them.

They found Japanese soldiers in among the group of dead women. The soldiers were dressed as women and had rifles with bayonets fixed. They forced the women to keep advancing on the Marine position.

My father talked about this incident many times. He felt terribly guilty about killing those women.

Chapter 115

Huey

By the final months of my tour, my capacity for feeling compassion toward the South Vietnamese people was at an all time low. Yet it was not gone altogether, my feelings were complicated by people like Huey. After we moved from Chu Lai to Danang, we ended up with a Vietnamese boy living on our combat base much of the time. We inherited Huey from the company that occupied Hill 60 before us. He didn't stay with us all the time; sometimes he would go home and stay with his family in Danang. I don't know how old he was but I would guess ten to twelve years old. He was sort of like a mascot except he did a lot more than a mascot, because he served as our interpreter when we needed one. The rest of the time, he hung out, bullshitted with the guys, and played poker. He was a good poker player and made a lot of money off young Marines who were not nearly as street savvy as Huey. In fact, he made so much money playing poker that he bought his father some cows, a sign of wealth.

It is strange to think back about Huey and how he lived with us. He was like a kid brother to everyone. He could swear and talk the jive as well as any Marine. And he was always out to take some of our money; he knew when payday was and would invariably be in the big poker game that followed. But you should have heard that kid talk, he had the foulest mouth I ever heard. I recall him trying to entice me into a poker game.

"Hey, tall and skinny, how come you don't play poker? You don't got no balls?"

I explained that I didn't like to gamble.

He laughed at me. "What the fuck you doing here then? Huh? You're just a pussy, a pussy Marine. I'm going to tell everybody what a pussy you are, that you got no balls to play poker."

I said something about how maybe I would scalp him and throw him over the wire just to show everybody I had balls—or something equally as stupid. I wasn't too great at the snappy comebacks with Huey.

Huey just laughed harder. "You're a piece of shit, man;

you're just a piece of shit. I bet you never got laid in the states, man. I bet you used to fuck your sister. Isn't that right, you used to fuck your sister?"

I just shook my head and walked off. Huey pretty much always got the upper hand in our interactions. And not just with me, he seemed to have the edge on everyone in the company. He was a smart little shit.

Despite Huey's larcenous nature, we placed a lot of responsibility on him. We could never tell when a Vietnamese was lying or telling the truth, so we were always dependent upon another Vietnamese to tell us, and most of us trusted what Huey said more than many of the official interpreters. Huey had identified VC for us, and we knew that his family had been targeted by the VC and had to live in a secure area because of their association with us.

We were pretty openly distrustful of most of the South Vietnamese. They rarely warned us of the booby traps that surrounded their villages, and there were countless stories of supposed civilians who turned out to be VC—even South

Vietnamese soldiers who were actually VC. We often had local South Vietnamese come onto our firebase during the day, performing domestic chores like doing our laundry or cutting our hair. I heard many stories about bases where they killed some VC in an attack, only to find that one of the bodies was a barber who'd been coming aboard the base during the day. It always felt a little eerie to get a haircut and have one of these guys holding a razor against my throat. Barbering was one of the easier ways to enter an American base and learn of its defenses. It was a common belief that all the barbers in Vietnam were VC.

My distrust of the South Vietnamese extended to their troops. The predominant opinion of the ARVN's was that they were generally worthless and could even be downright cowardly. Actually, I saw South Vietnamese Marines and Rangers perform heroically on several occasions. Nor did I think there was anything lacking in the Vietnamese character—I had plenty of respect for the North Vietnamese Army and the Viet Cong. But there were many incidents in which South Vietnamese troops broke and ran.

One such incident occurred during that same firefight at Nam O in which the Rangers distinguished themselves. It involved the loosely organized, and minimally trained, South Vietnamese Popular Forces, or PFs. The PFs were local villagers trained by the Marines to act as a militia to protect their villages. They worked together with a few Marines in special units, called CAP units (Combined Action Platoon), and were the Marine Corps' best effort at winning the war for the hearts and minds of the people in Vietnam. The Marines in the CAP units lived in the villes with the villagers and were integrated into the local community—unlike the rest of us who were more like intrusive invaders who dropped out of the sky and destroyed their communities.

When we hiked out into the dry rice paddies and set up the ambush outside Nam O, a detachment from the local CAP unit set up some distance behind us. It consisted of a Marine sergeant and three of his men, along with a couple dozen PFs. I believe they were deployed behind and to the side of us as an additional blocking force to catch the VC that got around our line. I couldn't see them but I talked to the sergeant on the radio during the firefight. After we ambushed the first bunch, we got up and started assaulting across the fields. This left the sergeant and his people out there on their own. And, sure enough, a number of VC had found their way around us and were moving across the fields toward the position being held by the CAP unit.

The sergeant called me on the radio as we were moving across the field on line. First he notified me that a sizeable group of VC had gotten around us and was headed in his direction. I told Captain Chamberlain, and he said to keep him informed. Then, as we were getting into the heavier fighting with the VC near the ville, I got another call from the sergeant. I can no longer recall his call sign, so I can't completely reproduce the radio transmission, but it went like this.

"Echo Six, be advised that my Papa Foxtrots are breaking for lunch, over."

I was incredulous. I responded with confusion, "What do you mean—breaking for lunch? Over."

He said, "They all just got up and left. They said it was time for their lunch, and they had to go home. I couldn't stop them without shooting somebody, over."

I told the skipper, and he asked what the situation was with the VC force that the sergeant had reported a few minutes earlier.

I asked, "What is your current situation? Do you still have

enemy in sight, over?"

When he responded, I could hear firing over the radio. He said, "We are engaging the VC right now. My men and I are holding the line."

That was his last transmission. I passed along what the sergeant said to the skipper, but there was nothing we could do about the situation. We had our hands full, and the sergeant and his squad were two clicks away.

When the PFs saw the VC coming across the fields toward them, they declared it was lunchtime, and they literally said that they had to go home to eat. I guess they weren't into well-developed excuses like we Americans are able to concoct. The CAP sergeant tried to stop them from running but was unable to do so. So he and his three Marines tried to hold the line without the PF's. The four of them were killed, and a unit from our firebase retrieved their bodies later that afternoon.

It was incidents like this one that gave the South Vietnamese their poor reputation. But, in fact, the Rangers fought well that same day. The PF's were just a pretty sorry lot, and no one ever really expected them to behave like crack troops in the field. Their job was primarily to defend their village compounds. Still, we were all hurt and angry about the deaths of that sergeant and his men, and so we tended to blame the South Vietnamese. But if you had a chance to get to know a kid like Huey, then it wasn't so easy to write off the South Vietnamese. Huey had as much grit as anyone I've ever known. I only met that sergeant a couple of times—I don't even remember his name—but I know he knew a lot of kids like Huey, and he chose to learn their language and live amongst them.

    I often wonder what happened to Huey when the North Vietnamese took over. It would not have gone well for him if they caught him. I sure hope he escaped.

Chapter 116

Shadows

The battle for Okinawa produced the most casualties of any of the islands in the Pacific campaign. It took three months to secure the island. Once more, the Japanese used the tactics they employed on Peleliu and Iwo Jima—they dug in and forced the American forces to come and get them. This was the longest period of daily combat that my father encountered in the war.

We took thirty thousand casualties on Okinawa. Eventually, my father was one of them.

Chapter 117

Getting Short

During the middle of my tour, I felt I would be in Vietnam forever—I couldn't even imagine the end of my thirteen month tour. All I could do was focus on getting through the immediate moment, literally watching my next step. I think this helped me to survive, because it is when your head is too full of thoughts that you fail to pay sufficient attention to where your feet are. Either you're looking too hard for an ambush and you step on the booby trap, or you're looking too hard for booby traps and you walk into the ambush. When you're in the zone of feeling that you're there forever, you quit thinking about anything but what's right in front of you. Then you're able to look everywhere at once and nowhere in particular. Your mind is not on what you might find—that's thinking about the future—you just take in what is there.

As I started to get short (short-timers have a short amount of time left in country), and began to think I might make it if I could just hold out for x number of days, then I began to get very anxious. I began to think about the future.

That's when people make mistakes.

Some guys got superstitious toward the end of their tours. They would take all kinds of precautions, avoid dangerous activities, et cetera. And yet, it didn't seem to make any difference. It seemed like a lot of people got killed when they were short. Obviously, I didn't get killed, but I sure felt the stress. In my final weeks, I developed several migraine headaches, something I had never had before, and I have never had since. And I was very watchful.

For some reason, there were several deadly incidents in those final weeks. These were the kind of incidents that seemed to shout out that who lived and who died was completely arbitrary. Two of these incidents involved landmines, and the third involved friendly fire.

Before Tet, we made a couple of forays from Hill 190—going up the river into the 'unoccupied' mountainous, jungle area west of us. After Tet, we were busy with the occupied valley of villages and farmland around our base. The enemy became more aggressive around our base, hitting our lines at night and attacking our patrols and vehicle traffic. One of the things the VC did during that period was to plant some big mines. Several were estimated to be in a range equivalent to a hundred pounds of TNT or more. There were two nasty incidents involving these huge mines.

    The first incident occurred when we had a detachment of amtracs bivouacked near our base. Amtracs are big, heavy tracked vehicles—like tanks but made to carry people instead of cannons. The amtrac detachment set up just east of Hill 190, where the flatland meets the base of the hill. The amtracs used the river a lot and simply driving back and forth between the base and the river had created a muddy corridor about an eighth of a mile long. This provided the VC with the opportunity to plant one of their big mines. They could plant it in the mud where it would have excellent camouflage, and they had an appropriately large target—an amtrac.

    One of the amtracs drove over it. When the mine detonated, the force of the explosion caused the vehicle to stand up on one end, which is an indication of how big the mine had to have been. I don't know the overall weight of an amtrac, but I heard the front ramp alone weighs two tons.

I heard the explosion in the radio shack; a moment later I got the call on the radio. Captain Chamberlain came into the radio shack right after I got the call.

He asked, "What was that explosion I just heard."

"Sir, I just got the call. One of the tracks hit a mine."

"How many casualties?"

"Sir, I don't know yet. All they said was that it was a really big mine cause it stood the track up on end. They're checking on the casualties right now."

"All right, Cathy, go get Doc Redondo and any other corpsmen in his tent. I want you to get down there and help them with the casualties. Keep me informed. Take what you need to run a medevac; there's going to be casualties."

"Aye, aye, sir."

I grabbed my rifle, radio and some yellow smoke grenades and boogied. We arrived just minutes after the explosion, and the place was in chaos. The amtrac had been right in the middle of the muddy path to the river. The commander of Second Platoon and the commander of the amtracs were busily trying to take care of the casualties. The lieutenant told me that they were still trying to determine exactly how many people were on the vehicle, but they knew that the driver was blown out of his porthole and another crew member on the other side was also blown out.

Everyone went into the mud.

I reported to the Captain over the radio. "Be advised we have at least 7 casualties, all Whiskey India Alphas, over."

"Roger, is that everyone, over?"

I replied, "That is still uncertain. All the casualties went into the mud and some of them were buried. Echo Two is getting an exact count, over."

"Roger, keep me advised. Six out."

We started retrieving bodies and putting them in one place for the medevac chopper. The survivors were so covered in mud that you couldn't tell how badly they were injured. Finally, the platoon commander said, "Okay, we got an exact count, and we still have two people missing. They've gotta be somewhere under that mud." Then he yelled for everyone to form up in a line at the rear of the amtrac. He made us all stand close to each other.

He said, "Okay, people, we've still got two men somewhere under that mud. We'll never find them just running around haphazardly. I want you all to stay on line, take short steps, and pay attention to what you're feeling with your feet. We're going to sweep all the way around the amtrac, then we'll make another circuit further out. Let's go, and stay on line."

I lined up in the mud with everyone else and started slogging through it, trying to notice any bodies. At the same time, I informed Six Actual what we were doing. We all knew that we had to find these guys quick or they would suffocate, if indeed they were still alive. We found the first guy quickly this way, but there was no sign of the second guy.

We made two circuits of the amtrac and still hadn't found him. The lieutenant broke us into smaller lines, and I joined a group that was making a second run through the mud right up next to the vehicle. We stomped around in that mud for at least five minutes before someone discovered the second guy's body. I helped pull him out of the mud. He was actually up close to the front of the track and several people had walked right over him before he was discovered. He was buried that deep.

Amazingly, he was alive!

Ever since the beginning of Tet, we had difficulty getting medevac choppers. This time, we had a bunch of casualties. I radioed back to the radio shack and asked Mike Bolton to contact battalion and get us a medevac, but battalion was unable to come up with anything. We were all terribly frustrated; there is nothing worse than having badly wounded people and not being able to say anything to them but "We're trying to find a medevac."

Finally, I saw a Huey flying by a few miles away; I switched my radio to a channel that often gave me access to the chopper pilots, and I made a general call.

"Chopper in the sky, chopper in the sky, this is Castilian Echo Six. Do you read me? Over."

The chopper pilot answered my call, and I told him our situation. He said he would be glad to help us out. I didn't give him coordinates or anything because he was in my sight. I just told him to head due West; our base was unmistakable.

We never used a Huey for a medevac; Huey gunships always served as fire support while the CH-34's did the medevacs. But these were not normal times. He flew over to our hill and came towards the yellow smoke that I tossed a short distance from the mudhole. I directed him in to land and looked at how little room he had. We had so many casualties that he couldn't carry them all. I reported this to the captain, then he talked to the lieutenant from Second Platoon. Finally, he talked to the pilot of the Huey. They decided to use the helicopter to move the less serious casualties to a nearby roadway where we would pick them up with one of our trucks (a six-by). The Huey would take the worst casualties on to the hospital in Danang.

    I was running around talking to the people on the ground, especially the corpsmen, the people on the hill (who were in communication with battalion headquarters) and the chopper pilot. They worked out this idea of ferrying guys over to the roadway because we couldn't get any vehicles down to the casualties, and we wanted to avoid carrying the more serious casualties. After studying his map, the chopper pilot announced that he hadn't gotten a good enough look at how the area was laid out, and now his chopper was too loaded to get high enough for a look. He decided he needed someone to ride in the chopper to show him where to go.

I was in some kind of three way conversation with the lieutenant on the scene, Captain Chamberlain back on the hill, and the chopper pilot. Suddenly, I was informed that I was going to ride with the chopper pilot to help guide him to where our trucks would meet him on the road.

That's how I got to take my only ride ever in a Huey, squatting between, and slightly behind, the pilots' shoulders while I pointed out directions to them. This was not your usual Huey flight, however, as the aircraft was really loaded down. In order to get into the air, the pilot had to tilt the rotor toward the ground in front of us and have a long running start. We zoomed along with the rotor just inches from the ground, and it seemed we stayed that low for an awfully long time. Finally, we were approaching a fence, and we still weren't high enough to clear it. I nervously gripped the pilots' seatbacks and watched as they waited until the last moment to lift the chopper up over the fence.

It was a harrowing ride; we never got very high off the ground. Plus, I was never very comfortable in helicopters after crashing into that firefight on Union II—not to mention the experience with the hotshot who crashed his chopper on us when we were getting resupplied in the mountains.

I believe Captain Chamberlain put the pilot in for a decoration.

The other incident with a big mine occurred a few weeks later, shortly before I rotated home. One of our jeeps hit the mine on its way from battalion headquarters. The jeep was within sight of our hill, and we all heard the explosion. The jeep was carrying two guys, one of whom was a short-timer returning from R&R. When people talked about the irony of that, they spoke in reverent voices, like they were in church. It was hard not to view it as fate and the curse of being short. No wonder I got anxious as my rotation date approached.

As usual, I went out to help deal with the casualties and run the medevac. But there were no living casualties to take care of. In fact, there were practically no bodies. They were blown to smithereens. We found two feet, still in their boots, in the remains of the jeep, and we looked a hundred yards around the jeep but found nothing that looked even remotely like a human being. Finally, someone found a piece of meat that looked like a big

Sunday roast. That's what got sent home.

That's why some caskets are best left unopened.

Around the same time, battalion sent us a jeep with a Zeon searchlight mounted on it, which we were told to place at the top of the hill. The Zeon searchlight was incredibly bright; it was so powerful we were warned not to get in front of it or we could be burned. It was turned on periodically to sweep the area around our base. Our whole approach at night was to try to be as invisible as the VC, so marking the top of our hill with a gigantic searchlight always seemed bizarre to me.

Perhaps others felt similarly, as the searchlight team only stayed a couple of weeks. During that time, we had a sniper team staying with us. They were equipped with the standard sniper rifle, a Remington 720 with a scope on it. One night, they stationed themselves on top of the hill near the searchlight. This was after the siege, but we were still getting some probes of our perimeter at night, so there probably were VC out there who had to hide when the searchlight came their way. On this particular night, one of the bunkers called me and reported activity outside the wire. A few minutes later, there was some activity reported by the next bunker up the line. It appeared that something was going on, and so the skipper sent a detail outside the wire to investigate.

A few minutes later, I got a call from the sniper team on top of the hill. They reported that they'd spotted a VC with their scope, and they had fired one shot and hit him. I reported this to the skipper.

His response was immediate, "Who the hell told those guys to be taking shots off the top of this hill at night?" Then he asked, "Do they know we have a patrol outside the wire?"

I called the sniper team and asked if they were aware that we had people outside the wire. They assured me that they could see our patrol, and the VC they shot was nowhere near it.

Then the patrol called me on the radio and requested a medevac, because one of their Marines had been shot in the neck. There was no firing other than the single shot fired by the snipers.

Obviously, the snipers had shot one of our guys. They swore that they'd shot a VC, but we knew what happened. Friendly fire casualties are the toughest to accept; you feel so strongly that it didn't have to happen.

The sniper team returned to battalion headquarters soon after this unfortunate event.

I don't know what happened to the guy they shot. I only know he was still alive when we put him on the chopper.

Chapter 118

Shadows

On Okinawa, the Japanese were dug in on the Southern end of the island, and the fighting intensified as the American forces zeroed in on this area. The worst fighting occurred along a series of ridges where the main forces of the Japanese were dug in much like in the Umurbrogol Cliffs on Peleliu. The name of the area on Okinawa was Shuri Castle. Much of the fighting for these ridges was back and forth, as the American forces took ground and then had to retreat from it.

During an attempt to capture one of those ridges, my father was shot. The bullet passed near his spine and paralyzed him. At the same time, the Marines were being beaten back once more, and they were forced to retreat in such a hurry that my father's comrades were unable to evacuate him. So they stacked enemy bodies around and on top of him and left him lying on the battlefield. He lay there in a pile of dead bodies all night long—

slipping in and out of consciousness. He didn't know if the enemy would find him, if his comrades would be able to rescue him, if he was going to survive or if he would ever regain the use of his body if he did survive.

It was surely the longest night of his life.

The next day, a tank drove out onto the battlefield. It drove right over the pile of bodies and the tankers pulled my father inside through a trapdoor in the bottom of the tank. He was evacuated to the Hospital Ship Hope and, within three days, began to recover from his paralysis.

The war was finally over for him.

Chapter 119

Twelve and a Wakeup

On March 10, 1968, I was twelve days from the completion of my tour. I was a full-fledged short-timer, "so short I could walk under a door". Mid-morning on the 10th, I got a call from Battalion Headquarters. If I could make it there within the hour, I would be on a plane home that afternoon. I raced around and got my stuff together, most of which was virtually packed all the time. I gave away the extra weapons I had somehow accumulated and had precious little time to make my goodbyes, only getting to say goodbye to a few folks. I rode to battalion and turned in my official weapons there. Next thing I knew, I was on a plane to Okinawa.

It was a strange experience at Okinawa. We had to go to a warehouse and retrieve the seabag of dress uniforms that we'd stashed there on our way to Vietnam thirteen months earlier. They were stacked up in the same warehouse where we left them, and a lot of those seabags were not being retrieved. They had a couple of corporals moving along the stack of seabags and reading the names off (which we'd placed on them with adhesive tape the year before). I retrieved my bag and heard them call out the name Bellon. I turned around and looked and, sure enough, there was Biff Bellon, one of my buddies from boot camp and machine gun school.

Biff and I had flown over together from the states, and now we were flying home together. In fact, it turned out that we had been on the same plane from Danang to Okinawa, but just hadn't seen each other. It was great to run into Biff! We went out drinking together that night, and we sat next to each other on the flight to the States. That made the trip home much better. Biff and I exchanged notes on what we knew about some of the other guys we had known in our training. Biff was on the hospital ship with Spiller, the honorman from our platoon in boot camp, when Spiller died. Biff was lucky to make it home himself. At Khe Sanh, he was manning a machine gun bunker that was overrun. Biff got trapped under a section of collapsed sandbags when the NVA threw grenades into the bunker. The NVA then took over the bunker and manned it with their own machine gunners for several hours while Biff remained hidden in the back of the bunker. Biff was sandblasted but otherwise unhurt.

I don't think many guys survived that don't have some amazing stories, usually involving a lot of luck.

While we were in Okinawa, they made us turn in the weapons that people were taking home as war trophies. They ended up with a pile of AK47's, SKS submachine guns, Chicom grenades and the like. I contributed a couple of potato masher type Chicoms that I had picked up somewhere. They told us that we would be searched thoroughly by U.S. Customs and put in the brig if we were caught bringing anything in. So everyone unloaded their trophies. Well, guess what happened when we got to the U.S.—they didn't open anyone's seabag. I could have brought back an arsenal of weapons.

I'm sure many guys did bring stuff home, especially those dudes at Okinawa that gave us the scare talk. After all, they had to do something with those big piles of weaponry.

We arrived at Travis Air Force Base in California about

seventy-two hours after I left Hill 190. Biff and I joined with some other guys to share a cab from Travis to San Francisco International, where I could catch a plane to Dallas. I called my parents from the civilian airport and surprised them with the news that I was home and would be arriving on such and such a flight.

Something happened on that cab ride that left me with an image that captures my feeling about returning to the states. We drove past a man wearing bermuda shorts who was pushing a lawnmower in his front yard. He looked totally ordinary, yet the whole scene seemed surreal to me, and I found myself feeling intensely angry at this man, though I knew it was irrational. Our young men were dying in droves on the other side of the planet, and this man seemed to be unaware, unconcerned, and untouched by it all. I could not reconcile the image of this man blithely living his ordinary life with the images of death and pain that filled my head. How could anyone approach life in an ordinary way when such things were happening?

I didn't know it at the time, but it would be many years before I would feel anything approaching ordinary myself.

For all the furor that went on during the sixties over the Vietnam war, I never got the feeling that the reality of what was happening in that war really touched the vast majority of Americans, despite their avowed political concerns.

Chapter 120

Shadows

The official name of the operation to take Peleliu was Stalemate, which was an especially fitting name, because it also reflected the dynamic between key members of the American high command. General Douglas MacArthur insisted that the invasion of Peleliu was essential to his strategy for retaking the Phillipines. Admiral Chester Nimitz disagreed. Nimitz wanted to bypass Peleliu and just starve them out, but MacArther took a strong stand with President Roosevelt and got his way. The consensus of historians is that Nimitz was right: The capture of Peleliu contributed nothing to the campaign to liberate the Phillipines.

It could have been bypassed.

Colonel Chesty Puller's First Marines spent six days making costly, frontal assaults of Bloody Nose Ridge without ever fully securing it. He was finally ordered to withdraw, but the fighting in the Umurbrogol Cliffs continued for ten weeks. The

Marines did not secure the area until the airfield was operational and Marine Corsairs arrived. The planes fired rockets and dropped napalm into the caves day after day until they finally obliterated the Japanese emplacements.

Chesty Puller is possibly the most famous of all Marines. He was a mustang—meaning he started out as an enlisted man—and he was highly respected by his men. He won five Navy Crosses and was an indomitable opponent who never considered backing down in a fight. But Puller lost 60 percent of his troops at Peleliu, the highest losses by a regiment in the history of the Marine Corps, and he was criticized for refusing to accept reinforcements when they were offered.

K Company suffered the highest losses in the regiment, and Captain George Hunt received the Navy Cross for his defense of the Point. K Company lost two thirds of their personnel in the process of taking and holding the Point. After the war was over, the Marine Corps built an exact duplicate of the Point on the grounds of the Officer Candidate School at Quantico, Virginia. It was used to teach future Marine commanders how to assault a heavily armed defensive position.

My father recovered from the paralysis of his wound on Okinawa. He rejoined the First Marines and participated in the American Expeditionary Forces that temporarily occupied China after the Japanese were required to withdraw. He was discharged from the Marine Corps and arrived back home in Dallas in February of 1946. I was born in December of that year.

Part III

Casting My Own Shadow of War

Chapter 121

How Much is a Generation?

It was another manhood ritual. I'd been home about a week when my dad invited me out for a beer on a weekday afternoon. We went to a nearby bar, and my dad ordered a pitcher of beer. I didn't even know beer was sold in pitchers.

My dad opened up the discussion. "So how does it feel? Being back in your own bed with clean sheets and a hot shower."

I grinned at that thought. "It feels great, especially taking a shower every day. What a luxury, just standing in the hot water. And I get to do it every day, I don't even have time to get dirty. Our only shower was a fifty gallon drum full of cold water, when we had access to it at all. I went months without a shower at times."

He nodded, "Yeah, it was the same in the islands." Then he raised his glass, "Well, here's to your return. Semper Fi, Marine."

I smiled, took a drink of beer and volunteered, "Actually, it feels a little weird. I haven't really settled in yet, I guess."

He nodded, "It takes a while."

"I mean, what feels weird is being around the people back here. I just feel kind of strange around people, around the whole world here—people driving around in their cars and everything so normal. It just doesn't feel right."

"Well, that's not surprising. This is a whole different world from the way you've been living."

"Daddy, I feel like, I don't know, like I'm in an unreal world. Do you know what happened at that basement brunch at the church on Saturday?"

He shook his head.

"An old lady asked me if I killed anyone in Vietnam. And I mean a really old lady, one of those shrunk-up little, blue-haired ones. I didn't know what to say to her. I couldn't believe she was asking me such a thing."

He nodded, "That's something you're going to encounter for the rest of your life, Son. People will look at you differently because you've been in combat. Some people will wonder if you've killed people and whether you're safe to be around. And some men are going to envy you because they still don't know how they would have handled it."

I frowned and said, "I do feel different from other people, but not because I was in combat. It's just that everything is so normal here, like nothing's ever changed. I'm used to a world where everyone is…" I searched for the right words, "like everyone is in it together, like we're all doing what we're doing for a reason." I wasn't doing a very good job of conveying what I wanted to say.

My dad added, "and you know how to take care of yourselves and how to survive in the worst possible conditions. You're different from most of these people."

I said, "Yeah, but I feel like I'm the normal one, and the people back here are the ones that are abnormal. I mean, how can people just go about their lives like nothing's going on? It just seems like it's not right, like people should be…," I struggled with my words, "like people should be concerned about what's happening on the other side of the world. It seems like most people back here aren't even aware of it."

My dad poured us both more beer and sounded

philosophical, "You're going to find that most people don't care too much about what's going on over there and what you've been through. Everyone's involved in their own little lives. The ones that have never been in combat, never slept in the mud and lived with the mosquitoes and the cold food, they'll never understand."

I felt frustrated at my inability to express myself. My dad was talking about people back here not understanding, but I felt like my dad was not quite understanding. He went on, "For the rest of your life, you'll look back on what you went through in the war, and you'll always feel different. But that's not a bad thing, you'll know some things about what life is about that the average person can't even imagine."

I nodded, "I guess that's true. But right now, all I know is how much it hurt. All the people dying over there…" My eyes began to mist up, "My friends, Daddy, my friends that were killed—"

"I know, I know, Son. You've got pain that civilians will never understand. For the rest of your life, that difference is going to be there. You're one of a special breed now." He raised his glass as though making a toast, "Welcome to the club, Son. It's a hell of a club to get into, and I wouldn't wish it on anyone, but you're in it now. And no one gets into this club without earning it."

This was not what I wanted to hear. I wasn't interested in how being a combat vet made me different, and I didn't want to be in any special clubs. I had finally earned my dad's respect, and he was treating me more like an equal, but I still felt a great gulf between us. I was trying to understand something very difficult. I couldn't put it into words at the time, and he didn't recognize what it was that I was struggling with.

It was war itself that I could not come to terms with. I couldn't understand how humanity had allowed something this awful—the time honored tradition of war—to persist into modern times. I could no longer see anything noble about war, yet my dad seemed to be looking back at his combat experience with a feeling of nostalgia for the glory that was past. I felt no glory, only pain, and I wanted to know what I was supposed to do with all the pain.

Maybe my dad was answering that—as best he knew how.

Being home and out of the war was great at first, and then not so great. I found it was harder to leave the war behind than I'd expected. I remained in the shadow of the war longer than it seemed I should. My dad didn't warn me about this, and it was not immediately apparent to me but, in fact, that shadow grew larger. Instead of becoming increasingly accustomed to being back in the world, I became increasingly aware of how I didn't fit in this world.

I was looking for something from my dad that day. He understood the rotten conditions in which I'd been living, and he understood the changes I'd gone through. But the thing I most needed to talk about—I'm not sure how much I was aware of this at the time—was the pain. I wanted to share that pain, the pain of Bill's death and Lieutenant Johnson's death, the pain of watching so many people die, the pain of watching men be confronted with injuries that would change their lives forever, the pain of watching myself become insensitive to human suffering when it occurred in a different skin. I wanted to talk with someone who understood all this and could tell me how to live with it. I wanted to know that I was not alone with this pain inside. I wanted to feel that my dad understood, but he was unable to give me that understanding.

My dad lived with pain that exceeded my own, but it was

sealed away and unavailable to him, which is too bad. Remaining in touch with our pain helps keep us from distorting our memories. It is critical that warriors never forget the pain of war—else they may too easily consider war a viable option. There is no one in all the world who better understands how hard we should work to avoid war than the veteran.

Chapter 122

A Different World

Coming home from war will always be a disconcerting experience. The psychological change from living in constant danger to living in relative safety does not occur overnight. In my case, my homecoming was disconcerting for another reason. The world I returned to did not even resemble the world I had left. That is undoubtedly the experience of everyone who has ever gone to war; however, that's usually more because of changes in the warrior. In my case—and in the case of the other men and women who were in Vietnam in the late sixties—the world changed quite abruptly as well.

I graduated from high school in 1964, just months after President Kennedy's assassination. I went to college at Texas A&M, an all-male, military college that not only had no girls, but no long haired boys, no drugs, and no anti-war rhetoric. When I left A&M at the end of the summer of 1966, I left a world that is more often referred to as the fifties these days.

When I came home from Vietnam in 1968, the culture of the United States had undergone one of the most radical changes imaginable. At the airport, my parents proudly showed me a bumper sticker on their car—it was a peace symbol with the words, "footprint of the American chicken". The antiwar movement had become a significant factor in American politics, and the peace symbol represented the antiwar attitude. My parents' bumper sticker was declaring those against the war to be acting cowardly. But all of this was new to me, and they had to explain what it meant. I didn't even know what a peace symbol was.

In Vietnam, we referred to the good old USA as 'the world'. We just couldn't wait until we got back in the world. We talked about the world as though it was the same place for all of us, the place that was normal, where everyone was friendly and supported each other, where we knew who we were and what we were doing there. The world was the place and the people we were fighting for, so it was quite a shock when I came home and discovered that I fit in better with my fellow Marines in Vietnam than I did with the people back in the world. I found more friendship and support in the Marines than among these strangers in America.

I was living in the shadow of war, and I struggled to find myself in the darkness. I knew exactly who I was and what I was doing in Vietnam, but I didn't have a clue who I was or what I was doing back in the world.

Throughout my tour, I felt connected to the Marines I was with. Several times, my comrades changed and each time I made new connections and re-achieved that sense of family. I do not know if I would have had the strength to face what I faced without those connections. But when I went off to have another try at college in January of 1969, I had no sense of family with the people around me.

I registered for school at North Texas State University. They had a separate line for veterans who were using their GI Bill funding to pay for school. At the end of the line, I came to a table staffed by two short, muscular guys with Marine haircuts. Their sign said Ex-Marine Association. What was this?

One of them said, "You an ex-Marine?"

"Yeah, I was separated in September."

"Nam vet?"

"Yep."

The other one asked, "Who were you with in Nam?"

"Seventh Marines. Echo Company"

"No shit. We got a guy who was with Seventh Marines." He told me he was with some transportation outfit out of Chu Lai.

I nodded. "So what is this…," I pointed at their sign, "association?"

The first one grinned. "We Marines are still hanging together. We got about twenty guys here on campus."

I nodded again. "What do you do?"

"Well, we help guys deal with the system. Like getting your veteran's benefits or dealing with problems here in registration."

That sounded helpful, but I didn't see why they needed an association. "Sounds like you must do more than that."

The first guy spoke up. "Oh, we do a lot more than that. I guess you could say some of it's sort of like a fraternity. We get together and have meetings, and then we might tap a keg or go out to eat together or something. We see to it that no ex-Marine shows up on campus without he's got some people to answer questions if he needs it. Sometimes we make political statements. There's a group of anti-war people here on campus. Sometimes we debate them. We like to have a couple guys in the audience whenever they give speeches so there's someone there to offer another point of view."

I didn't know quite what to think about it all, but I was turned off by the military haircuts. More than that, there was something about these guys recruiting members that I didn't like. Also, he shouldn't have compared it to a fraternity—I didn't care for fraternities. At Texas A&M, fraternities were viewed with great disdain. What it all added up to was I didn't really want to be in these guys' club.

I stalled a bit, "So you got like dues and stuff?"

The first guy shrugged. "Yeah, just twenty bucks a year. It's not about the money."

I nodded again. "Yeah, well, thanks. I guess I'm not too interested. Maybe later."

The first guy gave me a look like he knew for sure I was

never coming back. "Yeah, whatever, man."

I was tempted; it seemed like a ready-made set of connections. But when I first arrived at North Texas, I didn't know how unconnected I was going to feel there. I was still riding on the connection with my family in Dallas. These guys representing the association did offer connection, but it looked like they were still trying to be Marines. I would have stayed in the Marine Corps if I wanted that.

When I had to choose an area of study, I picked government. I'd never had the slightest interest in the subject before, but I'd never seen people die for governments before either, and I wanted to make some kind of greater sense of what I'd seen in the war. So I started taking classes in government. We were assigned a lot of reading, which was hard—I found it extremely difficult to concentrate enough to do the reading. Indeed, my life was not conducive to being a serious student. I lived in a tiny place off the beaten path—a little one-room bungalow outside the edge of town that was sparsely furnished to say the least. All I had in the way of possessions were my clothes and my shotgun—no TV or stereo. I had a telephone, but it never rang. The place was dark and quiet and reminded me of my radio shack in Nam.

During that first semester, no human being other than myself entered my little hooch.

I had trouble reading and studying, but I was still interested in what was being said in my classes—at least some of them. In fact, I was astounded at some of the things being said. The class that most interested me was one of the government classes. There was one student in the class who had extremely long hair and was forever challenging the teacher. Surprisingly, I found his comments to be very interesting. One day, the news was about some anti-war people destroying government property. The teacher talked about the incident, and then he and the long-haired student got into it over the right to protest.

The student said, "Jefferson said that freedom must be won anew by each generation. That doesn't mean only fighting other countries. I think he was talking about the forces within our own country that would erode our rights."

The teacher said, "Perhaps, but Jefferson also established a constitution that allows for how we conduct our internal struggles. Expressing your differences is your Fourth Amendment right, but attacking government facilities is not a right."

"What if the government is doing something wrong?"

"Then you talk to your representatives in Congress, and let them do something about the wrongs."

"But what if that's not working?"

"Democracy is sometimes slow, but it eventually gets the job done."

"But those representatives are the government. They may be profiting from the way things are; they may not have any reason to want to change things."

"Still, they are your legitimate avenue to change. Violence only leads to a breakdown in order."

"Yeah? What about the Boston Tea Party?"

The teacher hesitated, "Well...that led to reprisals from the British government."

"So they shouldn't have done it?"

Now the teacher was looking irritated. He said, "I'm not saying that. The Boston Tea Party was part of a revolution over a lack of representation in the government that was making decisions about people's lives."

The student replied, "Isn't that what we're talking about here?"

The teacher frowned and said, "We already have a democratic government. If we want to keep it, we have to abide by the rules that make it work."

"But what if it's not working? What if it's evolved into something that isn't really a democratic government?"

And on it went. Over the course of that semester, that one student challenged the teacher a number of times. I could tell it was bugging the teacher. He just wanted to teach and not have to defend the government. I never got to know the outspoken, long-haired student, or any of the other students in the class, and I certainly didn't agree with many of the things he said, but I found his comments thought-provoking. He made the class more interesting than the teacher did.

Some of the students had incredibly naive ideas. When we talked about the civil rights movement, more than one student seemed to seriously believe that all the people who were successful in our society were simply smarter and/or worked harder than the people at the bottom. Their capacity to deny the influence of social forces—much less just plain luck—was phenomenal. It was as though I were to claim my survival in Vietnam was due to my being a superior warrior—and all the guys that died were just not as skillful. That is not only ridiculous; it is insulting to all the people in the world who are less fortunate for a variety of reasons.

I myself only spoke up one time in that class that I recall. I remember it clearly because I felt like an idiot afterward, even though what I said was fundamentally correct. The class discussion had gotten into the struggle between democracy and communism, and the teacher said something about the Viet Cong being Communists.

I raised my hand.

"Actually, sir, most of them aren't really Communists. They may accept the Communist label, but that doesn't really mean anything to them."

He gave me a patronizing smile and asked, "And how do you know what the Viet Cong really care about?"

I think I began to flush at about this point in the interaction. I stammered, "Well, uh, I don't know. I just, well…I just know that most of the peasants in Vietnam don't want anyone there—not the Communists or the Americans—and I think they regard both sides as barbarians. Most of the so-called Communists don't really care about Communism; they're just fighting another colonial invader. The true Communists simply capitalized on the opportunity by making the war seem to be about their ideology."

He said something about that being how a new ideology takes hold in a population. Then I made the mistake of trying to give an example of what I was talking about.

I said, "When my battalion wanted to establish a location for an artillery battery and base for their headquarters near Chu Lai, they decided on a piece of land that was owned by a local farmer. They gave him some money and told him that he didn't own his land any more. A few months later, they found the farmer on the wire one morning."

The teacher said, "On the wire?"

I looked around. Everyone in the room was looking at me. I hesitated for a moment and then said, "His body was on the wire, the concertina wire," I gestured the loopy form of concertina wire with my hands, "the barbed wire that encircled the perimeter of the base."

The teacher just kept looking at me, along with everyone else in the room.

I explained, "I mean he was killed one night trying to attack their lines. I don't think he was VC before that. At least, I heard he probably wasn't VC." I paused, wishing I hadn't gotten into this subject, but it seemed too late to stop. "What I mean is we made him join the VC by coming into his home and taking his land." Again, I paused. Why didn't anyone have anything to say?

I added, "To him, it wasn't about ideologies; he wasn't a Communist. He was just fighting for his home, and we were the invaders."

All the teacher said was, "I see", and then he resumed his lecture. I felt like a total fool, and I felt everyone's eyes on me after that. I had never said anything in the class before, certainly nothing that identified myself as a veteran. Now here I was talking about bodies on the wire. I could imagine the other students' thoughts. Who was this weird guy who talked about killing in such a heartless fashion? I felt like they regarded me as not belonging there, and I was acutely uncomfortable. I didn't feel accepted by either the anti-war folks or the pro-war folks, who seemed to equate patriotism with supporting whatever the government did.

Meanwhile, there were talks and rallies being given by the radical anti-war people on campus. I usually stood on the periphery of the crowd and listened to the speakers, but I never listened very long. I felt embarrassed to be listening at all. After a short while, I would go home to my depressing little hooch. I never went to the movies, or out to bars, or practically anywhere. I didn't drink, other than an occasional beer, and I didn't smoke pot or use drugs. The only entertainment I had was to study my school books, and they didn't capture my attention.

At night, I dreamed. Most nights, it was the same dream.

I was in the hot LZ on Union II, and I was separated from my squad. I was on my knees, trying to peer through the smoke surrounding me, desperate to find my squad, and then I would see figures walking toward me. It was hard to make them out in the smoke, but they were carrying rifles and wearing helmets and looked like Marines. I had my rifle in my hands, but I didn't point it at the men coming toward me. As they got closer, however, I began to see more detail and, at some point, saw them clearly enough to realize that they were wearing pith helmets. They were not Marines, they were NVA soldiers! At that point in the dream, I would try to raise my rifle to fire at them, but I was always excruciatingly slow, and as I slowly raised my weapon, they would all fire at me.

Sometimes I would wake when they started firing at me. Other times, I would look down at my chest and see it pierced with holes oozing blood. Then I would fall backwards, knowing I was dead, until I woke up highly aroused with my heart pounding and my sheets usually wet. Sometimes, I was confused, and I would inspect my little hooch in the darkness, trying to get a stronger grasp of where I was. Of course, it was always very difficult to go back to sleep after waking from that dream.

I dreamed the dream over and over with little variation. Sometimes I had a .45 pistol instead of my M16. Sometimes the period of looking for my squadmates went on for a long time. And sometimes it seemed to take forever to decide that the shadowy figures were not Marines. But it was basically the same dream, and I dreamed it more than a hundred times. I had dreamed it a few times when I spent those months in Dallas with my folks, but I dreamed it repeatedly in that little isolated hooch outside Denton.

Chapter 123

The Way Home

That winter and spring in Denton was a very depressing time. The anti-war people wanted to bring all the guys home, and so did I. Perhaps then I wouldn't have to feel bad about having left my comrades to fight the war without me. Over the course of several months, my political stance swung completely in the direction of being against the war and wanting it to stop. Even during those few months when I had lived with my parents before going back to school, I had wanted the war to end. I voted for Nixon in the fall of 1968 because he said he would halt the war and do it with honor. At that point, I didn't have strong feelings about the war being a mistake, I just wanted it to end. However, over time, I came to feel that we probably never should have gotten into the war in the first place. That was difficult to accept, since I'd seen so many people die in that war. Did this mean that their deaths were in vain?

I occasionally encountered guys from the Ex-Marine Association on campus, hanging out with other guys with a similar look. One afternoon, at one of the political rallies, some of those guys were loudly heckling the speakers.

I walked over to where they were standing and spoke to them. "Hey, why don't you guys give it a rest so we can hear what these people are trying to say."

One of them was the guy from the registration table; I thought of him as the club president. I could tell he knew me from that encounter. He nodded toward the speaker and said, "This guy isn't saying anything; he's just trying to incite people."

I said, "Seems to me yelling at him is going to do more to incite people than just letting him say his say." I hesitated, then added, "Besides, a lot of these people are against the war."

He gave me a look that reminded me of the way he looked at me when I told him I didn't want to join his club. "Yeah? How about you, you against the war?"

It was a fair question. "I don't really know anymore. I know I sure as hell want it to be over with. I guess that means I'm against it."

"What about all the guys that died over there. If we just walk away and hand it over to the North Vietnamese, what does that say to those guys?"

I nodded, "Yeah, I know, it kinda sounds like their lives were wasted. But more people dying isn't going to change that."

He said, "It's not just more people dying. It's winning the war and accomplishing what we set out to accomplish."

I nodded again. "Yeah, I understand that's the idea. I guess I'm just not sure what the hell we are accomplishing any more." I looked him in the eye, "Anyway, I think you ought to let these people have their say without heckling them. I'm fine with you getting up there and giving the other point of view. But just trying to shout them down doesn't seem like a very smart way to disagree—not with these college kids." I indicated the crowd. "you just seem to be confirming that you don't have a reasonable argument of your own."

He nodded but didn't say anything. I said, "See you." and headed home to my dreary little hooch. I knew I could have joined in with the Ex-Marines and it might have felt satisfying, but I was uneasy with their hard line view of the war and the whole idea of joining them kind of disturbed me. I guess I had that Groucho Marx syndrome: I didn't want to be a member of a club that would have me for a member.

It was a bit of a shock to realize that I felt more sympatico with those weird guys with the long hair than with these ex-Marines. Not that I was friends with anyone from either group. But I understood what the anti-war people were saying, and I found myself agreeing with them more and more. Of course, this only made me feel even more like a fish out of water, because I couldn't relate to the weird-looking, long-haired guys at all. They seemed as foreign to me as the peasants had seemed when I arrived in Vietnam.

I lived on the periphery of society—suffering from frequent nightmares and feeling disconnected from the people around me—throughout that spring and summer. By the end of the summer, I was still attending classes, but my heart wasn't in it. I needed money, and so I answered an ad looking for an adult male to supervise a boys' dormitory at a nearby boarding school. The Selwyn School was located on a large campus outside of town, with stables and a pasture for horses. The job included the use of an apartment adjacent to the dorm. I loved the countryside and horses, so I applied for the job. When they learned I was a recently discharged Marine sergeant, they thought they'd found just what they were looking for.

I worked and lived at the Selwyn School for the 69-70 academic year. The first thing I discovered was that these kids were very different from the kids I'd known in high school. They looked weird—the long hair, beads, peace signs, bell bottom trousers, sandals, fringe jackets, etc.—and they behaved differently—burning incense, listening to the music of the sixties and displaying black lights and psychedelic posters in their rooms. They also thought differently—they were more politically aware than anyone I'd known in high school.

The second thing I discovered was that they were not so different after all, just normal kids living in a new era. But, of course, it took me a while to make that second discovery.

One Friday night, early in September, I came in after I'd been out drinking, and the boys were still up. It was well past their bedtime, but they were all hanging out in the lounge area watching

TV.

I went in and said, "All right, you guys, it's time for bed. You're up past lights out. Let's go, everyone off to your rooms."

They all ignored me.

I decided my authority was being challenged, and I didn't want to lose a battle this early in my time with them. I just nodded, stepped back outside, and immediately went into my apartment, where I got my shotgun and chambered one round. Then I put it at port arms and marched back into the lounge.

I spoke in a firm voice. "I said it's time for bed. Now get your asses into your rooms before I get upset."

One young man, Pat Farrel, said, "That thing's not loaded."

I pumped out the shell that I just placed in the chamber and said, "I'm not going to tell you again."

The room emptied in seconds.

Obviously, I had no business threatening those high school kids with a shotgun and, yes, I had been drinking or I'm sure I wouldn't have done it. My last billet in the Marine Corps was as acting platoon sergeant in Guantanamo Bay, Cuba, and I had come to expect people to follow my orders. I never had any difficulty taking orders myself. In the world I came from, you don't question orders from an authority figure, you just do as you're told. Those kids didn't have the benefit of my military background. I figured they were more likely to follow my orders if they thought I might do something a little crazy if they refused. So I put the shell in the chamber just so I could jack it out and convince them I had a loaded gun. Of course, I still deserved to lose my job over that little stunt, and I was lucky that I didn't. In fact, none of the boys complained, and they were always cooperative after that night.

The next time they were gathered in the TV room, they invited me to watch TV with them, and I did. I found myself hanging out with them more and more. We were only a few years apart in age, and this new world of theirs fascinated me. The school often had all-campus events, and I participated in these and gradually got to know the teachers and the other kids in the school. When the kids went off-campus to events, such as concerts in Dallas, I drove the school bus and chaperoned them.

I became part of the community.

Though I didn't recognize it at the time, this was something I desperately needed—to overcome my isolation and find a community where I could belong. I had been living on the periphery of human society, and I was starving for people with whom I could feel some connection. At the university, I felt no involvement in the community of students, and I was turned off by the Ex-Marine Association.

But, somehow, I connected with those kids. They provided me with the first real sense of community I'd felt since leaving my unit in Vietnam. I was in other units in the Marines after Vietnam, but none had that intense feeling of community that we had in Nam.

When I started working at the school, I thought these strange looking, undisciplined adolescents were from another planet. But despite the superficial differences, I discovered they were just a bunch of regular kids—in many respects, no different from my fellow Marines, just younger and bearing some different ideas.

Most of these kids were against the war, but they didn't reject me for having fought in it. Indeed, they were interested in talking with me about it. I ended up spending many hours talking with them about all kinds of things, from religion to politics to what was wrong with our values as a society. They introduced me to music. I had listened to the radio for years, but I'd never really listened to good music played on good sound systems. And, of course, the music of the era was great.

These kids had a very different way of thinking about life. They rejected much of the materialism and competitiveness of their parents' generation; they were trying to live by better values than those that ruled the land. They were idealistic certainly, but it was refreshing. To me, it reflected the same core values as the idealism that drove the civil rights movement and even the idealism that led me to join the Marines. In the early sixties, I was influenced by the civil rights movement and Kennedy's emphasis on individual sacrifice. Fighting for my country was the natural thing to do, because my country stood for the highest possible values—freedom and equality for all! The philosophy and idealism of these young people was the same as that espoused by the long-haired young man in my government class. And I was discovering it was the same as that I had grown up on; I felt it was precisely what made America great.

When I think back to the way I felt about the man mowing

his yard the day I arrived back in the states, I now realize it was the same as I felt about the old lady working in her garden the morning after I first stacked dead Marines on Operation Union II. In both cases, I had no idea how these people actually felt, but because they seemed to be so engaged in ordinary activities, I attributed a lack of concern to them. I viewed them as apathetic. It was apathy that angered me the most! I never resented any of the people who took strong positions about the war, whether it was to promote the war or to burn their draft cards. It was the people who didn't seem to notice or care that most bothered me. This war was a terrible thing; the least anyone could do was to have an opinion about it.

The kids at Selwyn had strong opinions and talking to them helped me to clarify my own thinking. My future was still unclear, but what was becoming clear was that I had to do something meaningful with my life. I could not pursue a career just because it paid well. I had to find something that would feel like a contribution. Otherwise, I would feel like Bill Rees and Lieutenant Johnson and all the others died in vain. This helped me to define who I was and, eventually, it helped me to determine where I was going with my life.

I was only at the boarding school for nine months, but by the time I left I'd begun to feel a connection to the world around me. That brief sojourn proved to be a major turning point for me. I'd finally found some common ground with the people in this strange world, and that was what I needed more than anything. Without it, I would still be adrift without a rudder.

Chapter 124

A Warm Welcome

After the year at Selwyn School, I took a job in Dallas and commuted to school in Denton. Though I'd found the beginnings of a sense of connection within the small community of the school, that faded when I tried to live in Dallas, a big city with a lot of people in a big hurry pursuing big money.

I was not very much in sync with the culture of Dallas in 1970.

I was living in one of the huge Dallas apartment complexes, working at a job in which I drove around Texas delivering securities, and commuting 30 miles away to Denton where I was carrying 17 hours of college classes. It was a colossal setup for failure, but I didn't recognize that fact.

My dad and I were beginning to clash over the war. He was still convinced that our involvement in Vietnam was absolutely necessary. We got into some heated discussions, not quite arguments, and found too many areas of disagreement. I still didn't know exactly what I thought about the war, so our discussions were kind of confused, but I had become much more comfortable with the idea that it may have been a bad idea in the first place and that even Nixon's policy of pursuing peace with honor may have just prolonged the killing.

I was going through a profound change, and my dad was aware of it and didn't much like it.

I remained in touch with some of the kids from the boarding school, but I had returned to living an isolated life, though this time was different. Instead of living alone on the edge of society, I was living with three guys my own age, as I had answered their ad for a roommate. These were normal enough guys, but I couldn't connect with any of them.

So now I had that painful experience of feeling isolated in the midst of people. My life was going nowhere: I was performing poorly in school; I was working at a boring job; and I again felt disconnected from the people around me. So when one of the former Selwyn students, Dean Singleton, came to visit, I told him of the rut I was living in, and we talked ourselves into breaking out together—we decided to go to Europe.

Within five days, I quit my job, dropped out of school, and sold my car to have money for the plane ticket. I sold the car for a pittance of what it was worth (I had bought it with money saved during my tour in Vietnam), and actually, I didn't quite drop out of school. I arranged for someone to withdraw me and he didn't get around to it until it was too late—so I ended up adding another 17 hours of F's to my record. My parents were out of town while all this transpired. They returned in time to discover that I was leaving for Europe the next day.

Needless to say, my dad was really pissed.

"Don, this is one of the worst decisions you've ever made."

I tried to explain, "Daddy, I'm going crazy living here. I hate this job I've got; I'm not making any headway in school; and I don't even feel like hanging out with the guys I'm living with. I feel like a fish out of water. I haven't felt like the world made much sense since I left the Marine Corps."

He said, "You'd be a helluva lot better off if you were still in the Marine Corps."

I didn't disagree, but that wasn't for me anymore. I

shrugged, "I just need to do something really different. I need to break out of the rut I'm in."

My dad snorted in disgust. "Break out? It's just the opposite. You need to bear down and stay at something. You'll never get anywhere if you just up and run off every time things get hard."

I said, "I know it seems that way, Daddy, but I just feel I have to do something different. This may not be the best decision I've ever made, but I know I have to change my life. If I don't do something to change the way my life is going—"

"If you don't do something to change the way your life is going, you're never going to get anywhere. That's right, but the solution isn't quitting. You have to stay at something, Don! So you don't like your job. Fine. Look for a better one. But walking out on school, selling your car… What the hell are you going to have when you come back? You're just digging yourself deeper and deeper into a hole that you could spend the rest of your life stuck in."

I couldn't make him understand that I already felt stuck in that hole, that my apparent running away was just a drastic attempt to get out of that hole. I knew I needed to do something radically different, and taking off for Europe somehow sounded like a way to do it. In some respects, it was the same kind of act as joining the Marine Corps. Both times, I impulsively decided to do something that was never planned.

Dean and I got on a plane to Europe early in November of 1970. Dean returned after two months, but I stayed for six months, working day labor jobs and moving on when I could afford it. I had been gradually letting my hair grow longer; now I quit getting haircuts altogether. I also discarded my comb and quit trying to straighten my curly hair. I lived a relatively Spartan life in Europe, yet a strangely rich one. I couldn't afford anything beyond the barest essentials, mostly hitchhiking to get around and sometimes sleeping in a sleeping bag outdoors. I saw some of the things that tourists go to Europe to see—the art and architecture—but mostly I saw many different ways that people were successfully living their lives. I guess it added to the cultural education I acquired in Southeast Asia—my sense of what was possible grew larger and my sense of how things had to be got smaller. Interestingly, my feelings of alienation decreased in the process. I was automatically an outsider because I was from a different continent, but those kinds of outsiders were easily accepted in Europe. The people were uniformly polite and kind, and the police were always a source of help, never a threat to me.

It was a mind-expanding experience, though painful at times, especially because I also went through a severe case of unrequited love. I fell in love with a beautiful American girl in Paris. She agreed to marry me, then woke up to the reality that I was in no shape to marry anyone. I had no visible means of support—no invisible ones either—and no plan for how I would live or what I was going to do with my life. Being more mature than me, she reluctantly dissolved our short engagement, and I sadly accepted her decision. After that, I spent some depressing months moving around Europe and trying to get over the girl. I didn't want to come back to the states until I felt I was sufficiently over the pain of that failed relationship, so it wasn't until May of 1971 that I returned to the states.

I used my return ticket to fly back to Miami by way of the

Bahamas, where my sister was living. I arrived in Nassau with no money to call my sister, who lived on a different island. So I tried to hustle some money in the airport by offering to sell some of my possessions. I found three young college students who were willing to listen to my offer.

"Look, I just need a few dollars to make a phone call. I'll sell you this sleeping bag or anything else here that interests you." The sleeping bag was a greasy thing I had picked up in a flea market in Athens. One young man was interested in my field jacket. It was one of the last carryovers from the Marines. I had worn it all through the winter in Europe, and I hated to give it up, but I was desperate.

I said, "Okay, how about ten bucks for it?"

The young man I was dickering with seemed ready to make a deal, but then one of his companions started chiming in. "Ten bucks? That's a ripoff, man." He turned to his friend, "You can get that thing in any Army-Navy store for five bucks. Man, don't pay this guy ten bucks; that's more than he paid for it."

The young man I was negotiating with nodded and looked down when he spoke to me, "I'll give you three bucks for it."

I argued, "It's worth more than that. It's really warm, and it'll last forever."

He shook his head. He had taken a stand and he refused to back down. His friend grumbled that it wasn't even worth two bucks. I took off my jacket and gave it to the guy for three bucks. I felt totally degraded by the way this guy's friend treated me. At that moment, I think I had a glimpse of what homeless people must feel like when they're treated like they're worthless and only out to rip people off.

I used the money to call my sister in Freeport. She arranged for me to have a ticket to make a side trip there and visit her and her husband for a couple of days. So I went to Freeport. It was strange to suddenly be staying in a nice place and eating well in a resort area. When it was time for me to fly on to Miami, she gave me ten bucks to help get me to Dallas.

I was in for quite a reception on my return. I was carrying a backpack and had long hair. When we arrived at the Miami airport, I was separated from the rest of the passengers and detained, searched, and held while they obtained the use of a fluoroscope to test some sugar cubes they found in my pack. They thought the sugar cubes might hold LSD. The sugar cubes were in my pack because I drank tea all over Europe and took to carrying sugar since it wasn't always available. I had nothing illegal.

I left the airport hours after the other passengers; then I was stopped and hassled by the Miami police before I even got out of the city. I hitched north and was again hassled by the Florida state police who gave me a hard time about where I was standing on the roadway. This time, the policeman locked me in the back seat of his car while he ran a radio check on my identification. Eventually I got out of Florida and headed toward Texas by way of Tennessee (you seldom get to take a straight line when hitchhiking). It was a long night, and early the next morning, I was standing on a roadway out in the middle of nowhere, somewhere in Arkansas. It seemed no one would pick me up. A trucker came by and gave me the finger in a particularly hostile manner.

Finally, two guys came by in a pickup and threw a half empty can of beer at me (this was very early in the morning). I gave them the finger. They slammed on their brakes, turned their truck around, accelerated toward me and then slammed on the brakes again and stopped about fifty yards down the road. Then they sat there gunning their engine. I'd been up all night and hassled repeatedly by my fellow Americans since arriving the previous day, and I'd had it.

I raised both my fists in the air and jumped up and down several times while I screamed at them. "Come on, you chickenshit mother fuckers! Come on! There's just me here, so come and get it, you fucking assholes!"

I was enraged and scared at the same time, and I was ready to fight. They turned around and drove off, probably decided I was crazier than they were.

The whole trip from Florida to Texas only took twenty-six hours. A number of people were very nice, driving out of their way at times to get me to a good spot for my next ride. The last man, a traveling salesman like my father, went off the highway and drove me to the door of my parents' house in Dallas. But I was singled out by the airport people, hassled twice by the cops, and treated with contempt and hostility by passersby on the highway—all in just twenty-six hours!

I had not encountered anything remotely resembling these events during my entire six months in Europe—yet this was the country I fought for.

One of the things I believed I was fighting for in the war was the right for people to be different, to disagree, question, and challenge the existing order. One of the platitudes that I grew up with was attributed to Teddy Roosevelt, "I may not agree with what you say, but I will fight to the death for your right to say it." I never resented the people who were questioning the course of the country in those days. I disagreed with much of what they said, but I always felt that our willingness to let them have their say just highlighted how great our country really was.

From the moment I first got home from Vietnam, I found a devisiveness in the U.S. that I'd not seen before. Ordinary people had "America: Love It or Leave It" stickers on their cars, and I'd never encountered this kind of intolerance before. I began to see the division when I went to college at North Texas and heard the anti-war rallies. When I was working at the Selwyn School, one of the teachers and I rescued a long-haired boy that some local cowboys had cut with a switchblade knife—just because his hair was long. But it was when I returned from Europe in 1971, looking like a hippie myself, that I really learned what was happening to my country. Just as my experience at the airport in the Bahamas gave me a small taste of how the homeless feel, that hitch gave me a small taste of what it feels like to be the recipient of prejudice.

This was what I was fighting against in the war, though perhaps it was different for others. It took a few years for me to realize that not everyone is fighting for the same thing, even when they're on the same side.

I'd been home from Nam for over three years, I was still having occasional nightmares, and I still hadn't found where I fit into this strange world that was supposed to be my home. Hitching through Europe with no money was hard but it was also an exhilarating experience. I was a stranger, but I was accepted. How ironic that it was in my own country, the one I'd fought for, that I felt I was not accepted.

Chapter 125

Still Dragging Baggage

One thing I figured out by the end of my stay in Europe was that living in Dallas was not for me. I still had no idea what I wanted to do for the rest of my life, but for the immediate future, I determined to live in Austin where I felt I had the best chance of finding a compatible community. It was beginning to sink in that I needed to be part of a community.

When I first walked in my parents' door the night I got home from Europe, my mother met me with, "Oh, my God!" Then she called back to my dad, "Honey, come here and see what your son looks like. At least, I think this is our son."

I hadn't had a haircut in over six months, but they didn't really freak out over how weird I looked. They were just relieved to see that I was still alive and okay. However, when I told them my plan was to go live in Austin, my dad and I got into it again.

"What are you going to do there?"

"Well, I don't really know. I know I can get a place to live with some of my friends. But I don't know what I'll do. I'll just have to find some kind of job."

"And what about school?"

I said, "I haven't given up on school; I still intend to finish college. But right now…" I shrugged, "Well, for now, school is just going to have to wait. The University of Texas is in Austin. When I'm ready, I'll probably try and go there. But for now, I have to find a job."

My dad looked down, sighed, and shook his head. I was still a big disappointment to him. I knew how important he felt it was for me to get a college education. He never finished high school, and he felt it had held him back all his life.

I thought about how my dad had wanted to be a naval aviator during the war. Yes, I knew his life would have been different with an education. Nor did I disagree; I wanted to finish college—it was just that I was having a hard time doing it.

I stayed only one day with my folks, and then I made my way to Austin, where I moved into a small house near the University of Texas with several former Selwyn students—Dean,

Jim Shuffield (and later his brother Mickey), and Rick Baldelli. These were great guys to live with, and we had that sense of family, but I was still struggling to find my niche in the world. I picked up odd jobs and again tried to go to school for a semester, but my academic efforts continued to sputter and no job held the promise of anything lasting. Though I felt a sense of belonging—without which I just didn't function worth a damn—I still didn't know where I was going or what I wanted to do.

I lived in, and around, Austin for seven years. Once more, it was working with young people that turned things around for me. I took a job at the Brown Schools, a residential setting for troubled adolescents. It was different from the Selwyn School because of its focus on a psychiatric population, but it was another small community where I found a niche. There was a large staff of paraprofessionals like myself, and I became close friends with many of them. I stayed at that job for six and a half years.

Interestingly, I eventually ended up living alone in the country again—for my final four years in Austin. But it was very different from the isolated experience I'd had in Denton. I chose to live alone because I wanted to make a truly serious effort at college, without a doubt my last chance at it. At age 27, after working in the mental health field for almost three years, I had finally found something that I truly wanted to do—I wanted to be a psychologist.

I had such an abysmal legacy of bad grades that the Registrar wouldn't let me into school at the University of Texas, except to attend classes in their night program, which was open to anyone. So I continued to work at my day job while I attended school in the evenings. For the first time in my life, I was able to concentrate and focus on my studies! Overnight, I developed good study skills: I sat up front and took careful notes in class; I read everything I was assigned and completed all my homework; and I studied for the exams. Suddenly, I was making A's. But though I had finally learned how to study, there were still obstacles in my path—all the result of my long history of failure in school.

One weekend in 1975, I was home visiting my folks in Dallas. Our combat troops had been out of Vietnam for two years; Saigon had recently fallen, and my dad and I had finally quit arguing about whether we should have been there in the first place. In fact, our relationship was improving steadily. The longer I stayed at my job and got promotions, the more he came to support the direction I was taking. I don't think my dad really cared what I chose to do with my life, only that I commit myself to something constructive. He was pleased to see me do well in the job, but what neither he nor my mom fully appreciated was that I had become fixed on the idea of getting a Ph.D. They certainly had a hard time taking that seriously, after all of my misadventures in college.

That weekend was the first time I revealed how I was doing in night school. They knew that I had been attending classes again, but they had learned to not get very invested in my periodic forays into college. I was sitting with the two of them in their den. I said, "You know I'm taking classes at the university."

My mother said, "Oh, yes, we heard."

I said, "Well, it's going a bit differently this time." They both smiled at me, like adults tolerating a child's preoccupations. "Actually, it's a lot different. This is my second year in night school, and I've made nothing but A's so far."

My dad said, "We always knew you could make A's. Glad

to see you doing it."

I continued, "Yeah, well, I guess what I haven't told you is the reason I've been doing this. You see, I've decided that I know what I want to do. I want to become a psychologist." They were both looking at me but not saying anything. "So I've got to go to night school until I bring my grades up enough to get into day school, because you can't get a degree unless you go to day school. Then I want to go for a Ph.D."

My dad asked, "How long is all that going to take?"

I said, "Well, getting the doctorate usually takes five or six years. At the rate I'm getting through undergraduate school while I'm working…" I stared off in the distance for a second, "all told, probably about ten years."

My mother put her hand over her mouth and shook her head. She said, "Oh my God." She laughed, "Well, I tell people my son is a professional student. I guess you'll just be going to college for the rest of your life."

Her response upset me. I felt very vulnerable telling them of my desire to get a Ph.D. and the last thing in the world that I wanted was to be laughed at about it. My eyes welled up with tears, and I burst out at her, "Mother, you don't know how hard it is for me to talk about this. I know I've let you down over and over with school, but this time is different. I'm really working at it this time—harder than I ever came close to trying before. I've finally found something I really want, and when you make jokes about me being a professional student—"

I wiped my eyes and asked directly for what I needed, a manner of operating that I'd learned in my work at the Brown Schools. "Mother, Daddy, I need you to support me on this. Not with money, I'm paying for it okay. I just need you to take this seriously. I'm obviously at the bottom of a big mountain and it's going to be hard enough to try to climb it. But it's a lot harder if you don't think I can. I've never worked at something this hard before. If it takes ten years to get to where I want to go, then I sure need to believe I can get there. But I do think I can do it, and I never thought that before. Please don't make jokes about it."

My mother began to cry. She said, "It isn't easy watching your child go nowhere with his life either. I didn't mean to hurt your feelings." Then she added, "And I've heard you make jokes about it, too."

I nodded, "I have, I know. It's just that this time is different; it really is."

She asked, "Do you know how many times we've thought you were going to finish school, and then you would fail again?" Now she was the one wiping away tears. She said, "Okay, I won't ever make jokes about it again. I promise."

My dad said, "Don, there's nothing in this world that I want more than to see you make a success of school. I know it's important to you to do it on your own. But if there's ever anything we can do—"

I nodded and said, "Thanks, Daddy." Then my mom and I hugged, and that was the last time I ever heard the term professional student.

After three years of making straight A's in night school, I was ready to go to day school to complete my final 30 hours, so I went to the Registrar's Office to register. The woman handling registration studied my record and said I had to go in and meet with the Registrar.

The Registrar was a middle aged man. He told me to be

seated, then he said, "I understand you want to be admitted to school. I've looked through your record," indicating my file sitting on his desk. "You've taken classes at four different schools and accumulated 60 hours of F's. You have failed courses at Texas A&M, North Texas State, SMU Division of Extension, and St. Edward's University."

He looked up and smiled. "Sixty hours of F's, that's quite a record."

He nodded toward his desk, "Now I know you've made some better grades in our evening program, but you're still a long way from having even a C average."

I said, "I've made 12 A's in night school. That's 36 hours. I have to take 30 hours in day school in order to graduate. If I make A's in all of those classes, that would be 66 hours of A's. That would balance off those F's."

He smiled as he shook his head, "I'm sorry, young man, truly I am. I can see that you've done some good work in the extension program, but it's not that easy in day school. More than that, though, I don't think you understand the depth of the hole you've gotten yourself into. We're talking about just getting to a C average. The only way you could significantly change your grade point average would be to go back to these schools where you made the F's and retake the courses. That way, the F's could be erased and replaced with passing grades."

He displayed an open hand. "As long as you carry these F's on your transcript, every A you make just balances an F and you end up with a C average. At best!"

I sighed, "Sir, there's no way I can go back to those schools. My job is here. This is the only place I have any hope of going to school."

It was his turn to sigh, "I'm sorry. My advice to you is to forget college. It's just not an option for you."

I nodded, got up and left his office and went outside. I had all of my grade slips from night school in my hand. I looked at them and thought about ripping them up and throwing them in the trash can. Somehow, I had never dreamed that they would still deny me entrance to school after I had had such success in night school. I stood outside the building for about half an hour, turning his words over in my mind. Then I determined to do something different and not just accept this man's pronouncement on my life.

Throughout my time in those many colleges, I never operated smartly. I never dropped out of a class if I wasn't doing well in it. I never sought to change or challenge a grade or otherwise tried to make things go my way when the system seemed to be going another way. I was always passive and just accepted things as they were. Sometimes, I was extraordinarily stupid in my passivity, as when I took 17 hours of F's when I left North Texas University and went to Europe. This time, I determined not to passively accept the obstacle in my path. I had made 12 A's, and that had to be worth something, so I decided to try something I never considered in all my years of college—going over someone's head.

I found out where the Dean of the Arts and Sciences department was and went to his office. The Dean was not in, but I was ushered into the office of the Assistant Dean, a neatly dressed man with a goatee. I laid my night school grade slips on his desk and I said, "These are my grade slips from the past three years in the Division of Extension. I just tried to register for day school and the registrar won't let me in because I have a lot of F's on my record from several years ago."

He looked at the grade slips, picking each one up and actually reading the course names. He looked at me, then he looked at the grade slips again. Then he picked up the phone, dialed a number and said, "I'm sending a student over to register for the fall semester. He has some problems with his record, but I want him registered."

That was all it took.

Chapter 126

You're Never Safe

One day, I was at work in Austin, and my dad showed up asking to see me. This was extremely unusual; he had only been to see me once since I started living in Austin, and he had certainly never been to the place where I worked. He told me that we needed to talk, and so we went out to the parking lot and sat in his car. He was agitated.

He said, "I came here because I didn't want you to hear this over the phone. There's no easy way to tell you, so I'll just say it. Your sister has been raped."

I gasped, "You mean Beth?"

He nodded, "Yes. He broke into her apartment in the middle of the night and held her at knifepoint, tied her up…" He looked down at the seat between us and I could see his eyes were full of tears.

"Is she okay? How is she?"

"She's okay. She's moved over to our house and is going to stay with me and Mom for now."

"Did he hurt her physically?"

My dad raised his hands in the air. "You tell me. He raped her. He didn't cut her with the knife or anything like that. But she was tied up, and he raped her."

"Well, how is she doing? I mean, how's her state of mind? How's she doing emotionally?"

I could see my dad gritting his teeth. "She's afraid to be alone right now. She seems to be okay when she's with Mom or me, but she won't go back to her apartment any time soon. She can't sleep if she's alone."

I nodded, lost in my own thoughts. I couldn't believe something like this could happen to my little sister. Finally, I asked, "Is there anything I can do? Did you have any thoughts about how I could help?"

My dad shrugged and said, "I don't really think so. Just call her and talk to her maybe." Then he changed the subject, "I'll let you know when they get him."

"Huh?"

"The rapist. The cops have his profile. He's been raping young women in apartments all over the north side. They say it's just a matter of time before they'll catch him."

"Oh. So this is like some regular thing? I mean, this guy has a record? He's like an experienced rapist or something?"

"Yeah, something like that. He always follows the same routine. They're calling him the gentleman rapist, because he speaks to the girls politely."

My dad paused and looked directly at me. Then he said, "I just wanted you to know, Don, that if they catch this guy and then ever let him out, I'll kill him. And if I catch him before the cops do, I'll kill him."

I gave him a wary look. "What do you mean? How could you catch him?"

He shrugged, "I don't know; I doubt that I can. But I offered a reward at the apartment complex for any clues that might lead to him." He paused and then added, "And I bought a shotgun."

I could tell he was serious. "Daddy, I understand your wanting to kill him. But that wouldn't be the best thing for Beth. In fact, that would be the worst thing."

"This guy should die for what he did. You should hear the details of what he did to her. Tied her to the bed with the phone cord. Put a pillowcase over her head. And raped her with a knife at her throat."

"Well, like I said, Daddy, I understand wanting to kill him. I wouldn't have any problem with killing him myself, if the law allowed it. But you know the law won't let you kill him. You'd just go to jail yourself."

"It might be worth it if I could kill that sonofabitch."

"No, it wouldn't, Daddy. Then Beth would have to watch her father go to jail. That would only make things worse for her, much worse."

"She deserves to be avenged."

"Daddy, if I know Beth, she doesn't care at all about revenge. What she needs now is just to be able to feel safe."

He said, "She'd feel a heck of a lot safer if she knew that sonofabitch was dead."

I thought about it. "Maybe. But maybe that's not even why you want to kill him."

"What do you mean?"

"Well, I guess what I mean is," I pointed my finger at him, "is that you'd feel better if you could kill him. I don't know if it'd make Beth feel better or not, but I think it would make you feel better."

My dad was quiet for a moment. I wondered if I had gone too far and really pissed him off. Then he said, "Yeah, I would feel better. Damn right I would. I've been completely useless through this whole thing." He stared at the seat between us and then again looked me in the eye, "You don't know what it's like, Son, to be a father. It's always been my job to keep you kids safe. I don't worry about you; you've been able to take care of yourself for a long time, but it was always different with the girls. And Beth, she's the baby of the family. I always had a special feeling for her. Oh, I loved Kay just as much, but I wasn't around when she was young. I've always felt I could make anything better for Beth, no matter what she was upset about."

He shook his head. "But not this time. I'm totally useless. I wasn't there to stop it; now there's nothing I can do…except kill this sonofabitch if I get the chance."

"Daddy, you're wrong. I think there's still a lot you can do. I know you've always had a special connection with Beth. We all know it. Well, right now it's probably more important than ever. I don't think you have to say or do anything in particular. She just needs to see that that special connection is still there, that you still see the same Beth you always saw. That's how she'll know that she's okay. She needs that from you; that's something you can do that no one else can do as well as you."

He looked at me with a neutral look. He wasn't convinced.

"Daddy, do you remember when we were at the end of my R and R in Hawaii? We were at the airport, and I got a chance to talk to you for a minute. I told you that I thought it was pretty likely I was going to get killed."

My dad nodded, "Oh yes, I remember that well. That's when I realized you were in more combat than you'd been letting on; you were just playing it down in your letters."

"Yeah, well, you helped me then, Daddy. You didn't do anything in particular; you were just cool about it when I told you. You just took it in stride. That helped me a lot. I remember I was feeling pretty scared to be getting back on that plane. But it helped to have you be so calm and strong."

He pursed his lips and nodded his head. I went on, "That's what you can still do for Beth. Be calm and strong for her. I think the less you're affected by what she's been through, the more reassuring it is to her." Now my eyes began to tear up, "You've always been strong for all of us, Daddy. Now you need to do it for Beth. Don't worry about this rapist, that horse is already out of the barn. Beth needs you to be there for her the way you always have, not protecting her like a little girl, but being on the other end of that special connection. That way, she'll know that she's still okay."

My dad looked down at the seat, then out the window for a bit. Finally, he looked up at me and said. "Thanks, Son. I'm glad I came to see you. I wanted to tell you in person because I thought it would be too upsetting for you to hear it over the phone." He smiled, "But maybe I needed to talk about it too." He chuckled and pointed his thumb back at the school, "I bet you're getting to be pretty good at what you do."

We grasped hands and he left.

Chapter 127

Lingering Shadows

I would say I finally rejoined the human race during those years in Austin, Texas. By the time I left there, I was on the course that I am still pursuing today—despite the many twists and turns that we all encounter on our paths through life. As in overcoming my record in school, the change in my life's path was gradual and took a long time. I was still emerging from the shell I'd grown in Vietnam. I encountered other veterans who seemed to be struggling with similar demons. Whether their particular mode was alcohol abuse, high adrenaline activities, or just reliving the scenes of horror, I saw the shadow of Vietnam hanging on tenaciously. As for me, I pretty much tried every mode.

Of course, I didn't realize how much it was still affecting me; I tried to live as though Vietnam was no longer relevant in my life. I had no television, so I never saw the nightly news clips from the war that so many people recall from the years of the Vietnam

War. I wasn't being reminded by external events, but the internal events had not stopped. I still had the occasional dream, and I kept thinking about what might have happened if I'd been there when Lieutenant Johnson was ambushed. Maybe the whole thing would have gone down differently if I had been there. Most likely, I would have been killed. How many times did I live that day differently in my mind?

Despite my intention to not feel guilty about that day, I felt quite guilty. I thought of Bill Rees every time I encountered a new opportunity in life. Here was something else that Bill might have enjoyed, if he had lived. I'm sure he'd have loved to be able to live in a place like Austin. When I was making my usual mess of school, I thought about what Bill might have done with the opportunity. My trips to see my folks up in Dallas heightened my awareness that I was not doing anything constructive with my life. Though the nightmares had declined, other after-effects of the war were just becoming visible.

I received a Bronze Star Medal for meritorious service in Vietnam. This was not a medal for valor but the citation did specify my performance in combat situations—so it included a combat "V" device—and the timeline began with my actions on the day Bill Rees and Lieutenant Johnson were killed. I left the medal at my parents' house in Dallas, and they kept it displayed in the room I used when I visited. Every time I visited, I would shut the case on the medal as soon as I walked into that room. I didn't want to look at it and never gave it much thought. I just automatically shut the case and left it shut throughout my visit. The next time I visited, it would be open again.

My father was immensely proud of my having been awarded a medal. He would often embarrass me by introducing me to people and mentioning it immediately. I got to where I didn't like being reminded of it. Whatever I did that day, my friends still died, and despite my many close calls, I was never wounded. I grew up trying to earn a Purple Heart like my dad's, by taking outrageous chances on the trees and cliffs and rooftops of Dallas. I would have gladly traded that Bronze Star for a Purple Heart.

I was still highly vigilant for danger. I could go from being sound asleep to totally aroused in an instant. This was an adaptation from the war that didn't seem to go away. Of course, there were times in Vietnam when I was totally exhausted and not in that state of readiness, like when I slept through the mortar attack on Operation Arizona. But most of the time I was only a step away from being wide awake, and this was still my normal mode of consciousness, even though years had passed since I'd left the combat zone.

When I first got home from the war, going around unarmed made me feel very vulnerable. I truly felt naked without my gun and took to keeping my old shotgun close at hand. I expected that vulnerable feeling to subside after I had been home a while, which it did—but only to a degree. So one of the things I did in Austin was to study karate, and I became relatively proficient at it after a few years. It helped some, though I knew that the greatest martial artist in the world cannot defend himself against high speed metal.

My dad reacted negatively when I told him I was studying karate. He said, "What do you want to waste your time doing that for?"

I asked, "Daddy, do you remember when you tried to teach

me to box? You got me boxing gloves for Christmas, and then we stood out in the front yard—by the magnolia tree—and you showed me how to hold my hands to protect my face, how to jab, how to throw a hook."

He nodded, "Yeah, I remember. You were only about eight years old."

I said, "What I most remember was that you couldn't get me to punch you. You kept telling me to, but I just couldn't bring myself to do it. Finally, you punched me in the nose, and it hurt like hell."

My dad chuckled, "I don't remember you getting hurt. I just remember you weren't much of a boxer."

"Well, at the time, I didn't understand why I was doing it, but I could tell you thought it was important." I looked down for a moment, then I continued, "Ever since I got home from Nam, I've felt really vulnerable walking around without a gun." I shrugged. "This karate training gives me the feeling that I'm not entirely defenseless. It may not change anything, and I doubt I will ever get in a fight with anyone, but it makes me feel a little more secure."

I looked my dad in the eye and asked, "Didn't you feel

something like that after you came home from the war?"

He wrinkled his brow and got a faraway look in his eye. Finally, he said, "I don't know, Son, maybe. For me, I think it seemed more like fate. When I got home, I just tried to leave the war behind me. Some of the salesmen I know carry guns in their cars. I've never done that...but I guess I understand."

My reflexive posture of watching out for ambushes continued, though it was many years before I realized the extent to which it permeated my life. Eventually, I became aware of how much I avoided crowds, didn't sit in the middle of the room without my back covered, and stayed highly attuned to any stranger who got behind me. It was a way of life. My last night in Europe, I slept in a youth hostel with a dozen other travelers, mostly Americans. During the night, two of these fellow travelers went through the hostel and stole everyone's passport—except mine. Trusting soul that I am, I slept with my passport clutched in my hand and my hand tucked inside my shirt.

Throughout my years in Austin, I continued to be prepared for a crisis—prepared in practical ways, such as carrying materials for a crisis in my car, but more importantly, prepared in emotional ways. I could launch into a state of mind that would allow me to function no matter what was going on, and I expect I'll be able to do that to the day I die. Combat veterans become more active in crises; civilians are typically passive, waiting for someone to tell them what to do.

I spent a lot of time outdoors in the countryside around Austin. I still found it impossible to walk in the woods without slipping into that state of mind I learned in the jungle—highly attuned to my surroundings, taking it all in, seeing everything while focusing on nothing in particular. This was not particularly unpleasant, it was just the way it was. I grew up hunting in Texas, and I've always loved the outdoors. I hunted ducks when I lived in Austin. I had particularly wanted to go deer hunting as a young boy, and my dad promised to take me, but it never happened, one of the big disappointments of my childhood. While living in Austin, I could have gone deer hunting if I wanted, but I discovered I'd lost the desire. Something about shooting a large mammal turned me off; perhaps it was too close to shooting people. And I couldn't forget the water buffalo we had to shoot so many bullets into.

That led me to a new understanding of why my dad never took me deer hunting. It probably wasn't because he didn't want to spend the time with me, which was my fear. He too may have lost his passion for killing mammals. He'd hunted deer before the war and probably recalled it as pleasurable, so it was easy to feed my interest and make plans to take me and teach me what he had learned as a young man. But he may have found the thought of an actual hunting trip to be something for which he couldn't work up much enthusiasm.

I suppose the oddest part of the war hanging on with me were the times I found myself missing it. There was a black and white clarity to life that was very appealing. Everyone was either a good guy or a bad guy. Life was a game of life and death, and you either made it or you didn't on a daily basis. As long as you made it, your only concern was making it again tomorrow. You didn't give serious thought to any future beyond that, because it was just too distant from the reality you were living. Sometimes I missed the intensity—not just the fear and the excitement, but the laughter, the friendships, and the profound appreciation of the simple pleasures of living. Clean sheets, a hot shower, a refrigerator full of food—these are the true luxuries of life. Lodging at the finest hotel is only an elaboration of these.

But the thing I missed the most was the connection I had with my fellow Marines. That sense of belonging is priceless—it is that, and the great sense of pride, that make the Marine Corps a family that men will die for. The more connected I became with the world around me—my friends and co-workers in Austin—the less I longed for the war.

Of course, I didn't reveal my longing for the war to many people. I doubt they would have understood.

Chapter 128

The Long Shadow of War

I left Austin in the late 70's to come to Chicago to work on my Ph.D. During graduate school, I married a wonderful woman—my dad was my best man in the wedding—and in the late 80's, we were blessed with two wonderful children. Life has only gotten better over the years.

Yet the shadow of war persists.

I had been living alone for almost ten years when I started living with Kim. One of the first things she had to learn was to not speak to me when I was falling asleep at night. If she said something when I was in that fog state between consciousness and sleep, I would come instantly awake in a state of hyperarousal and be unable to go back to sleep. I had stopped dreaming about Vietnam, but I had one very vivid dream shortly after we married. I was in a firefight, lying behind a rice paddy dike, and Kim was next to me. She wasn't shooting; she was just there with me. Throughout the dream, my anxiety focused on her. I was afraid she would raise her head too high and get hit. I put my helmet on her head and kept insisting that she understand how important it was to keep her head low.

I had rediscovered my vulnerability. I could watch out for myself, but I couldn't always protect my loved ones. This feeling was heightened when we had children. I could understand why my father went out and bought a shotgun after my sister was raped.

The most troubling and lasting feelings from the war are not about the moments of fear that I endured. The moments that haunt me most involve my inability to keep others alive. Several years ago, at our cottage in Wisconsin, some of our neighbors asked my help when their dog was giving birth, and the first pup was born dead. The rest of the pups were okay; but I spent a long time trying to revive the deadborn puppy and, despite my efforts, I could not bring the puppy to life. Afterwards, I went off and cried for a long time. The incident with the puppy had stirred up memories of trying to keep wounded men alive and watching them die. I felt tremendous pain that night, a pain that I had sealed away a long time ago.

For me, the greatest pain in war is not about killing people and it's not the fear of getting killed. It's the pain of being unable to stop people from dying.

I thought I'd gotten over my guilt and deep sadness over the deaths of Bill Rees and Lieutenant Johnson—until I started a business and invited a friend of mine to join me. He had been at his current job for many years and was near the point where he would get his pension and be financially secure for life. Instead, he gave up that security and joined me in the business. Unfortunately, it turned out to be a struggle for him, and he didn't do very well for a long time. I felt bad for talking him into leaving a secure situation. I felt I had gotten him into a mess. One day, I was talking about the situation with another colleague, and he asked why I took so much responsibility for my friend's decision. I realized that he was right; I was taking undue responsibility for my friend's decision.

I was still trying to save Bill Rees from getting himself killed.

I relived that day in October over and over for years, yet

thinking about it never made it come out any differently. I finally began to accept the fact that I had inherited the gift of life when Bill and Lieutenant Johnson and others did not, but acceptance alone was not enough. I still owed them something.

I had to make that gift meaningful.

What I finally concluded was that I owed it to all of them—to every one of the more than 58 thousand men and women on the Wall—and I now had a responsibility to make the most of this precious gift. I was given the opportunities that they would never see—so I had a responsibility to make the most of those opportunities. Part of my abrupt change from F's to A's in school was because I finally realized what a precious opportunity I'd been given to be there at all. All I had to do was take advantage of it.

I have found peace where I used to feel guilt. I've learned to live with the fact that I survived instead of some people I loved, and I make it okay by taking advantage of the opportunities that they will never have. When I come to important crossroads in my life, I think about the fact that I've been given the opportunity to be there instead of someone else. That way of thinking has helped me make more responsible decisions and stay on the right track at times when I might have gone in another direction. My mission is to make the most of the precious opportunities that come with not only being alive, but with being a member of the most highly privileged group of people in human history—an American citizen.

My reaction to my friend's struggle with the job change helped me to recognize that I tend to approach my work with a heightened sense of responsibility. One thing I will never do is to let someone else do my job for me.

Chapter 129

Breaking the Mold

It should be apparent by now that my dad was enormously important to me. He was a worthy role model, a man of integrity, courage, strength, generosity, and honesty. He was a hard worker and was respected by his peers. I respected and admired him, and I have tried to emulate him throughout my life. Most of all, I wanted to be close to him, to know him from the inside as well as the outside. That was difficult, because his insides were hard to reach, but that changed over time.

In the mid-80's, my dad and I had several meaningful talks about ourselves and our relationship with each other. We talked about what we each wanted out of our lives. One day, I told my dad that I wanted something to be different between us. He asked what.

I said, "You used to kiss me when I was a little boy. Do you remember?"

He nodded, "Sure, I remember."

"Well, these days, I don't get to see you very often. When I come down here, Mom and I kiss and hug, but you and I just shake hands."

He nodded again, "Yeah, it's been that way ever since you were in about the fifth or sixth grade."

I said, "Well, that's what I want to change. I want us to be able to kiss each other like we did when I was a kid. It's just not right that we shake hands like it's no big deal seeing each other." I glared at him, "I want to be able to kiss my dad!"

It was one of the few times I ever saw my dad tear up. He kind of lost his composure for a second, gripping his hands together and looking down. Then he looked up at me and nodded silently. Finally, he said, "I would like that very much, Son. That's what we'll do from now on." Then he added, "And if anybody can't handle two Marines kissing, that'll be just too damn bad."

We hugged each other and kissed then. Actually, it was a little awkward and felt strange at first, but we got used to it, and after that I kissed my dad right along with my mom whenever I arrived or was leaving.

Another talk that stays with me occurred one evening in 1985 when my dad and I were alone up at Lake Dallas. During my training, I had developed a specialization in the treatment of Posttraumatic Stress Disorder and had been working with Vietnam veterans suffering from the disorder. Upon graduation, I was offered a position running a program treating vets but turned it down and went to work elsewhere. We talked about why I had turned down the position.

I said, "That two years was intense, and it got me more personally upset than anything I've ever done in this field. When I went home at night, I couldn't stop thinking about my clients and how bad their lives were."

He asked, "Their lives now or their lives during the war?"

I reflected on his question for a moment. "I guess it's really more about their lives now. I've heard some horrendous stories about things that happened to them during the war, but that doesn't really get to me so much by itself. It's when I think about how much those things still bother them—that's more what gets to me."

He said, "So it's not the horrors they lived through, it's how they can't get over it."

I thought about the implications of what he was saying. "You know, I hadn't really thought about it in quite that way, Daddy. But that's right, it's not what happened to them; it's how damaged they are from it."

I thought about one of my clients, a man who'd been with 5th Marines, the unit that I had briefly joined on Operation Union II when I first saw extensive casualties. This man wasn't even in-country at that time, yet I carried the feeling that his suffering was so great because his unit saw so much action, and I felt I'd gotten off easy in comparison.

"You know, it's strange," I commented, "what bothers me is how much these guys continue to suffer. I could handle hearing their war stories easier than hearing about how their lives continue to be so haunted. Of course, hearing their war stories still stirred up my memories of the things that happened to me."

"It stirred up your memories of the war?"

I nodded, "Yeah, it did. I found myself talking about it with Kim all the time. She was a good listener, but sometimes I just overloaded her. One night, she said she felt like I'd just gotten back from the war. We watched this series about Vietnam on PBS that ran an hour a week for thirteen weeks, and I ended up in tears after most of the episodes. It was like my thirteen months condensed down into thirteen weeks, and it was just too much."

My dad nodded, "I guess we all keep that stuff buried. Hearing guys talk about it every day, I can see how that could bring it all back up. Maybe that's why I was never interested in joining the VFW. To me, that just sounded like a bunch of guys sitting around a bar telling war stories."

Meanwhile, my mind was working on what he had helped me to see more clearly. "But this is interesting, Daddy. Working with those guys didn't bring back the fear for me, it brought back my feelings of guilt. We call it survivor guilt—feeling bad that you survived when others didn't make it. That's what working with those vets stirred up in me, except I didn't feel guilty because I survived, but because I survived in so much better shape than they did."

My dad nodded and asked, "Why do you feel so guilty about it, Son?"

His question reminded me that I had never really talked to my father about the deaths of Lieutenant Johnson and Bill Rees and what that had done to me. Indeed, we had discussed few details of my experience in the war. I spared my mother most of the details of the horrors I had seen, but I had told her about the deaths of Lieutenant Johnson and Bill Rees and the powerful impact that had on me. My dad never asked about my specific war experiences, and I had never volunteered anything—perhaps for the same reason that he didn't want to go to the VFW and hear war stories. Maybe it was part of how he kept his own painful memories under control—but he was asking now.

"Oh, I know the answer to that, Daddy. It's all about one particular incident, the one that's mentioned on my Bronze Star citation."

He looked thoughtful for a moment, then he said, "I know—the part about your company commander getting killed…and your friend was killed subbing for you."

I was taken aback. I had told him the essentials of the story, but somehow I didn't expect him to remember it so distinctly. I said, "I'm surprised you remember that."

His mouth formed a smile but he wasn't really smiling. "Mom and I talked about it a couple of times. I know it got to you.

I guess I hadn't thought about you still feeling guilty, but I understand." He paused, then he said, "You know, I have things from the war that I still feel guilty about too."

I nodded, "Yeah, I know, the women you had to machine gun." He first told me the story when I was young. On Okinawa, Japanese soldiers disguised themselves in women's clothes and then advanced on the Marine lines hidden within a group of women villagers. Daddy was in charge of the position they advanced on. He ordered the women to stop, but the soldiers had bayonets at their backs and made them continue. Finally, he ordered the machine gun team to shoot them. I knew this was a source of great pain for him as soon as I saw the look on his face the first time he told the story.

He face tightened and he nodded quietly, "That's right. That was the hardest thing I ever did."

I looked down at his tightly balled fist, but I didn't say anything. It would have been completely superfluous to tell him that he'd only done what had to be done in the situation. He knew that—just like I knew that it was not my fault that Bill Rees grabbed my seat in the PC. Some things cannot be made better by reminding people that it wasn't their fault. Survivor guilt isn't really about fault; it's more like a reaction to feeling two things at once—terrible about someone dying and thankful that it wasn't you.

    I don't recall what was said after that; we changed the topic soon after. But I do know that I felt better. I'd finally had the conversation with my dad that I'd been wanting ever since I got home. Interestingly, it was not a conversation with a lot of answers. I simply felt that my dad saw some of my pain—indeed, he knew more about it than I'd known—and I saw some of his. It was interesting that we each felt something similar, but the important part was simply that we talked and shared our pain with each other.

Part IV

Shaped by the Shadow of War

Chapter 130

Lessons

I was born in December of 1946, the year my father returned home from the war. Twenty months before the day I was born, my father lay paralyzed and helpless on a barren battlefield in the midst of enemy territory, protected only by the dead bodies piled on top of him. I do not know what that night was like for him, but I have some idea what it did to him—because he raised me to be prepared for war. He put weapons in my hands and taught me to fight at a young age, and he always emphasized the importance of being able to remain strong in the face of fear. I was his only son, so I received the entire focus of his training in what he considered to be the essential skills of manhood. The difference in raising boys and girls was pronounced in our family. I was the one who got beat with the belt, and I was the one expected to run off wild animals and protect my mother and sisters when my dad was gone.

I now understand that my dad's reaction to my small size stemmed from his concern that I might not be able to hold my own against an enemy. Small size was a weakness that someone could exploit. I believe that was why he pushed the food on me, he wanted me to grow stronger and larger.

He imposed a great deal of discipline on me as well, much of it right out of the Marine manual. He believed self-discipline was a major advantage in life, and he acquired his own self-discipline from his Marine training. This is how it works. First you adhere to the discipline being imposed on you from the drill instructors. Then, over time, you develop an internal strength that is able to maintain that state of discipline without the need for the external structure, the drill instructor. My dad felt that the self-discipline he developed in the Marine Corps benefited him tremendously throughout his life.

As I look back on my childhood today, I view many of the painful moments with my father as *lessons*. My father was trying to prepare me for the worst. He came from a world in which a man is likely to face the greatest depths of fear and horror and loss, and so he set about toughening me up. I know that my experience with him doesn't differ from that of many, maybe most, members of my generation. Boys were raised that way back then. However, I don't think that is an accident. We all grew up in the shadow of war, and we were raised by the men who survived. How could they not pass on the lessons of survival to their sons?

Chapter 131

Generations

After following in my father's footsteps and surviving my own experience of war, I was able to see the myriad ways in which the shadow of his combat experiences had colored and shaped the life of our family. I recognized traits in myself that I'd seen in him and never understood. Indeed, I've found these traits to be common among combat veterans, which means there's a lot of families out there whose lives have been shaped by the shadow of war.

I don't like crowds. Crowds are dangerous, in part because individuals fail to appreciate how dangerous they become when packed into a crowd. When in public, I usually prefer to sit where I can see potential avenues of threat…and escape. In my car, I carry a large pack filled with bandages and medical supplies, as well as well-maintained tools. Like my father, I take immediate action in emergencies.

I enjoy fireworks displays but I generally stay indoors on the Fourth of July. As long as I know what's coming, fireworks are fine, but if I'm surrounded by a bunch of yahoos who think throwing firecrackers is fun...

After the war, I developed more of a temper and exploded many times. More than once, I vented my frustration by punching a wall and hurting my hand. Interestingly, this wasn't a significant problem until I married—fourteen years after my return from the war. I'd avoided the challenges of intimacy and getting along with others by living alone for many years. Marriage, of course, forced me to confront that and get better control of my emotions. When my children were born, I was tested anew. My temper is under control these days, but I shall always regret the times that I lost control when my children were present. I fear my kids may have learned to fear me as I learned to fear my father.

I can still numb out and be insensitive to the suffering of others. I have worked on this for years, and I don't think it's happened in a long time, but I doubt it's gone for good, because numbing out is a critical part of what happens when my 'threat detection system' gets activated. I suspect most combat vets remain capable of the same thing. However, my personal therapy and my career as a psychotherapist have helped me learn to stay tuned in instead of tuned out.

I expect I will remain vigilant for the possibility of attack for the rest of my life. That vigilance can cause me to become hyperaroused and wide awake in an instant. I do not regret my hair trigger ability to launch into a vigilant state, as I believe it is an important part of staying alive, but hyperarousal is exhausting and is one of the primary symptoms of PTSD. Learning to keep arousal within an adaptive range is one of the key transition tasks for returning combat vets.

So, yes, my children grew up with some of the same traits in their father that I experienced with mine, but I had a different relationship with my war experience. I lived in a different time, and I had the luxury of recovering from the war in a world that was more accepting of young adults taking a long time to grow up. I was able to delay many of the responsibilities of adulthood, such as a wife and family, while I figured out who I was and where I wanted to go with my life.

Whereas I was born the same year my father returned home

from World War II, my first child was not born until eighteen years after my return from Vietnam, which gave me a lot of time to process my war experience and resume my development. I was drawn to the field of mental health, where I learned better habits for my own mental health. Lacking my father's familial responsibilities, I was free to spend my early adulthood as a lost soul seeking to find myself. It was easy to do such things in the sixties and seventies—there were a lot of lost souls out there looking for themselves—so you might say my extended adolescence was supported by the cultural revolution of the sixties.

    The result is that I had the opportunity to spend additional years searching for where I fit in the world, a luxury simply not possible for many. It was another of those opportunities I inherited with my survivorship, though I didn't understand that back then. It allowed me to find my niche, my identity as a civilian, and to leave the war behind and regrow some of my humanity. My life differed from my father's, and those of many of his generation, in that I was changed by my combat experience, but I am not haunted by it. Nor I do regard it as something too painful to talk about, which—ironically—means it seldom intrudes into my life.

Plus my kids didn't have to eat everything on their plate.

Chapter 132

An Old Marine's Passing

In March of 1987, my wife and I took our eight month old daughter and visited my folks in Dallas. My dad was not feeling well during the visit, but he and I did get the chance to go out together a time or two. One day, we drove up to the lake to check on his boat and, while we were there, we sat and talked.

My dad said, "You know, Son, you've taught me a lot about being a man."

I was stunned by the comment. How could I have taught him anything about manhood? He'd done more of the traditionally manly things than most men ever dream about.

I said, "I'm not sure what you mean, Daddy. What have I ever taught you? You practically wrote the book on manhood—Merchant marines at 15, Honorman in boot camp, D.I., and then you became a self-made man. You're the one who taught me about manhood."

He said, "That's one side of being a man, and you've handled that side just fine. But you've shown me more of the other side, the soft side. You've always had a really strong character, maybe that's why you can be soft without giving up your manliness." He smiled at me, "It's something I admire in you, and I've tried to be better at it myself."

I accepted it. "Thanks, Daddy. You know you've always been my hero."

Two weeks later, he died suddenly of an aortic aneurism. I didn't know it at the end of that visit, but I was kissing my dad goodbye for the last time.

Chapter 133

Vestiges

In my fifties, I developed a tremor and when I tried to jog, I kept injuring my ankle. I took these difficulties to be the normal calamities of aging, but I learned differently. At age sixty, my body's warranty ran out. Within months of turning sixty, I was diagnosed with prostate cancer, glaucoma, and CIDP—Chronic Inflammatory Demyelinating Polyneuropathy—all were conditions correlated with exposure to Agent Orange, the toxic defoliant used in Vietnam. The worst of these is the CIDP, a progressive neurological disorder that is slowly eroding my ability to use my limbs.

At the time of this writing, I am now seventy years old and, for most of the past decade, I've spent two days a month receiving intravenous infusions of gamma globulin (IVIG) to combat my neurological disorder. I work out a lot, and I'm still on my feet, though I use a cane. I still work professionally—doing psychotherapy with trauma clients and teaching at the university—and I've accommodated my lifestyle to my physical limitations. I certainly don't enjoy having the limitations with which I live, but neither am I bitter. I've had a wonderful life, and I know how fortunate I am to be here at all. But I did start thinking about this Agent Orange thing…

The Arizona Territory was the most barren place I saw in Vietnam. It was a virtual desert in the midst of the verdant Southeast Asian landscape—almost nothing was growing there. I never gave that much thought at the time, but now I wonder: Was that because it had recently been sprayed with the Agent Orange defoliant? If so, then maybe I never had the worms, maybe the bad water I drank on Operation Arizona was contaminated with Agent Orange. Maybe I poisoned myself when I gave in to my thirst and immersed my face in that urn of bad water. If that is the case, I might not be impaired today if I'd resisted the temptation to drink from that urn of bad water.

Of course, it doesn't really matter. We each live with the consequences of our decisions, big and small. Some decisions are big enough to show a visible impact at the time we make them, while others seem trivial until consequences appear later in life. War heightened my awareness of the profound nature of some of my most trivial decisions. Time after time, I made small decisions—from putting myself in line for the First Marine Division to zigging left when the next guy zagged right to sticking my face in an urn of bad water—and those small decisions changed the course of my life.

Life is not all luck, of course. I've worked hard to get to where I am. But the fact remains that I am alive and Bill Rees and Lyle Johnson and over fifty-eight thousand others died, at least in part because of luck or chance. I no longer feel so guilty about surviving when they died, and I do not think there is some deep meaning to my surviving. However, I do continue to feel that I owe it to them to make the most of this life I've been blessed to live.

Chapter 134

Spiritual Wounds

In the early 1980's, I was the primary clinician and administrator of a program treating traumatized veterans. I interviewed every veteran, assigned a therapist, and treated many of them myself in individual, family and group therapy. That experience led me to spend eight years participating in a therapy group with several other veterans who worked as psychotherapists. In the late eighties and early nineties, I served on a national advisory committee for the Department of Veterans Affairs, making site visits and interviewing veterans at VA Medical Centers and Vet Centers around the country. Over the years, I have interviewed hundreds of combat veterans, from those who withdrew from society and lived secluded lives to those with successful careers as VA staff, policemen, firemen, and a host of professions.

I have yet to meet a veteran whose spirit was not wounded

by his war experience.

The Western diagnosis of PTSD focuses on the terror of combat and the power of a conditioned fear response. Unfortunately, that is but one of many ways in which the human spirit is damaged by war. Every combatant is affected by war, as is every civilian in a war zone. My father had PTSD symptoms and continued to experience bodily effects of those terror-filled nights. Yet his worst trauma was not that night when he lay alone on the battlefield under a pile of dead bodies, nor was it on Peleliu when they assaulted the Point or even when they endured the hellish fighting on Bloody Nose Ridge. No, my father's worst trauma was simply giving the order to open fire on a group of women who were being forced to advance on the Marine position on Okinawa.

The term *combat stress injury* captures the many different ways in which combat damages the human spirit. I felt guilt for surviving when my friends died, and my father felt guilt for actions he took. Mine is called *survivor guilt*, but his guilt was part of a *moral injury*—witnessing or participating in activities that violate one's most deeply held beliefs. *Traumatic loss* accounts for many of the postwar difficulties manifested by veterans, which most certainly includes me. Individuals who experience combat together are in a highly interdependent relationship, in which the survival of the other is inextricably linked to survival of the self—hence, the common nature of heroic acts in which individuals sacrifice their lives to save comrades.

The loss of a valued comrade in combat is the violent end of a love relationship.

I discovered my urge to act out my rage through killing, and my father discovered that he was willing to kill someone innocent in order to protect himself and his comrades. These are deeply upsetting things to learn about yourself—*spiritual wounds*. After a moral injury, the challenge is in finding your spirit and recovering your sense of yourself as a decent human being. In successful cases, this leads to a better life—my father was a leader in our church and performed many charitable acts—but in unsuccessful cases, the survivor remains mired in self-hate. Some veterans spend the remainder of their lives trying to atone for the moral violations they committed during their war experience.

My experience of survivor guilt is common among veterans, far more so than occurs in civilian trauma, yet it is still difficult to look at directly. For me, the hardest part was my relief that I didn't die when others did. It feels so disloyal. Fortunately, I've learned how to manage this guilt. I can't change the fact that I survived, but I can control what I do with my survival.

I have tried to balance out my impact on the world. I found a healing profession and helped other veterans, as well as other people whose lives were impacted by trauma. Trying to protect others from trauma like your own can extend from minor activities, such as volunteer work, to a lifelong career, and it is called pursuing a *survivor mission*. The pursuit of survivor missions is probably as common as survivor guilt. Ever since the war, I've sought to remind others of the importance of finding non-violent solutions to our conflicts and differences. Most importantly, I've tried to recognize God's presence in every human heart I encounter. I do not want to dehumanize others again.

Wars fought among civilian populations produce more noncombatant casualties and more atrocities. My father's moral injury occurred because civilians were involved, but at least his was a war of liberation. Americans were not known for committing atrocities in World War II. Atrocities against civilians are generally committed by occupying troops, not liberators. That's because the local population is placed in a dilemma—they will be punished if they help the occupiers—and so they do not report the mines that are laid along the roadway, and the occupying forces become distrustful and harsh toward the locals. In Vietnam, we were the occupiers, and the same is true of our wars in Iraq and Afghanistan. When will America learn the moral cost of trying to occupy other countries?

I do not feel that life is unfair because I now contend with my neurological difficulties. People are fair or unfair, but life simply is. When high speed metal is flying around, there is no underlying reason that determines who gets hit. It is tempting to ascribe meaning to who survives and who doesn't, but I do not think God works like that. I cannot believe that every person in Hiroshima was deserving of a violent death. So I don't believe God decides who will survive; He just stands ready to help those that do.

War survivors inherit a responsibility to make the world a better place, and part of that process is becoming aware of how the shadow of war continues to shape our lives and the lives of our families—long after the war has ended. My father lived a night of terrifying helplessness and subsequently raised me with an intense focus on facing fear, which led me to spend my youth seeking fearful situations in which I could test my courage. I certainly value the development of courage, but I don't want my children to feel compelled to leap barefooted from rooftops, and so I've tried to give them a different message.

My father's horrors and his pain from his war experiences exceeded my own. He came from a family—and a generation—in which talking through painful events was not encouraged among men, thus he never fully processed his war experiences. So I've taken his story and finished it…for both of us.

Epilogue

Seven years after my father died, I was standing in my driveway teaching my four year old son to ride a bicycle. I took the pedals off the bike and taught him to balance it as he rolled down the driveway, which he quickly mastered. Then I put the pedals back on and we added pedaling, which was harder, especially when he tried to slow down and turn. He was starting to get the whole package, when he turned the handlebars too sharply and fell in a heap next to the bike.

He started crying.

I walked over to where he was lying, and I could see no physical damage—he was just crying over the abrupt meeting with planet Earth. I stood over him with the words in my throat, "You're okay, just get back on the bike," but they remained stuck there, and I said nothing. Then something melted inside of me, and I knelt down and pulled him into my lap and held him close while he cried.

Soon enough, he stopped crying. For him, it was a momentary hurt, but for me, a deeper hurt had begun to heal.

Made in the USA
Columbia, SC
17 May 2022